# News and Journalism in the UK

## Second Edition

Written especially for students, *News and Journalism in the UK* provides a comprehensive introduction to the political, economic and regulatory environments of British press and broadcast journalism.

Brian McNair surveys the industry in a period of radical change, taking stock of what the British journalistic media have come through in the 1980s and 1990s, and assessing where they are going.

Integrating both academic and professional perspectives on journalism, Brian McNair identifies the main issues now confronting the industry. The book includes separate chapters devoted to the social history and contemporary role of journalism; analysis of the impact of such key events as the 'Wapping revolution' and the establishment of Sky News on regional and national UK journalism; a review of current debates on media ownership and regulation.

This second edition is fully revised and updated to include discussion of such issues as the changing political allegiances of the Murdoch press; the impact of the newspaper price war on circulation; the fortunes of the Mirror Group post-Maxwell; key changes in press ownership such as the sales of the *Observer* and Thomson Regional Newspapers; and the increasing pressures being faced by broadcast journalists in their reporting of political affairs.

**Brian McNair** is Senior Lecturer in Film and Media Studies at the University of Stirling. He is the author of several books on journalism and the media, including *Images of the Enemy* (1988), *Glasnost, Perestroika and the Soviet Media* (1991) and *An Introduction to Political Communication* (1995).

# Communication and Society
## General Editor: James Curran

# News and Journalism in the UK

Second Edition

A Textbook

Brian McNair

London and New York

To the Mugwump,
for Making It.

First published in 1994 by Routledge
This edition first published 1996
by Routledge
11 New Fetter Lane, London EC4P 4EE

Simultaneously published in the USA and Canada
by Routledge
29 West 35th Street, New York, NY 10001

*Routledge is an International Thomson Publishing company*

© 1994, 1996 Brian McNair

Typeset in Times by Poole Typesetting, Bournemouth, Dorset
Printed and bound in Great Britain by Clays Ltd, St Ives PLC

*British Library Cataloguing in Publication Data*
A catalogue record for this book is available from the British Library

*Library of Congress Cataloguing in Publication Data*
A catalogue record for this book has been requested

ISBN 0–415–13176–6

# Preface to the second edition

The first edition of *News and Journalism in the UK* was completed in early 1993. Since then, many of the trends identified there have been confirmed by events. The broadcast journalism organisations – the BBC and ITN in particular – have continued to operate in strongly competitive environments, and to 'brand market' their output. Concern about the future of 'quality' public service broadcast journalism, both news and current affairs, continues to be voiced. The press, too, have been required to maintain an intensively competitive stance. Press regulation remains an issue, although the newly appointed Heritage Secretary Virginia Bottomley confirmed in July 1995 that self-regulation, with the Press Complaints Commission as the main vehicle for exercising pressure on newspapers, would continue to be the government's preferred approach.

Sections of this edition which deal with these subjects have been updated where necessary, but substantial rewriting has not on the whole been required. Where there have been significant developments, these have been reflected in this edition. For example, in July 1993 competitive pressures led to the opening of a ferocious price war, involving most of the British national press, which continues as this edition goes to print. For some titles the price war was the last straw, and there have been a number of changes in the ownership structure of the British press since 1993. There has also been a major shake-up of the regional press, and the Scottish press in particular, with the sale of its newspapers by the Thomson Corporation. Most intriguingly, perhaps, in the sphere of press journalism, has been the shift in political allegiance since the General Election of 1992 of several

previously pro-Conservative newspapers, most notably those of
the News International stable. Such has been the extent of this
shift, indeed, that once routine references to a 'Tory press' no
longer seem entirely appropriate.

In the sphere of broadcasting, journalists have, since 1993,
been confronted with several challenges to their impartiality,
such as the BBC's decision (subsequently overruled by a Scottish
court) to show a *Panorama* interview with Prime Minister John
Major during the Scottish local election campaign in 1995. In
that same year the BBC's Director-General John Birt publicly
accused some of his journalists of adopting excessively confrontational styles in their interviews with politicians.

On a different note, in May 1995 the then-Heritage Secretary
Stephen Dorrell published a governmental Green Paper containing proposals for the far-reaching reform of Britain's cross-media
ownership rules.

Each of these developments, and their implications for the
future of news and journalism in the UK, is addressed in this
second edition which, like the first, is intended to provide students, academics and interested lay readers with a thoroughgoing
overview of the issues facing the British journalism industry as it
approaches the next century.

*Brian McNair*
September 1995

# Preface to the first edition

In 1981, when I completed my undergraduate degree in sociology, academics who studied journalism were primarily occupied with what is sometimes referred to as 'the ideological role of the media' – the part journalists were presumed to play in the reproduction and reinforcement of power and class relations in contemporary capitalist societies. The content analyses of the Glasgow University Media Group; the work of Murdock, Golding and others on the political economy of journalism; the analyses of crime reporting in Hall *et al.*'s *Policing the Crisis* – all were studies of how journalism functioned as ideology.

In the 1990s this remains a valid concern, and the great deal of work which has been devoted to it in recent years is reviewed in Part I of this book. Today, however, the media which are described in those seminal studies have changed fundamentally, as have the political, technological, and commercial environments in which they must work. The *Bad News* books were written in what will quite possibly come to be seen as the 'golden age' of public service broadcasting – a time when the values of neutrality and impartiality in news output were sincerely held by both consumers and producers, and when broadcast journalism was protected by the 'comfortable duopoly'. Now, the BBC and commercial producers of television journalism must coexist in a harsher broadcasting marketplace, competing for viewers against new entrants to the business. Independent Television News, since its establishment the sole provider of news to the ITV network, now faces challenges from other suppliers. The BBC, having survived three election victories by Margaret Thatcher's Conservative Party, had successfully convinced the Major Government of the case for renewal of its Charter in 1996, but faced a still uncertain future in the deregulated, digitalised, multi-channel system of the twenty-first century.

As for the press, in the early 1980s they were in a state of financial crisis, shackled (or so proprietors claimed) by overbearing unions hellbent on enforcing rigid restrictive practices. Electronic printing was still a technology of the future, and Fleet Street was still the centre of the British newspaper industry. Now the titles are dispersed, the unions vanquished, and newsrooms automated with huge consequences for the British press, at both national and regional level.

In the sphere of radio, new stations are being established across the country. Community radio has become a reality, as have national commercial networks, all broadcasting news. Like ITN, Independent Radio News must cope in the late 1990s and beyond with challenges to its traditional position as sole supplier.

This book is an attempt to describe these changes; to take stock of what the British news and information media have come through in the 1980s; what they are likely to become in the late 1990s; and the relationship between the two. It seeks to identify the most important issues and challenges for British journalism in the years ahead. What kind of journalism is the British audience likely to receive in the future? Will the arrival of Sky News, Cable Network News, and the other new providers of broadcast journalism force changes in the style and content of the existing terrestrial producers? If so, will they be negative changes, as feared by those who have long warned against the allegedly corrupting influence of Rupert Murdoch and American-style 'infotainment'? Or will the arrival of 24-hour dedicated television news channels lead to an increase in the quality, as well as the quantity, of journalism which is available to the British viewer?

Concerns have been expressed that in the new environment brought into being by the reformed system for awarding Channel 3 licences investigative journalism will be one of the first casualties of the pressures on ratings that will inevitably come to the fore. Are such fears justified, or are they merely the knee-jerk reaction of those who see their positions and commissions threatened?

In the newspaper industry, will the decline of trade union power and the introduction of new printing technologies lead to expansion, and with it more choice and diversity for the consumer? Chapter 7 assesses the debate between those, such as Cento Veljanovksi (1990), who believe that it already has, and those, more pessimistic, who assert that the economic fundamentals of the British press remain as they have always been – weighted in favour of existing, established proprietors.

In January 1991 the Conservative Government established a new body, the Press Complaints Commission, under the chairmanship of Lord McGregor of Durris, to monitor and regulate newspapers in matters of ethics. The PCC was the outcome of mounting public concern in the 1980s about the increasingly intrusive activities of the British press, and the tabloids in particular. Would the PCC succeed in restraining the tabloids, thus forestalling threatened legislation on privacy? Or would laws relating to the protection of privacy eventually be introduced, presenting, in the view of some, unacceptable risks to press freedom? What impact would the 'hot tabloid summer' of 1992, with its feast of Royal affairs, political resignations, and bugging scandals, have on the debate?

These are just some of the questions asked in the pages which follow. In attempting to provide answers to them, use has been made not only of the media scholar's familiar tools of analysis and informed speculation, but also of the views and assessments of those who are professionally involved with the news industries. In the past, it is fair to say, there has been little love lost between students of the media and those who work in them, a fact displayed most dramatically in the feud which developed between the Glasgow University Media Group and the public service broadcasters after the publication of the *Bad News* books. Although many journalists identified with the critique of impartiality contained in the GUMG's work, the BBC and ITN as organisations sullenly refused to cooperate with their authors for years afterwards. In part this was due to the sensitivity of the broadcasters, and their eagerness to defend the hallowed notions of impartiality and balance against anyone who might present a credible challenge to them. But it is also true that many in the academic community tended to display an excessive theoreticism, combined with a reluctance to engage media professionals in debate, preferring instead to rely on an instrumentalist view of the capitalist state and the media's role within it. The GUMG were certainly not the worst offenders in this respect but the reception their impeccably researched and presented findings met with suggests the depth of the hostility which many media workers felt towards all academics.

Relations between academics and media practitioners improved immensely in the 1980s, as the angry young men and women of the previous decade matured into professors and contract researchers and, more importantly, as the old certainties of both journalist and academic broke down under the assault of the radical right. Where before the concern of scholars had been to 'prove' the complicity of, for example, television news – and the public service system in general – in the reproduction of an unequal and exploitative society, in the 1980s it came to be seen as important that the public service ethos be *defended* against those who would happily have abandoned it in favour of deregulated, commercialised broadcasting.

In this sense there was a coming together of the academic and professional agendas in the 1980s. This book represents a conscious effort to contribute to and reinforce that trend; to assist in the cross-fertilisation of ideas and solutions between the worlds of the media professional and the student (increasingly, in any case, today's students of media are tomorrow's journalists and editors); to bring the professional experience of the practitioner and media manager to bear on the more insular process of analysis; and to encourage those who work in the media to absorb and use the analysts' findings.

As a textbook it aims to bring together, within one volume, sociological and professional perspectives on journalism studies, in the sincere belief that one may complement the other. The student will find here neither another manual on how to be a good journalist (many excellent books of this kind already exist) nor detailed textual analyses of the form and content of British journalism (Hartley's *Understanding News* continues to be useful in this respect), but an overview of the sociological, political, regulatory, and financial frameworks within which British journalism will be pursued in the late 1990s and beyond.

The first part of the book begins with a description of the British journalism industry as it was at the time of writing, and a review of the current state of knowledge on the social role of journalism. Chapter 2 investigates the origins of the central journalistic ethic of objectivity, and describes the efforts which have been made over the years to challenge it. Chapter 3 turns to the question of how news – objective or otherwise – is made, presenting a discussion of current academic debates in the sociology of journalism and its production. These chapters represent, as it were, 'the view from the Academy' – a summary of the fruits of the extensive research and analysis which have been done in the field of journalism by British and other scholars.

Part II turns to the professional agenda, and the challenges faced by British broadcasting and press journalism, at the national, international, and local levels. These six chapters, which form the bulk of the book, could not have been written in their present form without the cooperation of the many journalists, editors, and managers currently working in the British media who gave freely of their time. I gratefully acknowledge their help, and trust that they will feel their views to have been fairly and accurately represented here. I have highlighted their statements, often in the form of quotation rather than paraphrase or summation, in the belief that for the reader there is much to be gained in 'hearing it from the horse's mouth', to abuse a metaphor. Unless otherwise indicated, all statements attributed to media professionals were obtained by the author in the course of interviews.

Financial assistance to carry out the interviews was generously provided by the Carnegie Trust for the Universities of Scotland, and the British Academy.

Colleagues at the Film and Media Studies Department of the University of Stirling provided a supportive and calming environment during some difficult times. To Nancy, Philip, Peter, Dan, Mike, John, Richard, Tim, Kay and Suzy, I express my sincere gratitude.

And finally, to the class of 92, who were subjected to much of the book in its earliest drafts, thanks for your attention.

*Brian McNair*
January 1993

# Part I

# The view from the Academy

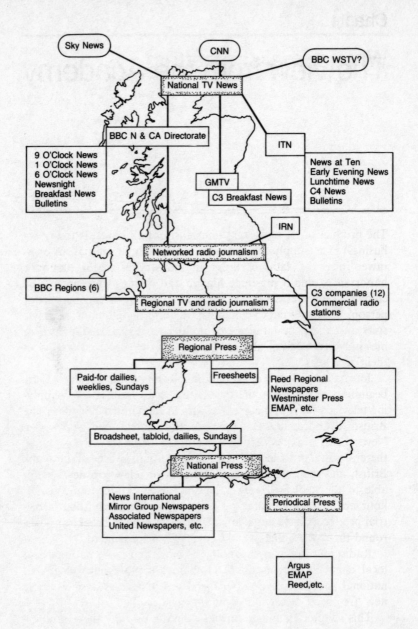

*Figure 1* A news map of the United Kingdom

# Chapter 1

# Why journalism matters

The production of news, and journalism of all kinds, is today big business. The supply of information (whether as journalism or as rawer forms of data) occupies an industry of major economic importance, employing huge human and financial resources, and enjoying high status. Across the world, top newsreaders, anchor persons, and newspaper columnists acquire the glamour of movie stars and exert the influence of politicians. Broadcasting companies judge themselves, and are judged, by the perceived quality of their news services.

Journalism is also an expanding business. In Britain at the beginning of the 1980s there were just two organisations supplying televised news and current affairs to the United Kingdom: the British Broadcasting Corporation and Independent Television News. Each provided around two hours of news per day. Now, there are five providers of television journalism accessible to the British audience. The number of hours of television news available to the dedicated viewer has increased exponentially as 24-hour channels have come on air, and as the established terrestrial producers have augmented their services with breakfast news, round-the-clock bulletins, and coverage of Parliament.

Radio journalism is expanding as more and more national and local channels are set up. And there are more newspapers, at national and local level, than there were ten years ago. A whole new 'freesheet' sector has come into being.

This chapter examines current thinking on how these proliferating journalistic media might affect individuals and social processes. Most of us assume that journalism matters, but does it really, and if so, in what ways? We begin, however, with a description of the British journalism industry: the types and structures of organisations which provide us with journalistic information; who owns them; the extent of their reach and the size of their audiences. In this way we can draw a 'news map' of the United Kingdom (see Figure 1), beginning with the most popular and pervasive medium, television.

## TELEVISION

The earliest provider of television journalism in the United Kingdom, the British Broadcasting Corporation, began life in 1922 as the Broadcasting Company. Originally a cartel of radio manufacturers, the Broadcasting Company was financed by a licence fee, and by a share of the royalties on the sale of radio receivers. The Broadcasting Company was nationalised and became the British Broadcasting Corporation in 1926, from which time it was licensed to serve as 'a cultural, moral and educative force for the improvement of knowledge, taste and manners' (Scannell and Cardiff, 1991, p.8).

Operating under the provisions of a Royal Charter, the BBC was constituted as a 'public service', funded by public taxation. It will continue to play this role until at least 1996, when the Royal Charter comes up for renewal.

From the outset the BBC interpreted its public service role to mean that it should be a major provider of information to the British people, devoting a large proportion of its resources to news and current affairs broadcasting, first on radio, and then on two channels of television. Today, about 17% of the BBC's network television output is devoted to news and current affairs. In 1990–1 BBC1 devoted 1,164 hours to news and current affairs, and 992 to the broader category of 'current affairs, features, and documentaries'. For BBC2 the figures were 268 and 1,384 hours respectively. The Directorate of News and Current Affairs – the department responsible for BBC journalism – had a budget in 1991 of £130 million (about 24% of total TV costs).[1]

Until 1955 the BBC had a monopoly on British television news. That year a commercial network was launched, producing its own news and current affairs. The independent television (ITV) companies shared out the making of current affairs and documentary programmes, while their news was provided by

Independent Television News (ITN). ITN was to be owned collectively by all the ITV companies, and run on a non-profit-making basis to supply them with news bulletins. This it did very successfully, winning the contract to provide Channel 4 with news when it came on the air in 1981. By 1988 ITN employed more than a thousand people to produce over twenty-five hours of news per week (Dunnett, 1990, p.132).

The bulk of the BBC's news and current affairs, and all of ITN's, is produced in London and networked throughout the UK. But both the BBC and ITV also provide regional news services. Since the merger of Yorkshire TV and Tyne Tees TV in 1992 there are twelve ITV companies covering the country, each with its own locally produced magazine, news bulletins, and current affairs output. In making their licence applications, the results of which were announced in October 1991, each company's 'bid' placed great emphasis on the continuing importance of regional television journalism, and made a clear commitment to provide it in the 1990s. Scottish Television, for example, one of the few companies for whom there was no competition in the bidding process, pledged itself to increase local news provision from its current level of 200 hours per annum to 370.[2]

The BBC also has regional branches producing television news and current affairs. In 1992 BBC South East and South West merged into one news and current affairs operation, BBC South, leaving the BBC with nine regional news centres in all.

From 1985 British terrestrial television had a third provider of journalism, TV-am, licensed to provide a breakfast service for the ITV network. TV-am comprised a consortium of banking and media interests headed by the former chief of Australia's Channel 9, Bruce Gyngell.

To compete with the arrival of TV-am, the BBC launched its own breakfast news TV service, as did Channel 4 with its *Channel 4 Daily*. In October 1991, TV-am lost its breakfast television franchise to the rival 'Sunrise' consortium – a group of media interests which included the Guardian and Manchester Evening News group, STV, and the Disney corporation. The new service began broadcasting on January 1, 1993, under the name Good Morning TV (GMTV).

In 1989 Rupert Murdoch's News Corporation launched Sky

News, Britain's first 24-hour television news channel, as part of its Sky Television service, transmitting from the Astra satellite. Sky News brought the number of UK national news providers to four. For a brief period of some six months there was another satellite provider of news – British Satellite Broadcasting – which launched fourteen months after Sky on the DBS system. Between April and October 1990 BSB and Sky fought an expensive battle for subscribers to their two completely incompatible systems, losing an estimated £1.25 billion between them. Neither Rupert Murdoch nor the consortium which owned BSB could sustain such losses for very long, and at the end of October 1990 it was announced that the two satellite networks would merge to form BSkyB, 50% of which would be owned by News Corporation, 16% by Pearson, 12% by Granada Television, and 3.7% by Reed International.[3]

Although Sky News has been, as we shall see, a critical success (perhaps surprisingly, given the widespread contempt in which the media establishment has held Rupert Murdoch's tabloid newspapers), in 1991 it was still suffering from the relatively slow take-up of satellite television by the British population, and the failure of cable to penetrate the British media market to any significant degree. Had it not been for the safety net provided by Murdoch's immensely profitable newspaper interests, Sky News's ongoing losses would, in the view of many industry observers, have been unsustainable. As this book went to press, however, BSkyB appeared to have entered a healthier phase, and with it Sky News. At the beginning of 1992 the *Observer* reported that the company was on the verge of profitability, with 100,000 dishes per month being sold, and 2.8 million homes by then being reached in the UK.[4]

Sky News was Britain's first domestically produced 24-hour television news service, but the US-produced Cable Network News, owned by American entrepreneur Ted Turner, has been available for a number of years to those with the appropriate receiving technology. Despite the global impact made by CNN with its coverage of the Gulf War, its audience in the UK remains small. In April 1992, however, CNN joined Sky News on the Astra satellite, thus gaining access to a potential market of some eight million homes, and signalling its determination to become a serious force in British television news. Also trying to break into the international television news market is the BBC's World Service. In November 1991, after years of planning, the World Service launched a global satellite television service – World Service Television News (WSTN) – which aimed to do for the global TV audience what the World Service has traditionally done for radio listeners. Moreover, the BBC hoped to make this service the base for its own 24-hour domestic TV news channel, which would compete with Sky News and CNN for the British audience.

Before leaving television, we should note the increasing importance of the electronic news and information services, Ceefax (produced by the BBC) and Oracle (its commercial rival). These are in effect subscription services, which enable the owners of specially adapted (and accordingly priced) television receivers to access 'teletext' data about everything from current events to transport timetables and recipes. Although the view of some observers that teletext services function as 'electronic newspapers' and will eventually make redundant the more familiar paper-and-ink variety is perhaps premature, they are of increasing importance as information sources, not least to the journalism industry itself. It has been estimated that some six million people use Oracle alone each day.[5]

Until 1992 Oracle was produced by ITN in London. In May of that year the licence was lost to Teletext UK, a consortium led by Associated Newspapers and Philips Electronics.

Taking all the above together, we can reasonably argue that television journalism in the United Kingdom was in a state of considerable health as it entered the 1990s. News, current affairs, and related information services had expanded both latitudinally, with new providers such as TV-am (and its successor GMTV), Sky News, and CNN coming into the market; and longitudinally, with the time devoted to journalism on television increasing relentlessly. On an average weekday in 1992 the BBC produced some six hours of news and current affairs, ITN about four. Viewers had access to another hour or so of local coverage, while those with Astra dishes or cable could watch the news for 24 hours per day, every day, if they wished.

## RADIO

Despite the expansion of television, radio has retained its share of the British audience and, in the commercial sector, of advertising revenues. Indeed, like television, radio has entered a period of expansion. *Broadcast* magazine reported in April 1992 that 'since 1986, radio listening has risen steadily as more stations have gone on air: from a low of eight hours forty minutes a week in 1986 it has increased to ten hours 26 minutes'.[6]

The dominant force in British radio journalism remains by far the BBC, which broadcasts some 4,000 hours per annum of national news, current affairs, and documentary features across its five channels – some 30% of its total radio output.[7] In addition, regional stations like Radio Scotland and Radio Ulster broadcast substantial quantities of their own news and current affairs output. The BBC also produces radio journalism, through the World Service, for an estimated global audience of 120 million people, with a 1992 budget of £143 million.[8]

At home, the BBC management in 1992 announced its intention to  establish by April 1994 a 24-hour 'rolling' news service on network radio.[9] 'Radio 5 Live' is now firmly established.

The supply of news to the commercial radio stations has traditionally been undertaken by Independent Radio News, the major part of which was until October 1992 owned by the Crown Communications Group. That month IRN merged with ITN and moved into the latter's headquarters in London's Gray's Inn Road. From here, a networked service of hourly news bulletins is transmitted to commercial companies across the country.

As a result of the 1990 Broadcasting Act dozens of small community stations on the one hand, and several new national channels on the other, have come into being, broadcasting news services as part of their programming. IRN continues to supply these stations, but has now been joined by rival providers, such as National Network News and Europe FM. The larger (and richer) local stations, such as Radio Clyde in Glasgow, produce a large proportion of their own news and current affairs.

## THE NATIONAL PRESS

If the story of British broadcast journalism in recent years is one of expansion, the state of the print industry is less clear. In the United Kingdom as of August 1995 there were thirteen national daily newspapers with a combined circulation of over 14 million (see Table 1.1). The largest circulations were achieved by the tabloids, with the *Sun* enjoying a significant lead over the *Daily Mirror/Daily Record*, and the *Daily Mail* and *Daily Express* coming a long way behind in third and fourth places (the death of Robert Maxwell in November 1991 had, of course, introduced a note of uncertainty over the Mirror Group's future). The fifth most popular newspaper was a broadsheet, or 'quality' paper – the *Daily Telegraph* – the only daily broadsheet with a circulation above 500,000.

Tabloids also dominated the Sunday market. Of ten national Sunday newspapers available to the British reader the five most popular in terms of sales were tabloids.

The 1995 figures provide only a snapshot of the national newspaper market as it was during the six-month period of January–June that year. Over the five-year period between 1988 and 1992 there was a consistent decline in the circulation of British newspapers, particularly those popular tabloid titles, like the *Sun* and the *Daily Star*, which operate at the more sensationalist end of the market. The figures for 1993–5 show that the decline is continuing for most titles, to a greater or lesser degree. Exceptions to the trend are the News International and Hollinger titles, which have also been the fiercest competitors in the newspaper price war which began in July 1993 (see Chapter 7).

Ownership of the British national press is concentrated in the hands of ten publishing organisations (see Table 1.2). The largest, News International, is owned by Rupert Murdoch, whose three daily and two Sunday newspapers account for 37% and 39% of total circulation respectively.

The Mirror Group, formerly owned by the late Robert Maxwell and now administered by a consortium of banks and other financial institutions, accounts for a further 23% and 30% of daily and Sunday circulation respectively. In November 1992 Mirror Group Newspapers announced the appointment as chief

Table 1.1 Circulation of British national newspapers, 1991–5* (000s)

| | 1991 | 1992 | 1993 | 1994 | 1995 |
|---|---|---|---|---|---|
| **Dailies (tabloid)** | | | | | |
| *Daily Express* | 1565 | 1538 | 1497 | 1367 | 1279 |
| *Daily Mail* | 1720 | 1689 | 1775 | 1794 | 1787 |
| *Daily Mirror/Daily Record* | 3719 | 3622 | 3435 | 3230 | 3266 |
| *Star* | 879 | 808 | 773 | 747 | 738 |
| *Sun* | 3693 | 3588 | 3517 | 4071 | 4080 |
| *Today*** | 490 | 495 | 538 | 587 | 566 |
| **Dailies (broadsheet)** | | | | | |
| *Daily Telegraph* | 1075 | 1044 | 1025 | 1080 | 1066 |
| *Financial Times* | 289 | 292 | 290 | 297 | 294 |
| *Guardian* | 431 | 418 | 416 | 403 | 400 |
| *Times* | 406 | 377 | 366 | 485 | 647 |
| *Independent* | 394 | 390 | 290 | 297 | 294 |
| **Sundays (tabloid)** | | | | | |
| *Mail on Sunday* | 1940 | 1960 | 2030 | 1984 | 1959 |
| *News of the World* | 4808 | 4725 | 4620 | 4774 | 4744 |
| *Sunday Express* | 1623 | 1692 | 1727 | 1563 | 1403 |
| *Sunday Mirror* | 2806 | 2768 | 2674 | 2567 | 2559 |
| *Sunday People* | 2338 | 2130 | 2032 | 2012 | 2068 |
| **Sundays (broadsheet)** | | | | | |
| *Observer* | 579 | 541 | 513 | 501 | 464 |
| *Sunday Telegraph* | 576 | 562 | 531 | 625 | 692 |
| *Sunday Times* | 1177 | 1203 | 1218 | 1221 | 1253 |
| *Sunday Independent* | 385 | 385 | 385 | 335 | 327 |

*Source:* Audit Bureau of Circulation
*Averages for January–June in each year.
**Closed in late 1995.

Table 1.2  Major proprietors and share of national newspaper
circulation (%)*

|  | Daily | Sunday |
|---|---|---|
| News International (*Sun, Today, Times, Sunday Times, News of the World*) | 36.7 | 38.8 |
| MGN (*Daily Mirror/Record, People, Sunday People, Independent***) | 22.6 | 30.0 |
| United Newspapers (*Daily Express, Star, Sunday Express*) | 14.0 | 9.1 |
| Associated Newspapers (*Daily Mail, Mail on Sunday*) | 12.4 | 12.7 |
| Hollinger (*Daily Telegraph, Sunday Telegraph*) | 7.4 | 4.5 |
| Newspaper Publishing (*Independent on Sunday*) | – | 2.1 |
| Guardian and Manchester Evening News (*Guardian, Observer*) | 2.8 | 3.0 |
| Financial Times Ltd (*Financial Times*) | 2.0 | – |

*Source*: Audit Bureau of Circulation
*Calculated on average figures for January–June 1995.
**MGN holds a 43% share.

executive of former *Today* and *News of the World* editor David
Montgomery. This appointment heralded major changes in the
management of the Mirror Group titles, including new editors for
the *Daily Mirror* and *Sunday People*, redundancies, and changes
in employees' working practices. The objective of the changes was
to improve the Mirror Group's profits (which at the end of 1992
were considerably lower per employee than those News
International's management had achieved). By January 1994 this
had been achieved, with the share price having risen from £0.50
in October 1992 to £1.70. Pre-tax profits in the 1994 financial year
were a respectable £198 million, greatly assisting MGN in its
efforts to acquire control of the *Independent*.

Other major owners include United Newspapers plc (the *Express*
titles), Conrad Black's Hollinger group (the *Daily* and *Sunday
Telegraph*), Associated Newspapers (the *Daily Mail* and *Mail on
Sunday*), and David Sullivan's Apollo Ltd. Sullivan's reputation
and fortune were built upon the production of pornographic magazines and sex aids, but he now owns two national newspapers: the
*Daily Sport* and the *Sunday Sport*. By September 1992 he had also
launched a regional newspaper, the *Sunday News and Echo* (see
Chapter 9).

The *Guardian* remains 'independent' in so far as it is not owned by any of the afore-mentioned corporations, but by shareholders organised in such a way as to guarantee the editorial integrity of the paper. In 1991 the *Independent* and its sister publication, the *Independent on Sunday*, found themselves in such financial difficulties that they were required to modify their constitutions and allow foreign investors to purchase substantial stakes in the papers. In 1994, as already noted, control of the *Independent* passed to new owners, prominent among them Mirror Group Newspapers.

The *Morning Star* (formerly the paper of the Communist Party of Great Britain) struggles on in the post-communist world, owned by its readers and relying upon them for funds to sustain its print run of about 10,000 copies. In the new·political environment of the 1990s, and without the subsidies once provided by the Soviet Communist Party, its long-term survival must be in doubt.

## THE REGIONAL PRESS

For the regional press, like broadcasting, the 1980s and early 1990s were a period of expansion, particularly in the market for small, community-based papers funded entirely from advertising revenue – the 'freesheets'. There are now dozens of companies publishing hundreds of these newspapers across the country. Although their main function is to advertise local businesses and services, most contain a certain amount of local news with which to attract the attention of potential readers, and so can legitimately be included in any discussion of British journalism.

In addition to the freesheets, of course, there are hundreds of paid-for newspapers being produced outside London, ranging from the large circulation Scottish titles such as the *Daily Record* and *Sunday Mail*, the *Herald* and the *Scotsman*, to smaller circulation titles targeted on small towns and rural communities. To the Scots, of course, these newspapers are not 'regional' but 'national', as is *Wales on Sunday* to the Welsh, and the *Belfast Telegraph* to the Northern Irish. For the purposes of this book, however, all newspaper production outside London will be discussed within the context of regional journalism (see Chapter 9).

Like the national press, ownership and control of the regional newspaper industry in Britain is concentrated in the hands of a small number of companies, predominant among them Reed Regional Newspapers (RRN), the Yellow Advertiser Group, East Midlands Allied Press (EMAP), and Westminster Press. Some national proprietors are also significant owners at regional level, such as Associated Newspapers, United Newspapers, and the Guardian and Manchester Evening News group. Until 1995 Thomson Regional Newspapers was a major regional proprietor. In July that year, however, the parent Thomson Corporation announced that it was selling its British newspaper interests, in order to raise investment capital. The English and Irish TRN titles were taken on by Trinity International Holdings, the Scottish titles by the enigmatic Barclay brothers (the *Scotsman*) and Associated Newspapers (the *Aberdeen Press and Journal*).

## THE PERIODICAL PRESS

No overview of the British print media would be complete without some reference to the periodical sector: those weekly, fortnightly, and monthly publications which straddle the boundaries between journalism, leisure, entertainment, and business. Some periodicals, like *Private Eye* and the *Economist* (both among the most successful publications in the country, if measured by circulation and advertising revenue), have a clearly journalistic emphasis. The satirical *Private Eye*, in particular, has investigated and uncovered many political and business scandals in its relatively brief life, which have subsequently gone on to make the mainstream news agenda. The *Economist*, as its name suggests, provides background, analysis, and commentary on the domestic and international economic situation.

The great majority of periodicals, however, operates in what the Audit Bureau of Circulation calls the 'specialist consumer and business markets'. This includes such titles as *Exchange and Mart* and *What Car?*, dedicated to providing practical information for buyers and sellers of goods and services; magazines such as *House and Garden* and *Good Housekeeping*, containing ideas for DIY and home decoration enthusiasts; the *Face* and *i-D*, which cover style in clothes, music, and popular culture; listings and review magazines, like *Radio Times* and *Sight and Sound*; *Cosmopolitan* and *Woman's Own*, addressing the female audience; and *Management Today*, which attempts to keep professional managers informed of issues relevant to them.

In June 1995 there were nearly 3,000 periodical titles being published in the United Kingdom, with 389 titles launched in the first half of 1994 alone, indicating that periodicals comprise a relatively healthy segment of the print industry as a whole (see Table 1.3). Ownership of periodicals is concentrated, like that of national and regional newspapers, in large companies such as Argus, EMAP, and Reed but the sector is one in which many relatively small, independent companies are thriving. Some, like Pressdram, which publishes *Private Eye*, are well established. Others, such as those in the rapidly expanding computer magazines market (Future Publishing, for example) are recent entrants who have exploited the changing technology and economics of publishing ushered in by the 'Wapping revolution' (see Chapter 7).

## THE 1995 GREEN PAPER

In May 1995 the then-Heritage Secretary Stephen Dorrell published a governmental Green Paper on the future of media cross-ownership in Britain.[10] As reported in the *UK Press Gazette*, 'the Government believes that the media's ability to influence opinion and engender political debate means it cannot be left purely to market forces'.[11] The essence of the proposals, which will be sub-

Table 1.3 Top ten UK periodicals by circulation

| Title | Publisher | Circulation |
|---|---|---|
| *Reader's Digest* | Reader's Digest Association | 1,784,733 |
| *What's On TV* | IPC | 1,651,507 |
| *Take a Break* | Bauer | 1,505,069 |
| *Radio Times* | BBC Enterprises | 1,441,280 |
| *TV Times* | IPC | 998,378 |
| *Bella* | Bauer | 991,300 |
| *Woman's Weekly* | IPC | 785,604 |
| *Woman* | IPC | 769,364 |
| *Woman's Own* | IPC | 757,569 |
| *TV Quick* | Bauer | 713,644 |

*Source*: *Media Week*, September 23, 1995; Audit Bureau of Circulation.

ject to extensive consultation lasting some years, was to treat the UK media market as a whole, reflecting its increasingly inter-dependent nature. Rather than inhibiting ownership across media sectors, as at present, the proposed new system would limit proprietors to 10% of the total UK media market, 20% of any regional market (Scotland, Wales, Northern Ireland, and the English regions), and 20% of each media sector. Exceptions to these limits would be allowed only in the public interest.

Clearly, were such legislation eventually to make its way on to the statute book, the implications for most current proprietors would be significant. Rupert Murdoch, for example, would have to relinquish some of his national newspapers, while being allowed to buy up to 20% of the television sector. The same would be true for the Mirror Group.

The consultation process would be completed, and the new rules implemented, it was predicted, by 1997.

## JOURNALISM'S SOCIAL ROLE

The journalism industry, taken as a whole, is a dynamic, growing sector of the economy in Britain, as in every other advanced capitalist society. For that reason alone, it would be worthy of close study. Journalism, however, is not just of economic import-ance, but arguably one of the key social and cultural forces in our society. In Britain, 80% of adults read at least one national newspaper, while 75% read a Sunday. A 1990 survey established that TV and newspapers come ahead of friends, family, politicians or other sources of information when it comes to influencing opinion, and that television journalism in particular is the main source of people's information about the world. Twenty-four cat-egories of public issue were mentioned to respondents, and 'tele-vision news was shown to have the greatest influence among the largest number of people. And when it wasn't first as an influence it came second or third.'[12] 'On average', writes Barrie Gunter, 'around two thirds of the mass public of modern industrialised societies claim that television is their main source of national and international news' (1987, p.7).

However, if it is true that audiences, when asked, tend to cite TV as the most important journalistic medium, much evidence now exists to suggest that its centrality as an information source has been exaggerated. Robinson and Levy describe as a 'myth' the belief, based largely on public opinion data, 'that the public receives most of its information from television' (1986, p.15). While viewers may *believe* that they do so, and repeat this belief to researchers, a number of studies has shown that the efficacy of television as an information source is limited by its very nature as a medium. Televised information, and news in particular, is characteristically 'thin' in content. Many more 'bits' of information can be contained on the front page of a broadsheet newspaper than can be broadcast in a twenty-minute TV news bulletin. Furthermore, television viewing may be (though need not necessarily be in every case) a relatively passive experience – a 'domestic ritual', to use Morley's phrase (1990, p.126), carried out in parallel with other activities such as talking, eating, and reading. Gunter notes that television journalism 'constantly introduces new material before the viewer has been given a chance to grasp properly the visual and auditory material that has just been presented' (1987, p.47). He argues further that TV viewers do not have especially high levels of recall or comprehension of the news stories to which they have been exposed and that 'the largest gains in news information are associated with newspaper usage' (ibid.).

Some research has suggested that interpersonal communication may be just as important to an individual's absorption of information as exposure to any mass medium, be it TV, radio, or the press. Robinson and Levy do not deny that 'the public may be made aware of news stories more quickly from television, but [research] suggests that subsequent exposure, by reading in newspapers or magazines, or by interpersonal discussion may be required for the point of those news stories to make a lasting impression on the viewers' memory' (1986, p.130).

The question of the efficacy of individual media as information sources is one which may be resolved in time by audience research in media studies and social psychology (although the difficulties associated with empirical surveys of this type should warn us against expecting an answer in the very near future). Of equal, if not greater importance is the broader issue of the effects of what the information media communicate on individuals and on society. What is the relationship between the products of journalism and wider social processes? If modern journalism's purpose is to supply information to a mass audience (leaving aside for a moment the extent to which that information is comprehended) what social significance does this information have?

At the simplest level, journalism presents us with an ongoing narrative about the world beyond our immediate experience. This narrative is asserted to be 'true'. The stories told us by journalists are factual, rather than fictional. For this reason, journalism performs a unique and essential social function. For most of us, most of the time, journalists are the main source of our information about the world beyond our own immediate environment. We may, on occasion, be participants in events that become the subject matter of journalism – in which case we may be better informed than any journalist about the event concerned – but this is exceptional (and most people would rather not be). Journalism, consequently, is often said to be our 'window on the world'; our means of contact with a world which, though shrinking, is still largely beyond our direct, personal experience. It provides the information from which we draw our 'cognitive maps' of reality.

Beyond this basic social function, journalism is said to perform an important political role in liberal pluralist societies, feeding and sustaining the democratic process by supplying citizens with the information which they require to make rational electoral and economic choices. Journalism, according to this viewpoint, underpins democratic institutions by keeping voters informed about the things they need to know. The task of journalism is 'to make information publicly available' (Bruhn-Jensen, 1986, p.31), this being 'one basic ingredient of the public sphere . . . required for public participation in discussion and decisions'.

This view of journalism's social role as essentially benevolent is underpinned by the 'uses and gratifications' approach to media effects, which asserts that the media in general have only a limited impact on the audience, who 'use' their content to 'gratify' particular needs, such as 'surveillance of the environment'. News is used for information purposes, but does not have significant power to tell us what to think. Its social impact, in this sense, is benign.

A more complex analysis, but one which shares the basic optimism of the 'uses and gratifications' approach is provided by the advocates of journalism's 'agenda-setting' role. Agenda-setting asserts 'a direct, causal relationship between the [journalistic] content of the media agenda and subsequent public perception of what the important issues of the day are. This is an assertion of direct learning by members of the public from the media agenda' (McCombs, 1981, p.211). The basic hypothesis of this approach is that 'through their routine structuring of social and political reality, the news media influence the agenda of public issues around which political campaigns and voter decisions are organised' (ibid.). In the agenda-setting hypothesis, journalistic news values act as a cue for the audience, alerting them to the importance of an issue, and encouraging them to place it on their personal agendas of important issues.[13]

The empirical evidence for this thesis is ambiguous, but since this is the case for all effects hypotheses, that is no reason to dismiss it. Denis McQuail notes that agenda-setting has the status of 'a plausible but unproven idea' (1987, p.276). Iyengar and Kinder are more confident, expressing strong support for agenda-setting on the basis of their own audience research (which applies only to American TV news). They assert that 'the verdict is clear and unequivocal . . . By attending to some problems and ignoring others, television news shapes the American public's political priorities' (1987, p.33).

## JOURNALISM AS SOCIAL REPRODUCTION

Approaches which assert an essentially benevolent social role for journalism, such as the theory of agenda-setting, are challenged by 'critical' theorists, who draw on Marxist and other analytical frameworks to argue that journalism's function is essentially one of social reproduction, in the service not of society as a whole, but of its dominant groups and classes. From this perspective the information media are viewed, like other cultural institutions in a class society, as producers of ideology, representing the interests of an elite minority to the subordinate majority.

There are 'strong' and 'weak' variants of the social reproduction thesis, corresponding to wider disputes in materialist theory about the nature of ideology, the audience, and the communication process. The structuralists, for example, inspired by the work of Jacques Lacan, Louis Althusser and others, would argue that the linguistic structure of journalism 'positions' the audience in a subordinate position *vis à vis* the dominant class of capitalism. This 'interpellation of the subject' operates at the level of the unconscious so that the individual member of the audience is, practically speaking, powerless to resist the ideological message. As Van Dijk puts it, 'the structures of news reports at many levels condition the readers to develop [dominant] interpretative frameworks rather than alternative ones' (1988, p.182). Ideology, to put it another way, is 'produced' in language, at the level of the unconscious.

The 'dominant ideology' thesis as expressed in these terms has come under some attack in recent years. On the one hand, it is argued that the hypothesis is primitive, underpinned by a mechanistic model of effects which has long been discredited. Paddy Scannell observes that 'for all its seeming sophistication the Theory of Ideology says something very simple indeed; something not very different from what Leavis was saying in the 1930s: the media are harmful and the function of theoretical critique is to expose them in that light' (1989, p.158).

Another position asserts that there is no such thing as a 'dominant ideology' or a 'ruling class', but rather a constantly shifting alliance of classes and social strata, who *struggle* to dominate ideologically, but do not necessarily succeed. Even if there is a dominant ideology, those such as Umberto Eco in Italy and Stuart Hall in the UK draw upon the theoretical concepts of semiotics and the political sociology of Antonio Gramsci to emphasise the possibility of oppositional and aberrant decodings of journalistic messages on the part of the audience. They would accept that there can be a dominant ideological message present in journalism, but that no inevitability attaches to its being transmitted successfully to the audience. For this group of theorists, ideological struggle is a *hegemonic* process, to which journalism contributes by 'reproducing consensus about social order' (Ericson *et al.*, 1990, p.19). News organisations are said to play a strategic role in hegemonic struggle, functioning as 'a site of contest between competing social forces rather than as a conduit for ruling class ideas' (Curran, 1990, p.142).

For John Fiske journalism functions 'as discourse, that is, as a set of conventions that strive to control and limit the meanings of the events it conveys' (1987, p.282). Starting from the assumption that news, like all texts, is polysemic, i.e. contains a plurality of meanings, Fiske argues that the news text 'is engaged in a constant struggle to contain the multifarious events and their polysemic potential within its own conventions' (ibid., p.286). Journalists work, semiologically, to select aspects of the real world, then to present them in a narrative form which allows them to be made sense of but also prevents potentially disruptive readings of events being made by the audience. Journalism can thus be analysed in terms of the 'strategies of containment' which it deploys.

Regardless of the sophistication with which the social reproduction thesis is put, it is always based on the assertion that members of the audience obtain from journalism information which will tend to support an ideologically loaded view of the world; one which will contribute to the reproduction of an unequal and fundamentally antagonistic social system without dysfunctional conflict.

Given the immense methodological difficulties attached to such a project, it is perhaps no surprise that attempts to demonstrate empirically such 'ideological effects' have been few. Those studies which have been undertaken are contradictory and inconclusive. Guy Cumberbatch's study of audience perceptions of television news coverage of the 1984–5 miners' strike appeared to show that viewers were generally apathetic or resistant to the 'dominant' message of the news, in so far as that message could be deduced from content analysis (Cumberbatch *et al.*, 1986). More recently, Greg Philo's audience research has claimed to demonstrate the opposite: that 'while differences in political culture and class experience have important influences on the interpretation of events . . . the media are providing a major input of information which seems to relate very directly to the beliefs of some people' (1990, p.56).

The social reproduction thesis can at times veer close to the conspiratorial presuppositions of earlier 'mass society' theorists, who assigned to all media a direct and powerful role in the subjugation of the subordinate classes of capitalism. The Frankfurt School's most important idea, as Richard Collins puts it, was to view the mass media – and journalism – as 'a "consciousness industry" propagating a "one-dimensional", "affirmative" culture in which the contradictions and barbarisms of capitalism are prematurely and falsely harmonised' (1976, p.49). In this form, it is clearly overly simplistic for contemporary purposes. Variants of the social reproduction hypothesis remain influential, however, not only among Marxists, but feminists and others concerned with the sociology of culture.

## JOURNALISM AND THE SOCIAL CONSTRUCTION OF REALITY

A different approach to the social role of journalism asserts that it is not simply 'a vehicle for objective facts about remote events' but tells us 'something about the structure of the world' (Davies, 1990, p. 160). In particular, it constructs the world for us in terms of categories, such as 'normal' versus 'deviant', or 'militant' versus 'moderate', which are then used to exclude or marginalise certain types of social actors. An important sociological study informed by this perspective is Hall *et al.*'s *Policing the Crisis* (1978), which argues that news organisations do not merely report events, but are active agents in constructing the socio-political environment which frames those events in the public imagination. Journalists, as reporters of news, are at the same time *social actors*, with a key role to play in shaping our perception of what news is, and how to react to it. If a large proportion of news may be said to comprise the reporting of problematic social reality, then journalists contribute substantially to the process whereby 'problems' are defined.

Another exponent of this approach, Jock Young, suggests that journalism 'can create social problems, can present them dramatically and overwhelmingly, and most important, can do it suddenly. The media can very quickly and effectively fan public indignation and engineer what one might call a "moral panic" about a certain type of deviancy. Indeed, there is institutionalised into the media the need to create moral panics and issues which will seize the imagination of the public' (1971, p.37). This approach, used in conjunction with what is known as the 'deviancy amplification model' developed by sociology, views journalism as an active social institution, working alongside other institutions such as the legal system and judiciary to regulate and negotiate morality.

Examples of how journalism can lead to deviancy amplification have included the celebrated battles between Mods and Rockers which took place in the south of England in the 1960s; the 'mugging' scare of the 1970s; and, in the 1980s, football hooliganism, 'Acid House' parties, and satanic child abuse. In all of these cases the media did not simply report events, but contributed to their emergence as problems in the public arena.

## CONCLUSION

The effects issue is one of the most difficult and contentious in media studies, despite the vast resources and energies which have been expended in trying to resolve it. This is no less true for journalism than for any other category of media output. In the end, it can be stated with certainty only that journalism matters because we believe it to do so. Whether or not the news and information media do indeed have the power to set agendas for the public at large, to reproduce ideology, to create moral panics, or to influence what we think, the fact that politicians, trade unionists, and other social actors *think* that they do some or all of these things means that they increasingly tailor their 'performances' to suit what their public relations and media advisers tell them are the requirements of the journalists. In the contemporary world, public figures and organisations actively seek out the media, even if they cannot always guarantee that their coverage will be favourable. For Rodney Tiffen, this is the only thing that *really* matters. In his view, 'the impact of news [and journalism in general] must be sought in its effects on how political life is conducted, how news practices interact with political processes and outcomes' (1989, p.6). From this perspective, the important thing is not the effect of journalistic output on individual attitudes and ideas, but the effect of the widespread *perception* of journalism's importance on the social process as a whole.

The increasing importance of information media in the political process was illustrated during the Gulf War when the leaders of the opposing sides used the news media, and the access which it gave them to each other's populations, to communicate their diplomatic and military messages. The American news channel CNN functioned as surrogate diplomacy for allied and Iraqi leaders in a conflict which was lived, as it happened, not only by people in the firing lines in Israel, Baghdad, and Dahrain, but by millions in Europe, Asia, and America, through the medium of television.

In domestic politics, too, the ability to use and manipulate news media – to set agendas and shape debates with the aid of photo-opportunities, sound-bites, and professional image consultants – is now generally accepted as a prerequisite of success. Political parties and pressure groups compete with equal vigour to manage the news, because they believe that, for the majority of the audience, news and current affairs is the key point of contact with the political process. For this reason, if for no other, journalism undoubtedly matters.

# Chapter 2

# Journalism and the critique of objectivity

To understand contemporary journalism, in Britain and in other capitalist societies, one must first know something about the two concepts which have historically underpinned its organisation and production: *liberal pluralism*, and *objectivity*. This chapter discusses the origins of these concepts, and the criticisms which have been made of them.

## LIBERAL PLURALISM AND PRESS FREEDOM

The invention of printing – which represented the birth of mass communication, and was the precondition for the emergence of journalism as a media form – coincided with the upsurge of religious, political, and social strife which accompanied the late medieval period. Medieval societies were *autocratic*, in that they were dominated by an aristocracy and led by a monarchy with absolute power, in cooperation with the institutions of the Church. These institutions exercised strict control over politics, ideology, and culture, powers which were claimed to derive from the divine will of God. The class structure and the privileges which it conferred on the small minority were believed to be divinely ordained.

The authoritarianism of the late medieval state was reflected in its control of the media. In sixteenth-century England the state monopolised publishing and printing rights. All publications were strictly censored by Church and state. In 1529 the English crown published its first list of prohibited books. Books had long been suppressed on religious grounds, but Henry VIII and the Tudors 'worked on the principle that the peace of the realm demanded the suppression of all dissenting opinion' (Cranfield, 1978, p.2).

Concern for 'the peace of the realm' derived from the fact that around the beginning of the fourteenth century the feudal establishment began to be threatened by the rise of a new social class, whose wealth and claim to power derived not from 'God', but from trade, commerce, and production. This rising capitalist class or bourgeoisie was, by the time of the invention of printing in the sixteenth century, becoming an important political influence in England and other European societies.

'News', in the sense of the dissemination of information about events, was already a familiar concept, dating back at least as far as ancient Rome. In the fifteenth century public announcements about official occasions, public hangings, and witchcraft became commonplace. But as merchant capitalism developed, the supply of information became an essential element of the wealth-creation process. The emergence of 'news', and media to disseminate it, thus coincided not only with the invention of printing but with the development of capitalism.

News was not merely an aid to trade in a developing capitalist society, but an important political instrument. Siebert notes that 'in most countries of western Europe the interests of the developing commercial class required limitations on monarchial powers and on the special privileges of the nobility. Capitalistic enterprise was incompatible with medieval notions of status and security' (1956, p.42). The early news media served as a channel through which the rising capitalist class could articulate and express these interests. This was the context in which the world's first weekly newspaper in English – *Curanto* – was published in Amsterdam in June 1618. In England in 1622 a syndicate of publishers began to issue regular bulletins of internal and foreign news, known as *newsbooks*, described by Cranfield as 'a single sheet of small folio, printed in two columns, and bearing no title' (1978, p.2).

In response to the growing threat posed by the emerging bourgeoisie and its embryonic information media, the authorities intensified their control over the printed word. On October 17, 1632, a decree of the Star Chamber in London (one of the most important institutions for the suppression of opponents of the status quo) banned the publication of all newspapers and pamphlets. In 1637 another decree limited to twenty the number of newspapers allowed to be published in London.

Notwithstanding these authoritarian measures the newsbooks survived by being circulated and read through informal networks, such as London's coffee house culture. The bourgeoisie, meanwhile, was increasing its economic strength *vis à vis* the aristocracy, developing and articulating further the ideological legitimation for its own political power. Enlightenment philosophers such as John Locke engaged in a philosophical critique of absolutism. The doctrine of divine right was incompatible with the rise of the bourgeoisie, which had to be 'free' from feudal authority. From this basic drive for power developed the political theory of liberalism and the bourgeois ideological concept of freedom: *economic freedom, political freedom*, and *intellectual freedom*, advanced in opposition to medieval absolutism as the precondition for the ascendancy of the bourgeoisie as a ruling class (McNair, 1995).

John Milton articulated the concept of press freedom as early as 1644, and pioneered the concept of 'the open market of ideas', which played an important part in the rise of bourgeois economic and political power. This was the revolutionary ideology of a radical, progressive class fighting against a declining absolutist and authoritarian order. Applied to the media, liberal and Enlightenment principles meant, primarily, that the sole guarantee of the victory of reason and truth in the public sphere was the free competition of ideas and opinions between diverse viewpoints; and that only by the flourishing and encouragement of such intellectual diversity could the truth emerge.

These principles remain fundamental to the working of liberal democratic societies. Tolerance and diversity continue to be regarded as essential for servicing a democratic political system, since such a system depends on rational choice; for enlightening and informing the public, who make the choices; and for allowing the media to stand as a Fourth Estate over government, thus preventing dictatorship. As Altschull expresses it, 'in a democracy, it is the people who rule. The voice of the people is heard in the voting booth. The decisions made by the people in the voting booths are based on the information made available to them. That information is provided primarily by the news media. Hence, the news media are indispensable to the survival of democracy' (1984, p.19).[1] John Keane argues that 'the call for press freedom is a distinctive organising principle of the modern European and

North American worlds . . . the theory and practice of publicly
articulating opinions through media of communication developed
endogenously in no other civilization' (1991, p.7). It arose most
vociferously in western Europe because it was here that the
'feudal components of the medieval *corpus politicum* relin-
quished their struggle against state builders only gradually and
unwillingly' (ibid.).

## OBJECTIVITY

If the term 'liberal pluralism' has defined the political environment within which journalism in advanced capitalist societies has
been practised, the concept of objectivity has become the key professional ethic; the standard to which all journalists should aspire.
Gaye Tuchman calls it a 'strategic ritual' (1972, p.661), which
mobilises the society-wide credibility and legitimacy sought after
by the journalistic profession. It is routinely 'used by journalists
in warding off charges of bias or distortion, or other criticisms'
(Schiller, 1981, p.3).

The concept of 'objectivity' is premised on the assertion that 'a
person's statements about the world can be trusted if they are
submitted to established rules deemed legitimate by a professional community' (Schudson, 1978, p.7). The key assumption underlying the concept is that 'facts are assertions about the world open
to independent validation. They stand beyond the distorting influences of any individual's personal preferences. [By contrast,]
values are an individual's conscious or unconscious preferences
for what the world should be; they are . . . ultimately subjective
and so without legitimate claim on other people. The belief in
objectivity is a faith in facts, a distrust of "values", and a commitment to their segregation' (ibid., p.6).

Objectivity in this sense, as Michael Schudson points out, is
a relatively recent concept. In the early part of the nineteenth
century journalism was partisan, openly representing the interests
of 'political parties and men of commerce'. Even by the 1920s
'objectivity' 'was not a term journalists or critics of journalism
used' (ibid.).

The precise origins of 'objectivity' as a professional standard in
journalism remain a matter of contention. Some trace it back to

the emergence of telegraph agencies such as the Associated Press in the United States. These 'wire services' supplied information to many clients simultaneously, so that their information had to be perceived as ideologically neutral if it was to be acceptable to all. Others have argued that objectivity was connected in some way with the process of commodification of newspapers which took place in the 1800s. In America in the 1830s the expensive, partisan newspapers began to lose ground to what was called the 'penny press' (and what was sometimes called in Britain the 'pauper press') – a cheap, commercial press which set out to serve an expanding reading public. This public did not comprise wealthy 'men of commerce' but small traders and artisans – the emerging urban middle class.

To attract and keep this readership (thus to gain advertising revenue) newspapers began to report crime, human interest, and other categories of news which today's readers would recognise as 'modern'. Journalists became the spokesmen for what Schudson calls 'egalitarian ideals in politics, economics and social life [the ideals of their readers, by implication]. The penny papers expressed and built the culture of a democratic market society, a culture which had no place for social or intellectual deference' (ibid., p.60).

Dan Schiller argues that the penny press expressed the ideals of a small-tradesmen, republican public, threatened by the encroachment of big business. It reflected the views of its readers that 'knowledge, like property, should not be monopolised for exclusive use by private interests'. While the elite press was widely perceived to be subservient and partisan towards the dominant economic class, the penny press successfully claimed to speak for the public as a whole, 'giving all citizens an equal access to knowledge and direct personal knowledge of impartially presented news' (1981, p.48).

The impartiality and independence claimed by the penny press successfully ushered in its stewardship of the pursuit of enlightened reason in the public sphere . . . The pre-emptive claim staked by the cheap journals to the defence of natural rights and public good was . . . the enduring foundation upon which the structure of news objectivity was built.

(ibid., 1981, p.75)

Another foundation stone of journalistic objectivity was the acceptance, by the late nineteenth century, of positivist epistemology and photographic realism, 'both of which claimed to reflect the world without reference to human subjectivity and selectivity' (ibid., p.11). The nineteenth century witnessed rapid technological progress, accompanied in the realm of philosophy by the beliefs in rationalism, realism, positivism, and empiricism. These philosophies of science stressed the 'epistemological primacy of scientific knowledge' (ibid., p.87), and the possibility of an objective, 'knowable' universe. The social sciences, such as history, also adopted this view of the world, encouraging further 'a general cultural acceptance of a reportable, objective world' (ibid.).

To these developments in epistemology Schiller then adds the invention of photography, the remarkable ability of which 'to represent reality – to depict, apparently without human intervention, an entire world of referents – bolstered the apparently universal recognition of it as a supreme standard of accuracy and truth' (ibid., p.92). These were standards to which journalism could also aspire.

Taking all these developments together, journalists at the end of the nineteenth century were encouraged to assume the existence of a world 'out there' which could be appropriated, or known, through journalism, with accuracy. The assumption was 'not that the media are objective, but that there is a world out there to be objective about' (ibid., p.2). Journalists now 'presumed a world prior to all imposed values, and the periodic construction of accurate and universally recognisable copies of events in this world became the newspaper's fundamental business' (ibid., p.87).

This concept of objectivity was challenged in the 1920s and 1930s by the emergence of fascist dictatorships, and the propaganda which came with them (and which was also used in the struggle to defeat them). This 'made journalists suspicious of facts and ready to doubt the naive empiricism of the 1890s' (Schudson, 1978, p.141). The new scepticism was reinforced by the emergence of the public relations industry, which asserted that absolute neutrality was unattainable. Facts were there to be manipulated: the only issue was, who did the manipulating, and to what ends?

By the 1920s, then, journalists had come to accept that 'there were no longer facts, only individually constructed interpretations' (ibid.), but asserted that these interpretations could be, and should be constructed in a methodologically objective manner, i.e. using professionally agreed rules which could minimise the impact of subjectivity on reporting. Thus, argues Schudson, the emergence of objectivity as a journalistic ideal came at the same time as a deeper loss of faith in ideas of rationality, absolute truth, and progress; reflecting the need, as it were, to reassert the *possibility* of a transcending truth in the face of twentieth-century propaganda techniques.

## BROADCAST IMPARTIALITY: A SPECIAL CASE

Closely related to, but distinct from the concept of objectivity is that of 'impartiality', a notion of particular importance to any discussion of British broadcasting journalism. Chapter 1 referred to the specific technical and formal characteristics of broadcast journalism which appear to make it more 'believable' as an information source. The perceived legitimacy and 'truth' quotient of broadcast journalism is also founded on the broadcasters' assertion that they are 'impartial'.

The proclamation of impartiality as a guiding principle of British broadcast journalism goes back to the origins of the BBC in the 1920s, and to the distinctive role which it was recognised to be playing in the developing 'mass society' of that period. By the early twentieth century, British society had become 'democratic'. Universal suffrage had been achieved and political rights extended to the masses. How, then, to ensure that these rights were exercised responsibly, in the national interest?

Part of the answer lay in the new medium of broadcasting, which was set up as 'a public utility to be developed as a national service in the public interest' (Scannell and Cardiff, 1991, p.6). The Crawford Committee, which led to the establishment of the BBC in its present form, adopted this 'Reithian' notion of public service broadcasting (after the founder of the BBC, John Reith) and promoted the development of the BBC as 'a cultural, moral and educative force for the improvement of knowledge, taste and manners . . . a powerful means of promoting social unity' and creating 'an informal and reasoned public opinion as an essential part of the political process in a mass democratic society' (ibid., p.8). Broadcasting was to take on the task of establishing a common culture amongst the national audience. Because 'the nation' was recognised to contain diverse elements (diverse politically, socially, and geographically) the BBC would have to be an 'impartial arbiter' (ibid.), independent of commercial and political interests.

Impartiality is not absolute, however. Broadcasting was established as a public service by the state, in accordance with what were seen to be the interests of the state – or the 'national interest', as it is more often put. Consequently, the rules of impartiality are withdrawn whenever 'impartial' journalism is perceived to threaten the national interest. As the BBC puts it, impartiality 'does not imply absolute neutrality, nor detachment from basic moral and constitutional beliefs. For example, the BBC does not feel obliged to be neutral as between truth and untruth, justice and injustice, compassion and cruelty, tolerance and intolerance.'[2]

The concept of impartiality was also imposed on the commercial broadcasting organisations when they were established in 1954. Journalism on commercial television, like that of the BBC, would have to be impartial with respect to controversial issues and events.

## THE CRITIQUE OF OBJECTIVITY: AN INTRODUCTION

Objectivity is the most important journalistic value. But it contains a fundamental contradiction. As Schudson puts it,

> while objectivity, by the 1930s, was an articulate professional value in journalism, it was one that seemed to disintegrate as soon as it was formulated. It became an ideal in journalism, after all, precisely when the impossibility of overcoming subjectivity in presenting the news was widely accepted and, I have argued, precisely because subjectivity had come to be regarded as inevitable. From the beginning, then, criticism of the 'myth' of objectivity has accompanied its enunciation.
>
> (1978, p.157)

Criticism of objectivity can be divided into two broad categories.

Firstly, there is the criticism, usually based on empirical research (content analysis), that journalism is *biased*.

As we have seen, liberal pluralism accords journalism a key role in the orderly reproduction of democratic societies. Jeffrey Alexander, for example, defines the social role of the news media in the following terms:

> by daily exposing and reformulating itself *vis à vis* changing values, group formations, and objective economic and political conditions, the media allows 'public opinion' to be organized responsively on a mass basis. By performing this function of information-conduit the news media provides society with the greatest degree of flexibility in dealing with social strains.
>
> (1981, p.21)

However, this flexibility (and thus the integrative social function of the news media) is threatened if journalists are not sufficiently autonomous from economic, political and other elites in society. As Alexander puts it, 'to the degree that the news media is tied to religious, ideological, political, or class groupings it is not free to form and reform public events in a flexible way. Without this flexibility, public opinion becomes "artificial" and "biased": it will be keyed to a part over the whole' (ibid., p.25). This approach is focused on 'how well or how badly the various media reflect the existing balance of political forces and the political agenda' (Collins, 1990, p.37). The underlying assumption of such criticism is that there is a *possibility* of objective journalism, but that it is not being realised.

A more fundamental critique asserts that there can in fact *be* no objectivity; that the concept is nothing more than a mystification, a legitimising ritual with no real validity. From this perspective, there are a variety of potential journalistic accounts of events, corresponding to the plurality of viewpoints which exist in the world. More than one of these accounts may have validity.

The starting point of this critique is the acknowledgement that journalism is not, and never can be, a neutral, value-free representation of reality. As Paul Willis put it back in 1971, 'once an item of news has been selected for transmission to the public there is already bias, some selective principle, some value, quite apart from the way it is presented' (1971, p.9). Roger Fowler states that 'news is not a natural phenomenon emerging straight from reality, but a product. It is produced by an industry, shaped by the bureaucratic and economic structure of that industry, by the relations between the media and other industries and, most importantly, by relations with government and other political organisations' (1991, p.222). Richard Hoggart argues that 'what its practitioners call "objective news" is . . . in reality a highly selected interpretation of events' (Glasgow University Media Group, 1976, p.x).

News and journalism, in short, are social constructions. The point (or something similar) has been made so often in the media studies literature that it has become a commonplace, but it remains central to the sociology of journalism: news is never a mere recording or reporting of the world 'out there', but a synthetic, value-laden account which carries within it the dominant assumptions and ideas of the society within which it is produced.

This view is rooted in the assertion that the categories by which we make sense of the world in consciousness are culturally specific. For example, in Britain, the United States, and other liberal democratic societies news tends to be about *conflict* and *negativity*. The negative – crime, industrial disputes, disasters – is more newsworthy than the positive. In the Soviet Union, on the other hand, journalists were taught an alternative conception of news values, which emphasised positive social phenomena. In Soviet news, until about 1986, crime was almost completely absent; there was no coverage of industrial disputes, or of such phenomena as poverty; or of forms of social deviance from the officially sanctioned norm, such as homosexuality, although such things existed. There was no coverage of Aids, none of aircrashes and other disasters, man-made or natural. Even the nuclear disaster at Chernobyl was hidden from the Soviet news audience until the last possible moment.[3]

These absences – strange and alien to the western audience – were not simply the result of the authorities' wish to silence and make invisible social and political problems. Rather, they were a direct expression of Lenin's view that journalism should perform a *constructive* social role: educating the masses with stories of exemplary production techniques; inspiring them with stories of industrial success; playing down crime and the deviant, rather than highlighting them. Instead of hearing about bad workers on strike, Soviet news audiences were told of the good workers who overfulfilled their production targets.

The Soviet news media had no need to concern themselves with winning audience share or making profits, so they did not consistently have to outdo each other with exclusives and shock–horror headlines. Western news media, by contrast, are required to win audiences with entertainment as well as information. Entertainment is often about drama, and drama is, more often than not, about conflict and negativity.

Soviet socialism and western capitalism represented two different political cultures, where different economic and ideological forces were at play, and where two very different concepts of what is newsworthy predominated. The question of which was the most appropriate is less important for our purposes than the recognition that news values can and do vary across cultures and, within a single culture, across media, so that in Britain *The Times*, the *Sun*, and the *Sport* each have their own definitions of what constitutes an important story. They are *value-laden*.

This is not the same thing as saying that journalism is 'biased', in the sense of 'deliberately shaping the content and presentation of the news so as to advance the cause of a particular party, candidate or ideology' (Ranney, 1983, p.34). Bias in this sense is common in the media, but the social-constructionist argument is rather different: it is that journalism, regardless of the integrity of individual journalists and editors, is always a selective, partial account of a reality which can never be known in its entirety by anyone.

## CRITICISING OBJECTIVITY

Notwithstanding the above, the 'objectivity assumption' remains powerful and prevalent amongst journalists.[4] Thus, media sociologists have sought to 'prove' bias, by means of content analysis. In this sense, the sociology of journalism has from the outset been concerned with 'establishing that [journalistic] information was produced: selected, organised, structured, and [therefore] biased' (Collins, 1990, p.20).

Most work of this type has begun from the assumption that

the media are inherently biased in favour of the powerful: the establishment, elite groups, the ruling class (or whatever one chooses to call those who occupy controlling positions in our society). An early example is contained in the work of Philip Elliot, James Halloran, and Graham Murdock (1970) on news coverage of student demonstrations in the late 1960s. This was the time of the Paris riots, which nearly brought down the French government; the shootings of students at Kent State University; and other manifestations of student unrest.

Elliot *et al.* asserted that the media play an important role in the 'labelling' of radical political action as deviant. When political groups (or other types of association, such as trade unions) go beyond the limits of normal parliamentary action (participating in demonstrations and strikes, for example) the media intervene to label these activities as deviant or illegitimate, marginalising them and diverting public attention away from the root causes of social conflict towards its epiphenomenal forms. The case-study used by these authors was the anti-Vietnam War demonstration which took place in London's Grosvenor Square in 1968. They show that weeks before the event media coverage built up an image of impending violence, caused by 'foreign' Marxist extremists such as Tariq Ali (then a radical student leader). Although the organisers of the demonstration had made their peaceful intentions clear the press nevertheless made sense of it in terms of the Paris riots – i.e. as a potentially violent, anarchical event. On the day of the demonstration itself, Murdock writes, 'there were relatively few incidents of confrontation between police and demonstrators, but having committed themselves to a news image based on this expectation, the newspapers proceeded as though the event had been characterised by street fighting' (Murdock, 1973, p.165). Moreover, this construction of the event was reproduced in all the national daily newspapers, as well as on television news.

In this way, 'the press played an indispensable role in the process of managing conflict and dissent, and legitimising the present distribution of power and wealth in British capitalism' (ibid., p.172). Murdock argues further that these features of news are present in other categories of coverage, including those of political, industrial and ethnic conflict, and of deviance.

The model employed by these authors is closely related to the 'deviancy amplification' framework of Jock Young and others discussed in Chapter 1. Hall *et al.*'s *Policing the Crisis* (1978), for example, attempted to do in the sphere of crime reporting what Elliot, Halloran, and Murdock did in relation to political demonstrations: specifically, to show that 'law and order' news tends to label certain groups – in this case, the young black population of inner London – as 'deviants', and in doing so, to contribute to the process whereby that labelling becomes a self-fulfilling prophecy (as measured in an increased incidence of the deviant behaviour).

## THE CRITIQUE OF TELEVISION NEWS

We have noted that television news is perceived to be the most important of all journalistic media, not least because of its reputation as an 'impartial' source of information. Consequently, a large number of studies within the critical tradition have been devoted to the 'demystification' of impartiality, i.e. the demonstration of television's 'bias'. The most ambitious of these to date has been the project begun by the Glasgow University Media Group in 1975 to analyse the output of British TV news over a six-month period. Their objective was to demonstrate, by means of quantitative content analysis and semiological techniques that 'the news is not a neutral and natural phenomenon: it is rather the manufactured production of ideology' (1980, p.viii), a 'sequence of socially manufactured messages which carry many of the culturally dominant assumptions of our society' (1976, p.l). To substantiate this hypothesis the GUMG examined television news coverage of industrial relations, at a time when this issue was at the top of the national political agenda.

Consistently, they concluded, in television news as a whole 'the ideology of one particular class is dominant and preferred' (1980, p.415). During the period of their study, they argued, television journalists were presenting events and the issues which underpinned them in terms favourable to the British establishment. The journalistic emphases – which the GUMG claimed to have documented – on wages as the cause of inflation; on strikes as the cause of Britain's economic crisis; on workers as the cause of strikes – made sense of these issues for the viewer in a manner which was biased towards capital and against labour.

The work of the GUMG was both influential and controversial. The broadcasters themselves rejected its findings (at least in public), while every anti-establishment group with a grudge against 'the meejah' used it as a weapon with which to beat the journalists. Consequently, it was the target of a sustained counter-attack, led by prominent members of the intellectual right such as Digby Anderson and Wes Sharrock. These authors set out to prove that it was the GUMG who were ideologically biased, rather than the broadcasters; that they were Marxist left-wingers whose evidence could not, for that reason if for no other, be trusted.

> Media men [sic] are treated as if they have signed up to be professional sociologists and have fallen down on the job. They are alleged to distort events (if not Reality itself) in their reports, where the measure of distortion is precisely the extent of discrepancy between their account and that given by the favoured sociological theories of the media scholars . . . In effect, then, charges of distortion [or bias] could equally well be formulated as statements that the media men disagree with their sociologically-minded critics.
>
> (1979, p.369)

Such studies do not prove bias, it was argued, 'they merely show that the media do not accept the same theories that are presently fashionable within sociology' (ibid.).

The methodological debates surrounding the content analysis of television news have been pursued more fully elsewhere.[5] Here, we might observe that the ferocity and frequency of attacks upon the GUMG's work, over a number of years and from a multitude of sources, reflects, at the very least, the success of their stated intention to demystify and deconstruct a major element of British journalistic output. For that reason alone, their work continues to deserve close scrutiny and attention.

## DEVELOPMENTS IN THE CRITICAL TRADITION

The GUMG were criticised not only from the right of the academic and political spectrum, but from within the critical tradition itself. A number of media sociologists shared the Glasgow group's basic thesis that television journalism performed an 'ideological role' in the wider process of cultural reproduction, but argued that their conclusions were too simplistic, since they implied a somewhat conspiratorial notion of bias. The GUMG, and the many similar studies which they inspired, were accused of *class reductionism*, since they appeared to equate the content of news with what was in the interests of the ruling class. Such an approach, it was argued, 'can in no way explain and analyse the inherent contradictions and varieties of permitted views, and the surface openness which exists across the range of broadcasting output' (Hartley, 1982, p.56).

In 1983 Philip Schlesinger, Graham Murdock, and Philip Elliot published *Televising Terrorism*, which took as its case-study the issue of terrorism and, in particular, the conflict in Northern Ireland. On the basis of this study, these authors rejected

> the commonplace radical characterisation of broadcasting as a largely uncritical conduit for official views. In opposition to these one-dimensional accounts we have drawn attention to the diverse ways in which television handles 'terrorism' and the problems this poses for liberal democracies. We have shown that some programmes are relatively 'closed' and work wholly or mainly within the terms set by the official perspective. Others, though, are more 'open' and provide spaces for alternative and oppositional views.
>
> (1983, p.166)

News programmes, they argued, were 'closed' in the main to all but the dominant official perspective on events, say in Northern Ireland. Documentaries and current affairs programmes, on the other hand, might well allow some discussion of the roots of the conflict, or the motivations of its protagonists, or even some critique of the state's position. Television had an 'uneasy, often abrasive relationship with the state, marked by struggle over the balance between autonomy and control . . . these conflicts produce a symbolic field which is a good deal more open and contested than [a] one-sided stress on television's legitimising role allows for' (ibid., p.161). They concluded, however, by emphasising that 'the extent of this diversity should not be overstated. Although television is the site of continual struggle between competing perspectives on "terrorism" [or, by extension, any other social phenomenon defined by the media as problematic] the contest is not an equal one. "Open" programmes appear far less frequently than "closed" ones and they reach smaller audiences' (ibid., p.l66).

The key development here was to view television journalism not merely as an instrument of class domination, but as a 'space' available to be competed for by the representatives of different ideological perspectives and explanatory frameworks. As John Hartley put it, 'the dominant class may have a privileged position with respect to the available spaces, but not a monopoly' (1982, p.55).

This approach was reflected in the author's own study of television news coverage of the defence and disarmament debate in the 1980s (McNair, 1988), which examined coverage of the concept of the Soviet military threat in the context of the publicly available evidence on such matters as Soviet military power and foreign policy objectives. It was found that news programmes tended consistently to reproduce without criticism or qualification the 'worst-case' official perspective on the Soviet threat. This position originated in the politico-military establishments of the US and British governments, and was deployed (in its many manifestations) in the early 1980s to legitimise the huge increases in arms spending which took place in those years. However, alternative perspectives on the threat – those not only of the Campaign for Nuclear Disarmament and peace campaigners but of former political and military leaders – *were* presented from time to time on minority audience current affairs programmes such as *Newsnight* or *Channel 4 News*. In an edition of *Newsnight* broadcast on October 18, 1983, the presenter announced that 'tonight we explore the case for regarding the Russians as perhaps less of a threat than they're sometimes made out to be'. The presenter then did what was not done on mainstream television news, labelling the 'Russian threat' perspective *as* a perspective, rather than objective reality, which could reasonably be set against other perspectives, of potentially equal validity. Specifically, he contrasted dominant western views of the Soviet Union as 'a very massive and threatening military power, stretching from central Europe to the extremes of Asia, poised to exploit any opportunities for expansion' with another

looking from the inside outwards, the view that sees the men
in the Kremlin swamped by Russia's own internal problems
and encircled by a whole range of external threats to their
security. The Chinese in the east, the unsettled Muslims to the
south, and the Afghans still unbeaten. Beyond that the
Americans deploying massively in the Indian Ocean. To the
west, beyond their own recalcitrant allies in eastern Europe, a
whole ring of the west's nuclear and conventional systems
pointing at them from Turkey around to northern Norway.

(McNair, 1988, p.67)

In this way the item created a rare, but significant space, in which
cold war assumptions about the scale and nature of the Soviet
threat could be contested, as on occasions did other minority
audience news and current affairs programmes.

## THE WORK OF CHOMSKY AND HERMAN

The work discussed above all relates to Britain. For a number of
years Noam Chomsky and Ed Herman have been documenting
the 'biases' of American journalism. For Chomsky and Herman
the American news media function as 'propaganda agencies' of
the 'national security state' (NSS). They seek to demonstrate
empirically

the capacity of western ideological institutions [principally the
media] to falsify, obscure and reinterpret the facts in the interests of those who dominate the economy and political system
. . . and the process of brainwashing under freedom as mani-
fested in the selection and analysis of issues by the media.

(1979, p.71)

As one of their case-studies, they take the category of 'terrorism'
and argue that 'among the many symbols used to frighten and
manipulate the populaces of the democratic states, few have been
more important than "terror" and "terrorism"' (ibid., p.6). They
argue, on the basis of detailed content analyses of American press
and broadcasting journalism that US journalists use these terms
in ways which serve the interests of the economic, political, and
military establishments.

Chomsky and Herman distinguish between three categories of terror: *constructive* – 'that which positively serves important domestic interests'; *benign* – 'that which is of little direct interest to the elite but may sometimes serve the interests of a friendly client'; and *nefarious* – 'that committed by enemy states (or by bearers of hostile ideologies)'. According to these authors, examples of 'constructive' and 'benign' terror tend to be ignored or marginalised in US news coverage of foreign affairs (Herman, 1982, p.146).

For example, when in the 1970s tens of thousands of people were killed in Central America by regimes armed and financed by the United States this was not defined by journalists, they argue, as 'terror', but tended to be ignored by the media. Violence by Arab groups in the Middle East, on the other hand, was highlighted by the media, labelled as 'terrorism', and condemned. Their point was not that 'terrorism' should not be covered, but that 'mass media attention to it is a function not of terror per se but of the relation of terror to larger national interests' (ibid., p.164.).

Chomsky and Herman have also studied human rights coverage, observing that here, too, human rights abuses in friendly states tend to be ignored by the US media, while those which occur in enemy states are highlighted.

## CONCLUSION

Is journalism biased, then? On the basis of the evidence gained by content analysts over a period of more than twenty years, we can state with some confidence that the news media of a particular society – press and broadcasting – tend to construct accounts of events which are structured and framed by the dominant values and interests of that society, and to marginalise (if not necessarily exclude) alternative accounts. In this sense, it might be argued, the evidence supports the materialist thesis that there is a link between the power structure of a society and its journalistic output; that journalism is part of a stratified social system; part of the apparatus by which that system is presented to its members in terms with which they can be persuaded to live.

On the other hand, as much of the work discussed in this chapter has shown, journalism clearly does provide spaces for alternative and oppositional views to be presented. Consequently, media sociologists have turned increasingly from the problem of proving bias to that of investigating the factors involved in the production of journalistic accounts of the world, and in particular the conditions under which openness – to accounts and interpretations of social reality which are not those of established elites – can be maximised.

# Chapter 3

# Explaining content
## Current debates in the sociology of journalism

Media sociologists have argued that journalism is not, and never can be, neutral and objective, but is fundamentally interpretative, embodying the dominant values and explanatory frameworks of the society within which it is produced. That observation is a necessary starting point in the critique of 'objectivity'. But if we wish to argue that journalistic media are in certain ways 'biased' we must then go on and pose the question 'how'? This chapter sets out the different approaches and theoretical frameworks which sociologists have adopted to *explain* media content, as opposed to merely describing it.

These approaches can be grouped into three broad categories: firstly, *politico-economic* accounts, which explain journalism in terms of the influence upon its production of economic and political factors; secondly, *organisational* approaches, focusing on the professional constraints acting on journalists; and thirdly, what James Curran calls *culturalist* (and Schudson calls *culturological*)[1] approaches, which locate the source of 'bias' in complex interactions between news producers and the external socio-cultural environment.

## THE POLITICO-ECONOMIC APPROACH

The politico-economic approach to the sociology of journalism asserts that the output of journalistic media is principally determined by the economic structure of the organisations concerned. It is founded on the *materialist* view of society (as opposed to pluralist) elaborated by Karl Marx and Friedrich Engels in the nineteenth century.

In a capitalist society such as Britain, the media generally take the form of privately owned business enterprises which, like other forms of capitalist ownership, tend to be concentrated in the hands of a small minority of the population. The essence of the politico-economic approach is that the journalism produced by these organisations is inflected in such a way as to serve the interests of that minority – to reproduce their ideas, values, and ways of seeing the world as part of the process by which society is able to reproduce itself. It emphasises 'the centrality of economic ownership, the individual influences exerted by the state, and the strictures and logic of the market' (Curran, 1990, p.139). Ralph Miliband succinctly articulates the politico-economic viewpoint when he states that

> Rather obviously, those who own and control the capitalist mass media are most likely to be men whose ideological dispositions run from soundly conservative to utterly reactionary; and in many instances, most notably in the case of newspapers, the impact of their views and prejudices is immediate and direct, in the straightforward sense that newspaper proprietors have often not only owned their newspapers but closely controlled their editorial and political lines as well, and turned them, by constant and even daily intervention, into vehicles of their personal views.
>
> (1972, p.205)

To assess the validity of the politico-economic approach we must examine two separate issues: firstly, is it *true* that ownership and control of the news media is concentrated in the hands of relatively few corporations and individuals? And secondly, do owners of media organs use their power to influence output in ways favourable to themselves?

As we saw in Chapter 1 four corporations control about 80% of the British press. A handful control the commercial broadcasting organisations. These are demonstrable facts, but what is their sociological significance? Do owners *use* their economic power as an ideological weapon?

The liberal pluralist answer to this question is that they do not, for two reasons. Firstly, it is argued that ownership and control of the media are no longer synonymous, if they ever were. This argument, which is frequently heard in relation to the capitalist economic system as a whole, states simply that, as a rule, no single individual or corporation holds enough shares in any particular media outlet to influence its editorial direction. Nowadays, it is argued, the majority of shares are held by pension funds, investment houses and, since the Thatcher Government introduced 'popular capitalism' and the 'share-owning democracy', even the people.

The simplest reply to this argument is that, if it were once true (a big if) it is no longer. The 1980s were a period of increasing concentration of ownership of the British media, spearheaded by Rupert Murdoch's News International but with equally aggressive empire-building by Robert Maxwell, Conrad Black and others. In commercial television the big players have fingers in several pies (Scottish Television, for example, has a major stake in GMTV), and there is growing cross-media ownership. And while it is true that many more people own shares than used to be the case, the small shareholder in the media, as in any other sector of business, remains virtually powerless against the weight of the large holdings.

There *are* some constraints on media ownership, but as the Thatcher Government showed in its dealings with Rupert Murdoch in the 1980s (see Chapter 7), these can be waived if it is politically convenient to do so.

This brings us to a second objection frequently made to the politico-economic approach. The pluralist may accept that there is excessive concentration of ownership in the media today, but will argue against this that 'journalists enjoy a considerable degree of independence from supervisory control' (Curran, 1990, p.143). In a recent articulation of this view journalist Robin Morgan points out that, during the Conservative Party leadership struggle in November 1990, the *Sunday Times*, under the editorship of Andrew Neil, supported Michael Heseltine, against the wishes of proprietor Rupert Murdoch. Such examples prove, he argues, 'the unpopular truth that proprietors concede a considerable amount of independence to editors and invest millions in their instincts and views with only one condition – circulation success'.[2]

There are many more examples to suggest the opposite, however. Both Rupert Murdoch and the late Robert Maxwell have taken a great personal interest in the running of their media properties, frequently intervening directly to impose a certain editorial line, or to prevent a story being reported. It is, of course, entirely routine for journalists to see their copy altered on grounds of stylistic inadequacy or lack of space. The interventions with which we are concerned here, however, are those which have their roots in the political or business interests of the proprietor.

In an interview shortly before his death Maxwell boasted that his ownership of national newspapers gave him the power 'to raise issues effectively. In simple terms, it's a megaphone.'[3] Anthony Bevins, political editor of the *Independent*, argues straightforwardly that 'dissident reporters who do not deliver the goods suffer professional death. They are ridden by newsdesks and backbench executives, they have their stories spiked on a systematic basis, they face the worst form of newspaper punishment – by-line deprivation' (1990, p.15). It has been shown that Murdoch's *Sunday Times* editors deliberately and without permission altered copy written by journalists on the *Death on the Rock* affair, in order to cast a bad light on the programme's producers and sources. The journalists concerned subsequently felt compelled to resign from the paper.

The main mechanism by which proprietors can exert such control is their power to appoint key personnel, particularly senior editors, who become the proprietor's 'voice' within the newsroom, ensuring that journalistic 'independence' conforms to the preferred editorial line.

These are hardly earth-shattering statements, despite the attempts of some commentators to assert the existence of journalistic independence, and its continuing role in the maintenance of a 'free press'. Few modern proprietors would bother to deny that they use their media interests not just to make money but to influence public opinion and the political environment. Robert Maxwell's views have already been quoted. Other proprietors, from Lord Beaverbrook on, have made similar statements, and many have shown a willingness to suppress or distort material which could have affected their business interests directly. Journalists and editors may attempt to resist such intervention, as in the case of the *Observer*'s dealings with the Lonrho company over a number of years, and guarantees of editorial independence are frequently written into take-over deals (such as Rupert Murdoch's purchase of the *Times* newspapers in 1981) but the economic interests and political preferences of the proprietor continue to be the most important determinant of a news outlet's editorial line.

Further commercial pressure is exerted, according to the politico-economic approach, by the constraints placed on journalistic content because of the need to attract and retain advertising revenue. There is evidence that such pressures exist. Companies do on occasion withdraw, or threaten to withdraw ads from publications of which they disapprove. The significance of this factor should not be overstated, however, since it is also true that commercial logic requires companies to advertise in popular media outlets, regardless of their political complexion.

The above points relate only to the privately owned media. The public service broadcasting system, as we have noted, was set up precisely to avoid the possibility that radio and TV could be abused by commercial or political interests. The BBC is 'owned' by the state, funded from public taxation, and has its political independence from the executive branch of government constitutionally guaranteed. The commercial broadcasters are allowed to make profits for their shareholders, but are tightly regulated to prevent outright political biases from surfacing in their journalism. The politico-economic perspective argues that such a system will nevertheless tend to produce output which is in the basic interests of the dominant economic group. In 1972 Miliband argued persuasively that the cultural institutions of capitalism tend to be staffed and managed by people drawn from the same elites which control the business, political, and military power centres. Coming from the same family backgrounds, going to the same public schools and universities, occupying similar places in the class structure, they share the same values.

It is possible to show empirically that those who control broadcasting in the 1990s *do* indeed tend to conform to the pattern Miliband described twenty years ago, as measured, for example, by the proportion of former public school and Oxbridge graduates who sit on the BBC's Board of Governors, or the Independent Television Commission. The dominance of a particular class in the supervision of broadcasting is not absolute, of course, and it may be that the links are weakening somewhat, but attendance at Oxbridge still counts for more in achieving power within the BBC than some other considerations.

But does the class profile of broadcasting's senior management mean that the organisations necessarily reflect a class bias in their output? The evidence here is contradictory. On the one hand, since the establishment of the BBC in the 1920s British broadcasters have frequently aligned themselves to a concept of the 'national interest' defined by the establishment. During the General Strike of 1926 the BBC refused to allow representatives of the trade union movement, or even of the official Labour Party opposition in Parliament, access to the airwaves to put the strikers' case. By 1926 the BBC had become part of the British state, 'with roles and functions delegated to it by Parliament, committed to cooperation with government and sharing its assumptions about what constituted the "national interest"' (Scannell and Cardiff, 1991, p.39). After their establishment in the 1950s the commercial broadcasting organisations were subsumed into the same system.

Yet there have been many examples of both the BBC and the commercial broadcasters coming into conflict with the British state, or with the government of the day. From the Munich crisis of 1938 (identified by Cardiff and Scannell as the first such instance) through the Suez crisis, the Falklands War, and the conflict in Northern Ireland, broadcasting journalists have often found themselves at loggerheads with politicians over the content of their coverage. Such counter-examples cannot be ignored, but have to be explained within a politico-economic framework, if that framework is to remain valid.

In *Putting Reality Together* Philip Schlesinger argues that the public service broadcasters occupy a special place in what he calls the 'ideological division of labour' within British capitalism, in which their formal independence and impartiality are crucial elements of their enhanced credibility in the minds of the audience. During the 1926 General Strike the BBC, faced with the problem of how to report its first major domestic social conflict, submitted to the government's desire that it should be employed as a channel of propaganda. 'But', argues Schlesinger, 'this mobilisation took place in a manner designed to maintain the BBC's credibility. Thus, it produced "factual" news, but this was linked to a clear-cut propaganda end – namely, the defeat of the strike' (1978, p.18). In the course of the strike Winston Churchill, then Home Secretary, wanted to take direct control of the BBC and use it openly as a propaganda tool. He was overruled in government by those who argued that this would undermine the very thing which made the BBC a valuable ideological weapon – its *perceived* independence. And having established its political independence on these grounds, the BBC has maintained it ever since, while always staying within the limits defined by the 'national interest'. John Hartley argues that 'the impartiality, objectivity, neutrality, and balance which form the bedrock of [British broadcasting's] editorial ideology are no sham. They are required if news is to act alongside the other agencies in naturalising dominant ideology and winning consent for hegemony' (1982, pp.61–2). And again, 'the relative autonomy of the [broadcast] news media, and their commitment to impartiality are the necessary conditions for the production of *dominant* ideological meanings' (ibid., p.55). Ralph Miliband has observed that

> this assumed impartiality and objectivity is quite artificial. For it mainly operates in regard to political formulations which while divided on many issues are nevertheless part of a basic, underlying consensus. Thus, radio and television in such countries as Britain and the United States may preserve a fair degree of impartiality between the Conservative, Liberal and Labour parties, and the Republican and Democratic parties, respectively: but this hardly precludes a steady stream of propaganda adverse to all views which fall outside the consensus. Impartiality and objectivity, in this sense, stop at the point where political consensus ends – and the more radical the dissent, the less impartial and objective the media.
>
> (1972, p.200)

As we shall see below, Schlesinger and others have moved away from this view of broadcast journalism as part of a propaganda apparatus, towards one which stresses the constantly shifting nature of 'consensus', and the possibility for dissenting voices to be heard in mainstream journalism. This 'culturalist' approach continues to adhere – in 'the last instance' – to politico-economic explanations in accounting for journalistic output, but recognises that the processes by which 'dominant ideologies' are constructed and then disseminated through the media are more complex and less mechanistic than Miliband's statement above might imply.

## ORGANISATIONAL APPROACHES

Organisational approaches to the study of journalism reject such analyses as overly conspiratorial, focusing instead on features of journalistic organisation in explaining output: principally, the limitations imposed by the news form; constraints imposed on journalists' ability to gather news; and the routine professional practices of journalism.

Bruhn-Jensen notes that 'the news form is at least to some extent a function of the organisational structure which is needed for large-scale communication of information to the public' (1986, p.46), while Paul Rock emphasises that 'news is the result of an organised response to routine bureaucratic problems' (1973, p.73), such as the need to produce material according to strict limits on space and timing. Both print and broadcast journalists must present news within certain confines of space and layout (in the case of the former) and, in television and radio, according to conventions on such matters as running order. These constraints, argues Rock, determine 'the rough system of priorities which will be allocated to the description of events; decide the proportion that these reports will occupy in the total presentation; and limit the entire volume of events which can evoke a journalistic reaction' (ibid., p.75). The availability of space, according to this perspective, is a basic organisational factor which may explain, better than any presumption of bias, why a certain newsworthy item is absent from a news programme or newspaper.

Time, too, is an important organisational factor. Galtung and Ruge (1973, p. 63) point out that events are far more likely to make it onto the news agenda if their time-frame 'fits' the rhythm of the news outlet concerned. Newspapers, for example, appear daily. They are therefore more likely to report events if they can be made sense of within a 24-hour time-frame. News has to be comprehensible to the audience as an 'event' with a beginning, a middle, and an end. Events which can be presented this way are more newsworthy than those which cannot. Rock suggests that western newspapers (and broadcast news outlets) are 'unable to contend with slow-moving historical cycles; they are far better equipped to accommodate rapid, unexpected change. They are generally incapable of reporting what seem to be indeterminate or fluid situations' (1973, p.77).

More 'fluid' and 'indeterminate' stories will be reported in the context of weekly current affairs programmes, or one-off documentaries, or in periodicals, but will tend to be absent from regular, daily news, until they 'explode' in such a way as to be unavoidable. The *process* by which famine in Africa came about and is perpetuated has largely been ignored by mainstream news outlets: only when Michael Buerk 'discovered' the refugee camps in Ethiopia in 1984, with all the picture-opportunities which they presented, and the individual stories which could be told, did the famine become 'news', and then only as an event, rather than a process.

Journalists, then, must construct their news in accordance with the scheduling and space requirements of the organisations within which they work. Not only does this help to explain why news is characteristically about events rather than processes, and effects rather than causes, it might also be thought to be part of the reason why news media tend, as content analysis shows, to favour the definitions of the powerful when constructing their accounts of events. 'Because of the demands of time and deadlines', argues Rock, 'journalists are inclined to position themselves so that they have ready access to institutions which guarantee a useful volume of reportable activity at useful intervals' (ibid.).[4]

A variant of the 'organisational' approach explains journalistic output in relation to the codes and conventions of the profession: what are often referred to as 'routine professional practices'. A famous article by Gaye Tuchman argues that the practice of objectivity is best viewed as a 'strategic ritual' performed by journalists in order to command authority and legitimacy in the view of the audience (1972, p.661). Like academic writers, journalists must be seen to be objective, and to this end they have developed a number of conventions which are used when constructing material.

To be 'objective', Tuchman argues, the journalist must present both sides of a story (or, in the case of a more complex debate, all credible sides); supporting evidence for any assertions made in the story must be provided; *authoritative* sources, such as politicians must be quoted (in this way the journalist is seen to distance him- or herself from the views reported, by establishing that they are someone else's opinions); 'fact' must be separated from 'opinion', and 'hard news' from 'editorial comment'; and the presentation of information must be structured pyramidically, with the most important bits coming first, at the 'top' of the story.

Taken together, the pursuit of these practices signifies 'objectivity'. In a TV news political story, for example, 'objectivity' would demand that the views of John Major be balanced by those of Tony Blair, and probably also by Liberal leader Paddy Ashdown; and that a recognised 'specialist' correspondent be enlisted to give an authoritative comment on the situation. The newsreader will *not* give his or her opinion directly, since this would break with the conventions of objectivity.

Organisational explanations of content tend to be opposed to the politico-economic, stressing the constraints acting on journalists rather than the ideological biases emanating from or acting upon them. Both sets of approaches are not mutually exclusive, however, and a third paradigm has emerged which actively seeks to integrate them.

## CULTURALIST PERSPECTIVES

The culturalist perspective links elements of both the politico-economic and organisational approaches within a framework which retains a materialist analysis but incorporates elements of the pluralist model. It has evolved as a result of the difficulties experienced by sociologists in trying to reconcile the materialist approach with the evidence of dissenting journalism. Consequently, it focuses not on who owns the news media, but on how those media are positioned relative to the power elites within society. It locates the source of 'bias' in the environment external to the journalistic organisations so that content is not simply a function of ownership, or of journalistic practices and rituals, but of the interaction between news organisations, the sources of their output, and other social institutions.

An early example of the application of this approach is contained in Hall *et al.*'s *Policing the Crisis*. This study argued, as we saw in Chapter 2, that the media tend to engineer moral panics and amplify deviance, using as evidence press coverage of the 'mugging' scare of the early 1970s. Having made this observation, at the level of content analysis, the authors went on to explain how they wished to 'draw attention to the more routine structures of news production to see how the media come in fact, in the "last instance", to reproduce the definitions of the powerful, without being, in a simple sense, in their pay' (1978, p.57).

They went on to map out 'structures of dominance' within which the representatives of power elites tend to enjoy privileged access to the media, as sources of information and, importantly, of the interpretative frameworks which journalists then use to construct their stories. These privileged sources become what Hall *et al.* called the *primary definers* of news. The journalists, who take on these primary definitions and then circulate them in their stories, become *secondary definers*.

An organisational account of this 'structured bias' towards the powerful would focus primarily on such causes as the pressures of deadlines. Hall *et al.* argue further that journalists harbour an ideological assumption that these are automatically the most credible, authoritative sources of information, and have privileged access to the media as of right. The powerless, on the other hand, are not seen as credible sources of knowledge and explanation, and tend as a result to be marginalised in journalists' accounts. In this model journalistic media are seen rather as neutral channels through which social power – what Schlesinger calls *definitional* power – flows. The journalists are not *necessarily* biased towards the powerful – but their bureaucratic organisation and cultural assumptions make them conduits of that power. From the culturalist perspective, journalistic output is shaped primarily by a combination of ideological, economic, and cultural influences acting on the news organisation from without. Journalists themselves are relatively autonomous from direct proprietorial and editorial control, but nevertheless reproduce preferred accounts and interpretations of social reality by internalising the dominant value structure of their society.

Philip Schlesinger has developed the culturalist framework in the direction of what he calls *source-centred* approaches, presenting a critique of the earlier *primary definition* model developed by Hall and others. For Schlesinger, this *hegemonic* model is too bound to the concept of dominant ideology, and fails to recognise that, in many instances, there is no single primary definition of an issue or an event's meaning; that structures of access to the media – through which primary definitions emerge – shift over time as the political environment changes; and that primary definitions are the product of complex processes of contestation and negotiation between competing social actors. The primary definition thesis, for Schlesinger, 'tends to understate the amount of conflict among those who principally define the political agenda in "polyarchic" political systems; it is largely atemporal; it ignores how new forces may reshape definitional space; and finally, overstates the passivity of the media' (1991, p.64).

In general, culturalist approaches are more optimistic than politico-economic models, since they imply that 'shifts within the power structure, and in the field of contestation in which the media are situated, can lead to space being given to definitions that are opposed to those that are dominant' (Curran, 1989, p.117). The relative autonomy of journalism highlighted by the culturalist approach means that subordinate or marginalised political actors can make the news agenda and influence public debate. It suggests that a struggle takes place, outside the media organisations themselves, for *access*, shifting the critical emphasis away from journalistic bias to the skill and entrepreneurship of social actors in winning this access.

The culturalists concede, however, that access to the journalistic media is not equitable: the powerful can call on greater resources to attract the journalists' attention than poorly funded pressure groups or political parties. The Prime Minister's office has far more power to shape the news agenda than that of the Opposition Leader. The Opposition Leader, in turn, has more 'definitional power' than the Green Party. But the general point remains: the news media in liberal democratic capitalist societies are relatively open to oppositional and dissenting viewpoints. From the culturalist perspective, indeed, such openness is the condition for the wider legitimacy of the system.

## PROPAGANDA VERSUS GATEKEEPER MODELS: THE CASE OF CHOMSKY AND HERMAN

To explore further the differences between the perspectives discussed above we can return briefly to the work of Noam Chomsky and Ed Herman, who reject the range of organisational and culturalist approaches – what they call 'gatekeeper' models, since they imply that journalists, rather than proprietors and owners, are the key actors in the production of news – described above. In a 1986 essay Ed Herman accepts that gatekeeper models, with their 'stress on the possibilities of dissent, openings and space' have contributed a great deal to the sociology of journalism, but criticises them for failing to reconcile theoretically the materialist hypothesis that the media have a reproductive social function with their apparent 'openness' to dissent. Gatekeeper models *do* tend to support the materialist view that the media are biased towards the status quo (explaining this with reference to external or organisational factors) but have not satisfactorily theorised the implications for the model of the presence of oppositional accounts of events within the news. They are, in short, something of a ragbag.

Instead, Herman argues for a 'propaganda model' of journalistic production: so called because it can be employed, as he puts it, 'to analys[e] the numerous and important cases where the mass media serve as instruments in campaigns of ideological mobilisation' (1986, p. 175). In using the term 'model' he signifies his intention to develop an analysis which can *predict* the way in which news and journalistic media will report particular events. Premised on a politico-economic framework the propaganda model assumes that the media's power to manage and manipulate public opinion will be used by elites in the pursuit of what they define as the 'national interest'. It also assumes that cases of media dissent are exceptional, and relatively insignificant when set against the more general tendency of journalists to reproduce dominant ideology.

The empirical case for the propaganda model comprises the observation that the US media tend to apply a 'dichotomous treatment' to coverage of international events, according to the political context within which they occur. During the period of the cold war, for example, dissidents in the Soviet Union and its satellites were covered far more intensively (if one considers the relative scale and frequency of the human rights abuses being reported) than those in 'friendly' countries such as Brazil, El Salvador, and Uruguay. US coverage of the imposition of martial law in Poland vastly exceeded that of a similar clampdown which took place around the same time in Turkey, a NATO ally. As Herman puts it, 'these dichotomies have great ideological signifi-cance' (ibid., p.177), and are the direct consequence of decisions by elites in the economic, political, and military sectors of American society, linked to parallel elites in the media, to high-light some phenomena, marginalise others, and manage public opinion in a manner which suits the 'national interest', or as Chomsky and Herman would put it, the interests of the National Security State.

They argue that the propaganda model can be used, system-atically, to explain the characteristics of particular news stories and media campaigns, such as the one which followed the shoot-ing down of a Korean airliner in late August 1983 (Herman, 1986). In the United States, as in other NATO countries, cover-age of the incident was unprecedented in quantity and quality. The Soviets were denounced by Ronald Reagan as 'terrorists', 'barbarians', and 'murderers'. It was alleged that they had known KAL 007 to be a civilian airliner when they ordered it shot down (it was later conceded by the CIA, that, in fact, the Soviets had believed KAL 007 to be a military spyplane, possibly the RC-135 which had been in the area on a top secret mission at the same time as the Korean plane). The US media reproduced the Reagan Administration's line virtually without qualification in a torrent of coverage. The resulting media image of the USSR as a 'criminal regime', and its impact on public opinion, contributed substan-tially to a mood in which previously contentious key adminis-tration arms procurements, such as the MX missile and binary gas weapons, were passed by Congress without protest. In Europe, too, the KAL affair effectively ended what had been up until then mass opposition to cruise missiles and other NATO deployments.[5]

The KAL 007 affair was a tragic and distressing incident. Herman points out, however, that coverage of similar incidents in the past, such as the Israeli shooting down of a Libyan airliner in 1973, with 108 lives lost, was much less aggressive and accusatory because, Herman suggests, the Israelis were an ideological ally, a friendly state in a strategic area of the world. The Soviets, on the other hand, were the 'enemy', whose existence was at that time the main justification for the US Defense Department's $300 trillion budget. Thus it was in the interests of the American 'National Security State' to highlight the KAL 007 disaster, firmly blame the Soviets for it, and marginalise any evidence which might have suggested a genuine error on the part of the Soviet military, or even worse, implicated the US government.

Herman's essay was published in 1986. Two years later, in June 1988, an opportunity arose to test the propaganda model. That month, in the Gulf of Arabia, the United States navy opened fire on an Iranian passenger jet, which had just taken off on a scheduled flight through international airspace; 279 civilians were killed. The American military, like the Soviets five years before, claimed that the Iranian airbus had been mistaken for a hostile military aircraft, which was probably the case. While the Soviet defence of their actions in 1983 was dismissed as the cynical propaganda of cold-blooded murderers, the official US account of what had happened to the Iranian plane set the news agenda from the outset. In this comparative analysis, the propaganda model correctly predicted how the media would report the two incidents.

Chomsky and Herman's work is important not only as a powerfully argued and thoroughly documented critique of how journalism works in a 'free' society. It also presents in quite a stark manner the central issue with which the sociology of journalism is concerned – the extent to which journalistic output is *closed* to alternative viewpoints, functioning in the interests of a political and economic elite, and the extent to which, on the contrary, it is *open* to contesting, dissenting voices. For Chomsky and Herman the answer is clear: journalism is propaganda. Exceptions to the rule are precisely that, and do not negate the main point: in the manipulation and manufacturing of consent which the elites of liberal democracies require, journalism is a key ideological institution.

Another US sociologist, Daniel Hallin, rejects this account of how, and why, journalism is produced. Hallin studied US media coverage of the Vietnam War, from which he concludes that while journalists generally adopted a pro-establishment interpretative framework for making sense of the conflict – a 'cold war' framework which saw it in terms of 'a swiftly encroaching Communist menace' (1986, p.53) – they became more diverse in their viewpoints, more critical of and negative towards the US government as the political consensus around the issue broke down at the end of the 1960s.

Coverage of Vietnam has always been important to those who believe that the US media, far from being ideological instruments of the state, are busily engaged in undermining and subverting it. The American Right still believes that the graphic and harrowing footage of the war shown on American TV in the late 1960s and early 1970s was directly responsible for sapping the morale of the American public to continue supporting the conflict. The war, they believe, was lost on TV (indeed, this belief has led governments ever since to impose strict limitations on journalists' freedom to report military conflict).

Hallin rejects this view, arguing that the US media, in the case of Vietnam and more generally, 'play the role of exposing, condemning, or excluding from the public agenda those who violate or challenge the political consensus. [They] mark out and defend the limits of acceptable political conflict' (ibid., p. 1 17). Cold war interpretations of the Vietnam conflict – that it was Soviet-inspired, as opposed to being an indigenous, popularly rooted, anti-colonial liberation struggle – were routinely reproduced, he points out, without supporting evidence. Ideological readings of the war became what Hallin calls a 'baseline reality' for journalists reporting the conflict, rather than being seen as opinions to be judged on their merits. In the media there was 'a tight consensus on the nature of world politics and the American role in it – the premise that the preservation of an anti-Communist Vietnam was a legitimate goal of American policy [was] never brought into question' (ibid., p.48).

Hallin also argues that the US media, far from highlighting and exaggerating US military atrocities in the conflict, actually played them down. The story of the My Lai massacre, for example, was not told until two years after it happened. In short, then, US reporting of the war was overwhelmingly biased in favour of the US establishment. Where Hallin parts company with Chomsky and Herman is in the significance he allots to the fact that, sometimes, political consensus breaks down; an issue arises which splits the elite, as Vietnam eventually came to do in the American case.

The split in the US establishment around the Vietnam War was not about the inherent correctness of the US government's anti-communist line, or its entitlement to pursue that line anywhere in the world, but on the tactical issues of how best to defeat the North Vietnamese, and what scale of losses was acceptable in that struggle. Hallin argues that after 1968 or so, as the Vietnam War moved from the 'sphere of consensus' into the 'sphere of legitimate controversy', so coverage began to reflect divisions within the US establishment. Tied – by adherence to the professional ethic of objectivity – to reflecting the debate, the US media reported criticism of the Nixon Administration; not for being anti-communist and militarist, but for being incompetent in its pursuit of the war aims. The media did not originate the critical coverage, in other words, they merely reported it. Hallin concludes that 'the behaviour of the media . . . is intimately related to the unity and clarity of the government itself, as well as to the degree of consensus in the society at large' (ibid., p.213).

While Chomsky, Herman, and Hallin share a critical, materialist framework, emphasising the pro-systemic bias of journalism, the last-mentioned allows for a degree of openness not present in the propaganda model. For Chomsky and Herman journalism is propaganda and the dissemination of dominant ideology. Hallin takes on the more Gramscian, 'culturalist' notion that the 'ruling class' is often split and divided, and that there is no single, unified 'dominant ideology' to be reproduced. Objectivity, if its role as a 'strategic ritual' is to retain validity, means that such splits, when they occur, will be reported by journalists, often to the anger of the parties being criticised. The Nixon Administration, and the American Right subsequently, blamed the media for America's defeat at the hands of the North Vietnamese Communists. In Britain, the Thatcher Government took offence when the BBC chose to report that some in the political and military establishments, not to mention public opinion, were opposed to a military solution in the Falklands conflict. In such cases, division amongst the establishment will be reflected in media output.

Philip Schlesinger cites Hallin's work in criticising Chomsky and Herman for being too deterministic. He rejects their view that media reportage of conflict among elites is 'trivial given the assumption of an "elite consensus" that can be imposed upon the public as a whole' (1989, p.302). For Schlesinger, Hallin's work can be read to suggest that 'the relative openness and closure of media systems is strongly dependent upon divisions within the political class' (ibid.).

Chomsky and Herman are also criticised for their tendency to generalise from the American experience to those of all liberal democratic capitalist societies, including Britain where, clearly, the political and economic environments within which the media work are very different. However, a comparative analysis of British television news coverage of the KAL 007 and Iran Air shootdowns shows some consistency with the propaganda model. In the case of KAL 007 the TV news agenda was set, from the outset, by the Reagan Administration. Ronald Reagan's view of the shootdown as 'a barbaric, terrorist heinous act', an 'atrocity', a 'massacre', and an 'unspeakable act of inhuman brutality' quickly became the *primary definition* of the event (McNair, 1988, Chapter 5). Since the Soviet account – that KAL 007 had been involved in some kind of US/CIA reconnaissance mission – could not be taken seriously, elaborate theories had to be worked up to explain how a jumbo jet, equipped with three independently functioning navigational computers and flown by one of the most experienced pilots in South Korea, could have accidentally penetrated 500 kilometres into Soviet airspace, by coincidence passing over one of the most sensitive Soviet defence establishments. The 'Marie Celeste' hypothesis was made the basis of one news item, for example – postulating that a sudden loss of cabin pressure had caused the plane's occupants to lose consciousness. Such efforts to explain the inexplicable reflected the journalists' adoption of the administration's framework for making sense of the incident – its primary definer status.

This privileged status was also evident in coverage of the airbus disaster. Here, however, the effect was to minimise media interest. On September 2, 1983, 48 hours after the KAL story

broke, the BBC's *Nine O'Clock News* devoted 19 of its 25 minutes to the incident. ITN's *News at Ten* gave the story 13 minutes.
At the same stage in the airbus shooting the story warranted only
5m 40s on BBC1, and 4m 6s on ITV. *Channel 4 News*, which has
almost an hour to deal with stories 'in depth' gave it 1m 51s of
news-time that day.[6] The US administration's definition of the
event as an 'understandable accident', for which the Iranians
themselves were largely to blame, was accepted uncritically.
Indeed, the Iranians were portrayed as cynically exploiting the
tragedy for their own ends.

In this case, then, the propaganda model seems to fit. Two very
similar incidents produced two entirely different patterns of coverage. This does not mean, however, that the propaganda model
is superior to the gatekeeper one, always and everywhere. The
extent to which journalism is open to alternative or oppositional
accounts of controversial events may be argued to be dependent,
firstly, on the politico-economic framework within which the
journalism is pursued (e.g. public service or commercial); the
extent to which elites are united behind one particular reading of
an event; and, as Schlesinger emphasises, the skill of the source-
strategies employed by the protagonists competing for access to
the media.

## CONCLUSION

Politico-economic, organisational, and culturalist approaches to
the sociology of journalism are not mutually exclusive. But they
are premised on profound differences as to the nature of the
state's functioning, of journalism's role, and the concept of ideology. From the politico-economic perspective the economic base
determines, in various ways (economic ownership, political control, advertising), the form of the cultural and ideological super-
structure, of which the journalism industry comprises a major
part. Economic, political, and managerial control of the means of
intellectual production by a dominant class ensures the percolat-
ing down through society as a whole of that class's ideology,
which thus also becomes 'dominant'. Subordinate or oppositional ideas are excluded by or marginalised in the mainstream media.
The culturalist perspective, on the other hand, asserts that the

cultural institutions of advanced capitalism are sites of struggle between competing ideological positions. Some groups have privileged access to these sites, by virtue of economic or political status, and thus their ways of seeing the world become 'hegemonic'. They are, however, frequently contested in the struggle to make sense of the events and issues thrown up by social and economic processes. In liberal pluralist societies, it is argued, the relative autonomy, objectivity, and impartiality of journalistic media must be taken seriously by journalists, who will preserve spaces in which subordinate ideas and dissenting explanations can be heard, even if only on the fringes of mainstream media output. Without such openness, characterisations of the system as pluralistic or democratic would be much harder to sustain.

The organisational perspective, finally, tends to absolve journalists from responsibility for their output by saying that the constraints and conventions imposed on their work – whether imposed by audience expectations, limitations on resources, or the demands of deadlines – are more important in understanding output than any concept of ideological class bias, no matter how 'open' one concedes it to be.

Each of these approaches has a contribution to make to the understanding of how and why journalism is produced. There clearly *are* proprietors who actively seek to influence the content and tone of their media, whether by the appointment of key editorial personnel, or simply by attempting to 'spike' stories which they do not like. Others adopt a 'hands-off' proprietorial style, content to view their properties as cash cows, rather than instruments of ideological and political influence. Some combine both approaches. Tiny Rowland of Lonrho, for example, whose efforts to influence the content of the *Observer* newspaper are well documented, was regarded by his former staff at the *Herald* offices in Glasgow (sold to a management-led consortium by Lonrho in 1991) as a relatively benign proprietor who left them to get on with the job. The *Herald*, of course, was not a national 'newspaper of influence' (in the all-UK sense). In addition, it made a profit for Lonrho, while the *Observer* has been (and remains) a financial loss-maker. Both factors may help to explain why Rowland felt entitled to take such a close personal interest in the latter.

Whether proprietors are 'nice' or 'nasty', the central argument of the politico-economic approach remains valid – that *power*, however it is used, resides with the owners of the media, and not their employees. The exercise of this power will vary from one proprietor to another, but the fact of its existence is undeniable.

Likewise, it is beyond argument that journalists are limited in their work by constraints built into the production process, such as deadlines, limits on space, and access to sources. All contribute to the shaping of output and the form of the final product. Any sociological account which fails to acknowledge the importance of these constraints is of minimal value in our understanding of how journalism is made. But neither can one allow journalists to refer all criticisms of their work to 'organisational factors' over which they have no control. Journalists hold beliefs and assumptions about who are the most authoritative and credible sources in the construction of a given story; about what is the most important story on a given day; and about how a story fits in with 'consensual' ways of seeing the world. These beliefs and assumptions are – inevitably – value-laden, and will tend to reflect the elite culture within which the journalist is working and has been – or wishes to become – professionally successful.

Thus, we arrive at the culturalist position, which stresses the dynamic, conflictual nature of the processes whereby journalists (and citizens in general) form their values and beliefs. When 'dominant values' begin to fragment – as has been seen in Britain since the re-election of the Major Government in April 1992 – the news media (even those traditionally most associated with those values) may move into an adversarial position *vis à vis* political and other elites, as they did in reporting the government's decision in the autumn of 1992 to close most of Britain's coalmines. They may become a site of dissent, contributing to the breakdown of a previously hegemonic worldview and its replacement by another. When the British establishment lacks unity and coherence the British media, like those of the US in the case of the Vietnam War discussed above, reflect that disunity, and become more open. This openness can be further stretched and widened by effective source strategies.

Each of the approaches described in this chapter, then, should be seen as being of potential value in dissecting the process of journalistic production. Determining the relative importance to be attributed to each requires careful analysis of the specific economic, political, and ideological contexts within which individual journalists and media are working. The influences and pressures operating on *Sun* journalists will be very different from those affecting the BBC. Journalists on the *Guardian* will not be subject to the same constraints as those on *The Times*.

Journalists, finally, like the rest of us, are products of their surrounding culture and environment. To understand their motivations and practices, the analyst must appreciate the dynamic, changing nature of that environment. In Part II, we move on to consider the impact on British broadcast and print journalism of the changing political, technological, and ideological environments of the 1980s and 1990s.

# Part II

# Issues

# Chapter 4

# Broadcast journalism
## The changing environment

From 1918 to 1979 Britain was governed by what Nicholas Garnham calls a 'tripartite corporatist consensus', which established a system of public service broadcasting as 'one of its institutional forms of political and cultural hegemony' (1986, p.28).

The organisation of British broadcasting in the form of a public service monopoly was the result of deliberations by two government-appointed committees: the Sykes Committee, which reported in 1923 and recommended that, given the potential social and political power of radio broadcasting in the UK, it should remain free of control by the government of the day; and the Crawford Committee which, reporting in 1926, called for broadcasting to be free of commercial domination. It was believed not only that it was innately desirable for a potent new means of mass communication to be exempted from harsh commercial imperatives, but that the fact of wavelength scarcity would tend toward a monopoly structure for the emerging broadcasting industry. That being the case, better that such a monopoly be held in public rather than private hands.

The British Broadcasting Corporation, as it was to be called, would be funded by its audience in the form of a licence fee. It would be universally available throughout the country, and free at the point of reception; it would play the role, consciously articulated, of promoting a sense of Britishness and national community, while educating, informing, and entertaining in the manner regarded as desirable by the establishment of the time. Most importantly, public service broadcasting would enjoy constitutional independence from the politicians, standing aloof from their partisan debates and self-interested policies.

Thus, broadcasting in Britain was defined from the very outset – in contrast to the United States, where development followed an uninhibitedly commercial path, or the Soviet Union, where broadcasting was commandeered by the Bolsheviks and put to use as a part of the propaganda apparatus – as something too serious to be left to the marketplace, or to the whims and manipulations of politicians. Its entertainment would be 'worthy' and enlightening, popularising and upholding the highest standards of British social and cultural life. Its journalism would be put to the service of British democracy, informing audiences about public affairs from a standpoint of political impartiality and balance. For the BBC, unlike the newspapers with their openly declared biases, there was to be no taking of sides.

Such a course was 'consensual', to return to Garnham's phrase, because it reassured each of the major political parties to know that none of its opponents could hijack the broadcasting system while in office. The existing media proprietors, on the other hand, had no wish to see broadcasting become a competitor for scarce advertising revenue, and so they had little objection to a publicly funded system. And public service broadcasting was an institution of 'political and cultural hegemony' in so far as it could be, and was used to disseminate throughout an increasingly enfranchised British society values, ideas, and information which contributed to its smooth and relatively conflict-free reproduction over decades.

The early British broadcasters regarded themselves as key players in the construction of a national culture – a culture which reflected, as it was bound to do, the unequal class and status structure of British capitalism, within which certain forms and means of expression were preferred over others; certain art forms and not others regarded as legitimate; and certain groups regarded as ideologically suspect, even subversive.

The public service principles laid down in the 1920s for the BBC were extended to commercial broadcasting when Independent Television (ITV) was set up in 1955. Although the ITV companies would operate on a fully commercial basis, deriving their income from the sale of advertising time, the organisation which they jointly formed to produce their national and international news, Independent Television News (ITN), was sub-

ject to the same constraints in coverage as the BBC's news and
current affairs service. Regional news, and network current
affairs, which were to be produced by the regional companies
themselves, had also to be impartial. Neither advertisers, nor
owners of the ITV companies, could exert pressure on ITN's editorial decision-making processes, although its survival and thus
the career prospects of its personnel clearly depended on their
ability to produce a service which would be popular with the
viewers.

As a public service, British broadcasting was only one of a
number of twentieth-century British institutions which embodied
such features as 'universality of provision', 'quality of service',
and the suppression of market forces. Education, health, public
libraries, and state welfare provision as they developed after the
Second World War represented the application of similar principles in other key spheres of social life, made possible by the emergence of Labour as a governing party, and the subsequent 'social
democratic consensus' which straddled the major political parties
throughout the 1950s, 1960s, and 1970s. The crisis of the public
services, and public service broadcasting in particular, stemmed
directly from the ending of this consensus and the coming to
power in 1979 of the Conservative Party headed by Margaret
Thatcher.

## THE CHANGING POLITICAL ENVIRONMENT

Some commentators have dissented from the idea that there ever
was any such thing as a 'social democratic consensus' in Britain,
but there can be no doubt that the Thatcher Government made a
conscious break with the recent past in consciously rejecting the
role which successive Labour and Conservative governments had
allotted (however reluctantly) to public service institutions. It
began to implement a political strategy of introducing market
forces and commercial logic into arenas from which they had
previously been excluded. The strategy was underpinned by
monetarist economic theory and classical liberalism, which
challenged the view that publicly funded bureaucracies were the
most efficient providers of services. In the case of public service
broadcasting the influence of radical *laissez-faire* economic theory

was complemented by the government's ideological hostility to what was seen by the Conservatives as a politically suspect cultural elite, fundamentally opposed to their radical reforming mission.

Relations between the broadcasters and the government of the day had never been without difficulties. From the General Strike onwards, Conservative and Labour governments regularly engaged in battle with the BBC over the content of its journalism. Winston Churchill, Anthony Eden, and Harold Wilson were all in their time persuaded that the BBC was insufficiently deferential to government and should be brought to heel. None succeeded in doing so, and the broadcasters learned to live with what were, in one sense, valuable opportunities for them to demonstrate their much-vaunted independence to audiences at home and abroad. ITN, being a relatively late entrant to the system and thus free of the 'voice of the nation' status which surrounded the BBC, had largely avoided these tiffs. Politicians appeared to think, furthermore, that as it was not publicly funded, ITV could less easily be censured on political grounds.

The hostility which quickly showed itself between the broadcasters and the Thatcher Government was of a qualitatively different kind, with roots in the changing social composition of the Conservative Party leadership and its most vocal supporters on the right of the political spectrum. The Conservative Party which came to power in 1979 was dominated by people who saw themselves to some extent as 'outsiders' in the British class system. Passionate believers in capitalism and the beneficent workings of the free market, they did not identify with the 'old' establishment – those such as Edward Heath, or Harold Macmillan, with whom were associated all the evils of consensus and public service. In their own private circles, and to the public, they presented themselves not as creatures of privilege but as self-made men and women. They were not, in the main, aristocrats, nor did the majority of them benefit from vast inherited wealth. Margaret Thatcher's father had been the celebrated 'grocer of Grantham'. John Major, her chosen successor as party leader and Prime Minister, made it a central element of his political identity that he had never been to university and could barely remember how many (or how few) 'O' levels he had obtained at school.

But if these politicians were not necessarily the products of

British class privilege, they were extremely zealous adherents of a capitalism 'red in tooth and claw'. While the old Conservative Party had espoused a humane capitalism, with itself cast as civiliser and reformer in the classic patrician sense, Mrs Thatcher's supporters demanded an end to all forms of liberal whingeing and attempts to prevent the market from doing its regulatory job. They opposed, and defeated, the consensual tradition in their own party, and on coming to power attacked it wherever else it was found, reserving a particular venom for the cultural establishment in the universities and in the media. The BBC, as the media organisation with the greatest reach and status amongst the British population, and with the most impeccable establishment credentials, was a natural target. Staffed largely by public schoolboys and Oxbridge graduates, some of whom were known to support the Labour Party, and committed to the intrinsically consensual concept of impartiality in its journalism, the BBC's ethos of fair play and its remit to inform the British people almost immediately clashed with the 'them and us' mentality of the new Conservative Government.

The story of the BBC's relationship with the Thatcher Government has been told elsewhere in great detail,[1] and we will deal here only with the key events. These are generally accepted to have been, firstly, the 1979 decision by a camera team from BBC2's *Tonight* current affairs programme to travel to the town of Carrickmore in Northern Ireland, at the 'invitation' of the Provisional IRA, there to film that organisation setting up a roadblock and demonstrating their military control of the surrounding area. The film of the 'Carrickmore incident', as it became known, was never broadcast, but the mere fact that the BBC had cooperated with the IRA in making it enraged Margaret Thatcher. On a subsequent occasion in the 1980s she would complain about the dangers inherent in television journalists supplying terrorists with 'the oxygen of publicity' by giving them access to the airwaves. The Carrickmore incident was particularly offensive to her because it occurred only a few months after the IRA's assassination of her close friend and political adviser Airey Neave.

A few months later *Tonight's* producers compounded their crime in the government's eyes by broadcasting an interview with the organisation which had admitted responsibility for the fatal bombing of Earl Mountbatten and members of his family while on holiday in the Irish Republic. The BBC attempted to defend the broadcast as a legitimate element in its coverage of Northern Ireland. The British people, it was argued, should be aware of the views of those who were taking up arms against the state. For the government, this was political naivety. To grant airtime to terrorists, under any circumstances, was to bestow credibility upon them, and thus to strengthen their cause.

The broadcasters' coverage of Northern Ireland continued to be an irritating thorn in the side of the Thatcher Government throughout the 1980s. The BBC's decision in 1986 to broadcast a documentary profiling two prominent Northern Irish radicals led to an intervention by the then-Home Secretary Leon Brittan and the subsequent banning of the programme by the BBC's Board of Governors. Although the politicians concerned were of Republican and Unionist sympathies respectively, and thus the programme was 'balanced', it fell victim to the government's view that there was no such thing as bad publicity for the 'men of violence'. No matter what might have been said of a critical nature about the featured individuals' involvement in paramilitary activities, their very presence on screen was argued to undermine the British state in Northern Ireland, making it undesirable for the programme to be shown. When the Board of Governors, led by former *Times* editor and prominent Conservative William Rees-Mogg, went along with this line of reasoning, BBC staff took industrial action. Under sustained pressure from a number of directions, *Real Lives* was eventually screened (in a truncated form), but the government's point had been made.

The same logic underpinned the government's decision in 1988 to introduce a ban on the broadcasting of statements by members of proscribed Northern Irish organisations and their supporters, including democratically elected members of legal political parties such as Sinn Fein. The measure was inspired by TV news coverage of the killing of two British soldiers at the funeral of the IRA unit killed by the British Army's SAS in Gibraltar in March 1988. It had been a longstanding concern of the government that representatives of Sinn Fein could be interviewed on television following a murder, attempting to justify the violence in political terms. The broadcasting ban sought to put a stop to this spectacle, leading journalists to develop alternative means of accessing these voices, such as the use of actors, subtitles, and paraphrasing. The broadcasting ban survived until late 1994, when the IRA ceasefire and dramatic improvements in UK government–Sinn Fein relations made it politically expedient for the voices of Gerry Adams, Martin McGuinness, Danny Morrison and others to be heard on British television and radio.

Coverage of Northern Ireland also resulted in troubles for ITV. Although, as already noted, ITV's news and current affairs programming had tended to escape the critical attentions of politicians, it had developed a strong investigative journalistic tradition with such programmes as *World in Action* and *TV Eye*. These programmes frequently targeted the excesses of big business and the political establishment and in 1988, following the Gibraltar shootings, Thames Television's *This Week* prepared and broadcast a programme which directly contradicted the official version of events[2] and hinted at a 'shoot-to-kill' policy by the SAS. Despite pressure from the Home Secretary Douglas Hurd the Independent Broadcasting Authority (IBA), whose members' job it was to supervise and regulate ITV's output, allowed the programme to be shown. A bitter and sustained attack on *Death on the Rock* and its makers followed, which saw both members of the government and the Tory press attempt to discredit the programme, its reporters, and its witnesses. The *Sun* newspaper led the attack by libelling a key witness to the shootings on its front page, describing her as the 'Tart of Gib'. For this libel the *Sun* had to pay substantial damages, as did other press supporters of the Conservative Party who had committed similar libels, such as the *Sunday Times*.

The government-commissioned Windlesham Report subsequently cleared the programme-makers of any professional misconduct (Windlesham and Rampton, 1989). In one sense, therefore, ITV won this battle to report an important issue with the full battery of investigative journalistic techniques. More than one commentator, however, has suggested that the radical restructuring of the ITV system unleashed by the 1990 Broadcasting Act (see below), which included the abolition of the IBA and in which the makers of *This Week* lost their lucrative franchise, was not entirely unconnected with the *Death on the Rock* affair.

If Northern Ireland was a recurring domestic source of tension between the broadcasters and the government in the 1980s, coverage of foreign policy also caused difficulties, particularly for the BBC. In 1982, when Margaret Thatcher was three years into her first term of office as Prime Minister, the Argentines invaded the Falkland Islands (Las Malvinas) and claimed them as their own. The government's response – dispatching a naval task force to the region – committed Britain to its greatest military challenge since the Suez crisis of 1956. And, as in its coverage of Suez, the BBC interpreted its journalistic role as being to represent 'the nation', rather than simply the government. When Britain was in a condition of total war, and the survival of the state threatened, as had been the case during the Second World War, the BBC willingly subordinated its output to the requirements of governmental propaganda and disinformation campaigns. Suez, however, had not been a matter of Britain's survival as a nation-state, and neither, it was felt, was the Falklands campaign. In both instances, domestic public and political opinion was split between those who favoured military action and those who did not, the latter arguing during the Falklands crisis for economic and diplomatic sanctions to be used against the Argentines. For the BBC, the Falklands conflict was one which could legitimately be reported within the framework of impartiality. Government policy could legitimately be criticised, and opposition to it reported. To do otherwise would have been to relinquish its public service role.

That said, the BBC was not anti-government or anti-British in its coverage. As the Glasgow University Media Group showed in its analysis of TV coverage of these events, the BBC frequently reported without qualification inflated claims of British military success (1986). Heavily sanitised military accounts of the conflict and its impact both on British troops and on the young conscripts who made up the Argentine invasion force were blandly reproduced. For the Prime Minister and those of like mind, however, this was not enough. The BBC (ITN under the editorial control of Alistair Burnet was enthusiastically toeing the line) had to demonstrate unquestioning support for the government and its policies.

At the height of the conflict on BBC2's late-night current affairs magazine *Newsnight*, presenter Peter Snow used the phrase 'the British claim' when referring to the contradictory claims of British and Argentine military sources about the progress of the conflict. The detached tone of the expression reflected the BBC's editorial commitment to impartiality in reporting the conflict, within the context of a situation in which the British government could not reasonably claim to represent the nation as a whole. For Margaret Thatcher, it was tantamount to subversion.

Foreign coverage was again the reason for a dispute with the government when the BBC was called upon to report the bombing of the Libyan capital Tripoli by US aircraft based in Britain. By this stage in Mrs Thatcher's second term of office Conservative concerns about the BBC had led to the establishment of a Media Monitoring Unit, under the auspices of Conservative Central Office and party chairman Norman Tebbit. Using comparative content analysis not dissimilar to the type employed by the Glasgow University Media Group in the 1970s the Media Monitoring Unit published its report on television news coverage of the Libyan bombing in April 1987.

The 'Tebbit dossier', as it became known, began from what was acknowledged to be the BBC's 'constitutional commitment to balance and impartiality' and concluded that, in contrast to ITN's 'impartial editorial stance', the BBC had taken 'a number of editorial and journalistic decisions the effects of which were to enlist the sympathy of the audience for the Libyans and to antagonise them towards the Americans'.[3] There was much more in this vein, most of it rejected as absurd by the BBC. Opposition politicians interpreted it as an attempt to put political pressure on the BBC in the run-up to a general election (which took place in June 1987). The Tebbit dossier may, indeed, have been an attempt to encourage self-censorship by the BBC in certain areas of its news and current affairs output, but it is entirely consistent with the pattern of the 1980s up until that point, in which the BBC was perceived by radical right-wingers such as Tebbit to be a major obstacle in the path of the Thatcherite revolution, and abused accordingly.

## THE CHANGING TECHNOLOGICAL ENVIRONMENT

Ideologically based Conservative Party hostility to the BBC, and the concept of public service broadcasting in general, would

always have been unpleasant and discomforting for the broadcasters, faced as they were with the prospect of having to argue
regularly with the government for an increase in the licence fee,
but it was made more threatening by the fact that Margaret
Thatcher's premiership coincided with important developments in
the field of communications technology. The thrust of these
developments was to remove the historic constraint on British
broadcasting of wavelength scarcity, and thus to challenge the
basis on which the public service system had operated for
some sixty years. In the course of the 1980s the fruits of the cable
and satellite 'revolutions' became ripe for commercial
exploitation.

By 1982 British public service broadcasting had already
expanded to four television channels, with a fifth possible, but the
coming of cable and satellite transmission into the UK and other
advanced capitalist societies promised the creation of a truly
multi-channel television system, with not four but forty-four
channels likely to become available to British audiences by the
mid-1990s. By the end of the 1980s cable television had not yet
become established as a popular and commercially viable means
of delivering television services in the majority of urban areas, but
the Astra, Intelsat, and BSB satellites were all providing British
viewers with channels to supplement the existing public service
terrestrial services.

In these circumstances the government's ideological assault on
public service broadcasting for being not only subversive and dissident politically but elitist, paternalistic, and unresponsive to the
demands of the audience was able to mesh with practical options
for change to the old system and the creation of what was
described as 'genuine choice, consumer sovereignty' in the broadcasting sector.

Demands now came for an end to the public service duopoly
and its privileges from those with commercial interests in the new
television channels coming into being. Some of them, most
notably Rupert Murdoch, were strong supporters of the
Conservative Government. Rupert Murdoch also owned some of
the most widely read and influential British newspapers. These
were used to echo and elaborate on the complaints of politicians
about the BBC, and to prepare the ground for a full-scale leg-

islative attack upon it. This attack began with the announcement by the Home Secretary in 1985 of the setting up of an enquiry into the future of public service broadcasting, with special emphasis on its financing. The enquiry would be chaired by Professor Alan Peacock of Heriot-Watt University in Edinburgh, one of a number of prominent 'free marketeers' and government supporters on the committee. Few within broadcasting or observing it from outside doubted that the Peacock Committee's job was essentially to be one of finding a convincing rationale for ending the licence fee system and fundamentally changing the status of the BBC as a public service organisation.

## THE BROADCASTING DEBATE AND TELEVISION JOURNALISM: 1986–91

The report of the Peacock Committee, when it appeared in July 1986, began from the assumption that the 'historic compromise' represented by British public service broadcasting – what was described as the 'comfortable duopoly' of the BBC and ITV[4] – had been outpaced by the coming of cable, satellite, video cassette recorders, 'piggyback' services such as teletext, and other developments on the technological horizon, such as multi-point distribution services, high definition TV, and new ways of collecting viewer subscriptions. The grounds on which the public service duopoly had been established and maintained were no longer valid, and it was time for a radical restructuring of the system.

The BBC, moreover, faced a deep financial crisis arising from the slowdown in the growth of its revenues from the licence fee. By the 1980s, the switch from monochrome to the more expensive colour licence had been completed, while broadcasting costs continued to increase faster than the retail price index. Peacock doubted whether it was politically possible for the BBC to meet its costs indefinitely from annual increases in the licence fee.

The committee also suggested that the existence of the duopoly had produced a system which was more costly and less efficient than it needed to be. For both the BBC and ITV, the arrival of a multi-channel system would erode audiences and, for the latter, threaten the security of its advertising revenue. This possibility led the committee to what for many, including the government, was its most surprising conclusion that, while change in the financing of the BBC would be necessary, it should not be in the direction of compelling the organisation to compete with ITV for advertising revenue. Charged also with the task of protecting the 'quality' of public service broadcasting the committee argued that

> competition for advertising revenue between the duopolists . . . would be bound to change their programme strategies . . . Both the BBC and ITV companies would look for revenue by scheduling programmes in order to maximise audiences in peak time, and probably at most other times. With more advertising 'slots' available, advertisers would be in a stronger position to influence programme content. We are not prejudiced by the claims of advertisers that it would not be in their interests to influence programme content. There would certainly be a risk that controversial drama, critical consumer programmes, current affairs programmes and satirical programmes which challenge conventional attitudes and prejudices would not be supported by them.[5]

To the relief of the ITV companies, and the anger of the Thatcherites in the government, the BBC would not be required to go down the road of selling audiences to advertisers in order to survive. Instead, the committee envisaged a future in which the BBC would be funded from the proceeds of a pay-per-view system. The BBC should join ITV and the emerging cable and satellite companies in a sophisticated market system based on consumer sovereignty. 'If we had to summarise our conclusion in one slogan', declared the committee, 'it would be direct consumer choice rather than continuation of the licence fee. Eventually we hope to reach a position where the mystique is taken out of broadcasting and it becomes no more special than publishing became once the world became used to living with the printing press.'[6]

The committee recognised that such a change could not take place immediately, not least because the technology which would make subscription TV possible was still in its infancy. The BBC would continue to be funded by the licence fee, while the British television system would gradually be extended to incorporate new channels. Then, when channels had proliferated, a subscription system would be introduced and the licence fee partially or wholly replaced, leaving a limited public service provision in those areas of programming which the market could not sustain, such as minority interest current affairs.

Described by the *Guardian*'s media critic as 'a muddled outcome',[7] the Peacock Report amounted to a stay of execution for the BBC. Although not legally binding on the government, the context within which the committee had been established made it politically untenable for its conclusions to be entirely ignored. So the BBC was secure from radical change to its funding base in the short term. On the other hand, the advocacy of a transition to subscription funding in the longer run set the BBC's management the task of reforming their organisation and legitimising its existence in the eyes of the audience. In this respect, the key date for the BBC was 1996, when the Royal Charter governing its operations was next due for renewal. This, and the period of negotiation which would precede it, was when the BBC's public service role would be most intensely scrutinised and, if the political will was present, reformed.

Peacock had little to say directly about the BBC's journalistic output. It was accepted that the provision of news and current affairs was a genuine public service and would have to be safeguarded in a competitive environment.[8] It was clear from this that a central plank in the future defence of public service broadcasting would be the maintenance of its reputation for the delivery of quality journalistic and information output. This would have major implications for the BBC's internal management and resource allocation decisions in the years following the Peacock Report's publication. In February 1987 Michael Checkland was appointed Director-General of the BBC, stating that one of his immediate priorities was to strengthen the organisation's news and current affairs provision. In what was widely perceived to indicate a significant upgrading of the role of journalism within the BBC's operations (and a reflection of management dissatisfaction with existing output), John Birt was appointed as Checkland's deputy and put in charge of the newly formed News and Current Affairs Directorate. From this position he began to encourage a new kind of journalism within the BBC, the details of which will be examined in the next chapter.

As for ITV, the Peacock Committee again had relatively little to say of a direct nature, being constituted primarily as an investigation into funding options for the BBC. A number of points were made, however, which would have serious implications for the commercial companies when the government later came to draft new broadcasting legislation. Most importantly, Peacock criticised the prevailing system for awarding commercial television companies licences to broadcast, on the grounds that it deprived the Treasury of its fair share of the 'superprofits' generated by commercial television. Lord Thomson's famous comment that the commercial TV business was 'a licence to print money' was recalled, prompting the committee to suggest that, in future, ITV licences should be subject to some kind of competitive tendering, which would require prospective licensees to pay a realistic price for the privilege of gaining access to the scarce and therefore valuable resource of airtime.

This proposal, when it was adopted and developed by the government in its subsequent broadcasting legislation (in the form of the imposition of an 'auctioning' system for the awarding of ITV franchises) meant, somewhat ironically, that the short-term consequences of the Peacock Committee's report would be considerably more far-reaching for the ITV companies than the BBC.

## The options for change

The report of the Peacock Committee, by common consensus, set the agenda for broadcasting reform in the late 1980s and early 1990s. In doing so it represented a defeat for the more radical opponents of public service broadcasting within the Conservative Party, leaving the BBC intact until at the earliest 1996. This (for the BBC at least) welcome news was confirmed in the other key document of the pre-legislative phase of the reform process. In July 1988, the House of Commons Home Affairs Committee published its report on the future of broadcasting which, by the government's own admission was, along with the Peacock Report, to play a decisive role in the shaping of the reform proposals.

The Home Affairs Committee began by reasserting the continuing relevance of the concept of public service broadcasting, clearly identifying it as a national asset to be used for the national good. Such a service should continue to exist, it recommended, universally available, free from government intervention in its routine operations, and catering for minority tastes. While the developing technological environment would inevitably lead to a proliferation of new channels delivered by cable and satellite, the committee was clear that existing public services should be maintained. On the specific question of journalism the committee noted that 'television is the principal means of receipt of news and other public information available to virtually the whole population.'[9] As such, the consumers of public service television (and of course radio) should continue to expect 'sufficient time' to be given to 'news and news features' and that such material should continue to be presented with 'due impartiality'.[10]

The report welcomed what it perceived as a trend towards regionalisation in production and predicted that, for the ITV companies in particular, regionalism would be an increasingly important asset 'in the context of the arrival of internationally-based services on satellite which will be aimed at an international, rather than national, let alone regional audience'.[11] This point emerged strongly in the debate, discussed below, about the future of ITV's news and current affairs provision, and the contribution to be made by ITN to that.

Another feature of the report, of particular relevance to the future of British journalism in the 1990s, was its acknowledgement that issues of ownership and control of the media were of central importance. According to the committee, 'it is an important democratic safeguard that no one should be able to control more than one major means of public information.'[12] The report consequently called for the government to include in its legislation measures to restrict the concentration of ownership within any media channel (such as commercial television), cross-ownership (simultaneous ownership of different media channels), and excessive penetration of the UK media by foreign entrepreneurs such as Silvio Berlusconi. In a recommendation specifically directed at Rupert Murdoch's expanding media empire, the committee stated: 'we regard it as imperative that ownership of extra-terrestrial services based outside, but receivable in, the United Kingdom [Murdoch's Sky News, for example] should be taken into account in any future provisions regarding ownership of the UK-based channels.'[13]

Like the Peacock Report this was far from being the endorsement of unfettered deregulation some in the Conservative Party
would have wished for. On the contrary, the committee's support
for the continuation of the BBC's public service status was unam-
biguous. 'As the future of the other television channels is exposed
to competitive pressures we see advantage in maintaining the BBC
as a more or less fixed point in a developing broadcasting
environment.'[14]

## The White Paper

Having obtained two weighty declarations of opposition to any
hasty reform of the BBC's financing or public service role, the
government, in its White Paper on broadcasting, when it
appeared in November 1988, had relatively little to say about the
corporation. There was, however, a clear signal of future intentions in the statement that 'it will be necessary to review the role
of the BBC when the present Charter expires at the end of
1996'.[15] With the exception of this reference to the BBC's future,
the White Paper was in essence a proposal for the root and
branch reform of the ITV network, beginning with the introduction of a competitive tendering system for the awarding of franchises. Pre-empting the objection that such a system would lead
to a deterioration in programme quality (since companies might
be required to cut production budgets if they were to make successful money bids for licences), the White Paper declared that
ITV would continue to be legally obligated 'to show high quality
news and current affairs dealing with national and international
matters, and to include news coverage (and possibly also current
affairs) in main viewing periods', a commitment which Home
Secretary Douglas Hurd repeated in Parliament when presenting
the White Paper on November 11, 1988.[16] There would also be
a statutory requirement for the companies to broadcast a certain
proportion of regional news and current affairs. Failure to provide these services could lead to the proposed new regulatory
body for commercial television, the Independent Television
Commission (ITC), withdrawing licences to broadcast from
companies.

The longstanding requirement of public service broadcast journalism to be 'impartial and accurate' on all matters of 'political or industrial controversy or relating to current public policy' would also be retained.

Channel 3, as ITV was to become, should continue to provide competition to the BBC in the provision of national news and current affairs, and to this end should support and have access to at least one organisation 'effectively equipped and financed to provide news'. Historically, this role had been performed by ITN, which was owned by the regional companies themselves. Most observers agreed that ITN had made a good job of competing with the vastly bigger and better-resourced BBC news and current affairs operation, and would in all likelihood continue to provide the service for the new C3, but some concern had been expressed about the rather cosy nature of its relationship with the companies. The White Paper, reflecting these concerns, proposed to alter that relationship fundamentally, by divesting the companies of a majority of their shares in ITN. In the future, it was suggested, the majority of shares in ITN, or whichever organisation might become the 'nominated provider' of news services to C3, would be owned by non-licensees. If the nominated provider 'failed to deliver an acceptable service'[17] the ITC would be empowered to withdraw its approval.

The White Paper also announced the government's intention to establish a fifth terrestrial channel, which would provide news and current affairs coverage on the same public service basis as C3 and C4. The first attempt to find a licensee for Channel 5, in 1992, failed due to industry uncertainty about the channel's financial prospects. Applications to run C5 were again invited in 1995, this time, however, with greater success. When final bids were submitted in May 1995 the Mirror Group, Pearson, BSkyB and Granada were among those included in the various consortia assembled.[18] Shortly before this edition went to press it was announced that Pearson had been successful.

## The Broadcasting Bill

The proposals outlined in the White Paper were fleshed out and elaborated in the Broadcasting Bill, which went to the committee stage of Parliament in February 1990. Significantly, they included a requirement for the new C3 to broadcast both news and current affairs at peak viewing times, thus answering one of the major objections to the White Paper. At the same time, however, David Mellor, the Home Office Minister responsible for guiding the legislation through to its conclusion, conceded that C3's requirement to provide public service broadcasting was less rigid than that of BBC 1 and 2, or of C4. To survive in the more competitive 1990s, he argued, C3 would not be expected to fulfil the public service remit 'as it has been commonly understood'.[19]

Concern as to the implications of this qualification for commercial current affairs television was expressed by several members of the committee charged with scrutinising the bill in detail. Regarding television news, the main point of contention concerned the future of ITN, and its relationship to the regional companies. As already noted, the White Paper proposed to force the ITV companies to divest themselves of the major part of their shareholdings in ITN. The bill made it explicit that a majority stake in the nominated news provider for C3 (be it ITN or any other company) should be held by non-licensees.

This element of the bill was resisted, firstly, on the grounds that it would deprive the ITV companies of financial and editorial control over ITN, with dangerous consequences for its quality of service. As Labour's Robin Corbett pointed out, the possibility clearly existed that future newsworthy events requiring the commitment of expensive newsgathering resources would not be adequately covered since the dominant commercial interests in C3's news provider could refuse to supply funds. It was pointed out that ITN's much-praised coverage of the Romanian crisis of December 1989 cost the organisation some £400,000 in excess of the planned budget for that year. In the system then prevailing, this money was made up by the regional companies which owned ITN and ran it not as a profit-making operation but a necessary element in fulfilling their public service responsibilities. In the new system proposed by the bill, different motives and competing interests would come into play. In Corbett's view, 'the new arrangement will have to cover newsgathering *and* provide a mark-up for the shareholders, most of whom will not be customers. That builds up tension between the management, the majority of the non-broadcasting shareholders, and the minority of licensee shareholders. In turn, that could lead to pressure to spend less on international newsgathering and to buy in film and voice-overs, which would be of lower quality.'[20]

Conservative John Greenway supported this argument, asking, firstly, 'how can the ITV companies guarantee quality . . . when they have only a minority shareholding in the news company?'[21] Secondly, if the non-broadcasting shareholders were to refuse the funds necessary to support quality coverage of a newsworthy event, would the ITV companies themselves be required to make up the difference?

A further objection voiced by Greenway related to the government's intention to transfer legal responsibility for the publication of programmes from the regulating authority (the ITC, as it would become on January 1, 1991) to the companies themselves. How, he asked, could the ITV companies be accountable in law, as publishers, for material produced by an organisation in which they had minority ownership and voting control?

A rather different objection was raised by Plaid Cymru MP Dafydd Thomas, who suggested that the commercialisation of ITN as proposed by the bill would threaten the editorial independence of the organisation. 'Journalists', he argued,

> who often report in difficult situations, must feel that they are supported by an independent [of commercial interests] line of editorial control, so that they can reflect the reality of the situation they may be in. That is a tradition of free speech and democracy, not just in the United Kingdom, but worldwide. By introducing a commercial element into the operation of the nominated news provider, we shall change the rules in a way that will undermine the tradition of independent journalistic practice.[22]

Labour's Tony Banks voiced the 'if it ain't broke don't fix it' position. 'At present there is control, diversity and quality [in ITV's news service], so why change the structure?'[23]

The issue of regionalisation, to which the Home Affairs Committee had drawn attention in 1988, was raised by Labour's Alistair Darling, who took on the implications of the White Paper's comments on the desirability of more regional production and developed them in relation to the future of ITN. Why, he asked, should all the regional companies be required, as at present, to broadcast simultaneously all ITN bulletins, at times and in conditions over which they had no control? Why could the companies not be enabled to use ITN's materials more flexibly? By way of illustration Darling cited the example of BBC Radio 4 in Scotland, which presents national and international news from a local perspective: in particular, that of the central and west-of-Scotland industrial belt, where the majority of the population is concentrated. Radio Scotland, he pointed out, uses the extensive newsgathering resources of the wider BBC organisation, but refracts its coverage through the local prism. ITN, Darling argued, could have the same relationship to the regional TV news providers of the C3 network.[24]

Mr Mellor's reply centred on the dangers inherent in such an approach: a nominated news provider deprived of its 'monopoly' position in supplying the C3 network would be unable to compete effectively with the BBC's News and Current Affairs Directorate.

Perhaps the most contentious issue to be raised at the committee stage of the bill, and certainly the one which received the most comment and coverage in the press, concerned its implications for the preservation of 'impartiality' in television journalism. For the Liberals, Robert Maclennan noted that under the bill's provisions editorial control over the C3 news provider would pass from the ITV companies to non-broadcasting shareholders. Moreover, the appointment of the news provider would be decided by the ITC, whose chairperson would be directly appointed by the government. Wouldn't this, he asked, 'greatly affect the purveying of news and current affairs?'[25] For Labour, Mark Fisher reminded the committee of the 'Tebbit dossier' and 'the Government's careless cavalier lack of respect for impartiality when it inconveniences them', and expressed concern that the bill contained no measures to prevent such 'meddling' from happening again.[26] Consequently, he proposed an amendment to the effect that news and current affairs programming should be subject to impartiality requirements.[27]

As was to be expected, given the size of its Commons majority, the government's preferred positions generally prevailed. Between the committee stage of the legislation and its final reading in Parliament the government's main addition to the bill was to insert into Clause 6, dealing with the responsibilities of the ITC in its monitoring of broadcasting 'impartiality', a set of guidelines specifying that the 'due impartiality' provision could be applied to a 'series of programmes considered as a whole', and that it should apply particularly to what the act described as 'major matters'. The act then issued the ITC with advice as to what its Code of Guidance for the C3 companies should address, such as the definition of impartiality itself, and the ways in which it could be achieved within programmes of different types. The ITC's Code should indicate that 'due impartiality does not require absolute neutrality on every issue or detachment from fundamental democratic principles'.[28]

Until this point the government's, and in particular David Mellor's, handling of the bill had drawn considerable praise from both broadcasters and opposition political parties, in so far as the worst fears of many about the extent of deregulation and the assault on public service broadcasting had not been borne out. The BBC had been left more or less as it was, and the ITV companies, though committed to a new system of allocating licences, were likely to remain profitable and privileged in the face of the coming extra-terrestrial competition. Now, however, alarm bells rang.

Objections to the proposals on impartiality were a response as much to their origins as to their content. Having passed through the committee stage of Parliament, the bill went to the House of Lords for further debate and amendment, at which point vocal right-wing forces made their presence felt. Throughout the period of the Thatcher Government, as we have seen, the public service broadcasters had been under attack from the radical right, always supported and often led by the Prime Minister herself. A prominent member of this lobby in the House of Lords was Woodrow Wyatt who, after consultation with Margaret Thatcher, introduced an amendment which sought to define the concept of impartiality in rather precise terms, and to police it far more vigorously than had been envisaged hitherto.

The 'Wyatt amendment', which the House of Lords discussed on July 11, 1990, proposed that programmes on current controversies 'lacking in impartiality' should be 'balanced' by means of a concluding studio discussion, fifteen minutes in length, in which alternative viewpoints could be put. It also proposed that any such programme would have to be balanced by another on the same subject, representing an alternative 'bias'. Former chairman of the IBA Lord Thomson denounced the proposals in the debate as 'impractical, extremely reactionary, and thoroughly illiberal',[29] while a number of speakers made the obvious point that one person's impartiality was another's bias, and asked who was to decide in the case of a specific programme which was which? Lords Wyatt and Chalfont (who strongly supported the Wyatt amendment) were accused of being 'stalking horses' for the Prime Minister, in that they placed on the agenda a measure dear to her political heart, while enabling her to avoid the need for heated Commons debate (or the scrutiny of the Standing Committee).

Following the debate in the Lords on July 11 the government introduced its own version of the amendment, and Lord Wyatt withdrew his. Though some of the Wyatt provisions which so alarmed the broadcasters were watered down in the clause which was eventually incorporated into the act, it still represented an unprecedented degree of legal intervention in an area which had traditionally been left to the broadcasters themselves to police. Henceforth, due impartiality would have to be achieved, not in a single programme, but within 'a series of programmes considered as a whole'. The ITC would specify what constituted 'a series' and 'a) what due impartiality either does or does not require, either generally or in relation to particular circumstances; b) the ways in which due impartiality may be achieved in connection with programmes of particular descriptions; c) the period in which a programme should be included in a licensed service if its inclusion is intended to secure that due impartiality is achieved'.[30]

For the liberal broadcasting establishment its purpose and likely consequences were clear. For John Pilger, 'control is the real aim. The amended bill will tame and, where possible, prevent the type of current affairs and documentary programmes that have exposed the secret pressures and corruption of establishment vested interests, the lies and duplicity of government ministers and officials.'[31] Citing *Death on the Rock* as the kind of 'one-sided' though necessary programme which the new impartiality regime was intended to stifle, Pilger predicted that 'charlatans and child abusers, Saddam Hussein and Pol Pot, all will have the legal right to airtime should they be the objects of "one-sided" journalistic scrutiny.'

Others argued that the new rules would leave broadcasting organisations vulnerable to legal attack from ideologically committed organisations, of right or left persuasion, who would drag companies through the courts every time they perceived a 'bias' in news or current affairs. Ray Fitzwalter, head of Granada TV's current affairs department, argued that '"impartiality" should not be the terrain of lawyers'.[32] Such a litigious regime would encourage confrontation, and make self-censorship more likely, especially for small companies lacking the financial resources to defend themselves in costly legal actions.

More pragmatically, the broadcasting organisations expressed the fear that, in future, they would be required to make series, rather than single programmes on particular issues. The BBC's then head of news and current affairs, John Birt, was reported as saying that 'impartiality is achieved by the steady exercise of good judgement at every link in the editorial chain and not by a rigid tit-for-tat formula which will stultify programme making and obstruct public understanding'.[33]

As was to be expected, none of these criticisms of the government's proposals was accepted by the Minister in charge, David Mellor. In his view impartiality was a longstanding element of broadcasting regulation. The interpretation of *what*, precisely, constituted due impartiality in particular contexts and programme formats remained with the independent regulatory body. The government, he maintained, was simply spelling out in more detail what the ITC's remit in the area of impartiality was to be. He rejected the pessimistic scenario presented by John Pilger and others as unjustified. The main reason for the changes, he argued, was that if as proposed in the bill the companies were for the first time to become legally responsible for their output, 'for clarity it is important that they and the viewer should be fully aware of what is expected of them in terms of impartiality'.[34]

The Broadcasting Act came into effect on January 1, 1991, and the ITC's Programme Code was published in February 1991. To the relief of the more pessimistic observers, the Code was less prescriptive than had been feared. 'Due impartiality', it stated, 'should be interpreted as meaning adequate or appropriate to the nature of the subject and the type of programme . . . It does *not* mean that "balance" is required in any simple mathematical sense or that equal time must be given to each opposing point of view'.[35]

One early casualty of the new Code was Austin Mitchell, the Labour MP who had a regular spot on LBC Radio's *Newstalk* programme. Since his appearances were not 'balanced' by those of another, opposing politician and since he dealt with matters of political and industrial controversy, they breached the ITC's Code and had to cease. On the other hand, Mr Mitchell's regular appearances on the Sky News satellite channel were acceptable under the act, since he co-presented the programme with Conservative MP Norman Tebbit.

The ITC recognised that different programme formats – news, current affairs, docu-drama – would require varying judgements to be made about the requirements of impartiality, and permitted individual journalists such as John Pilger to make 'personal view programmes' containing subjective opinions on controversial issues. Such programmes should, however, be clearly sign-posted so as to distinguish them from the companies' editorial stances. It was confirmed that 'due impartiality' need not be achieved within a single programme, but could be applied over a longer period. The requirement of due impartiality had to be met with particular rigour in coverage of 'major matters', as distinct from 'controversial matters taken as a whole'. Thus, broadcasters would have to take special care in coverage of major domestic political debates, general elections, and so on. Moreover, impartiality would have to be applied during the period within which an issue remained 'major' – normally a matter of a few days at most.

Finally, the Code explicitly enjoined the companies to apply their impartiality rules to organisations and individuals outside the mainstream political party system, noting that 'the obligation to ensure due impartiality related to issues, not parties, and some important issues do not divide opinion along existing party lines'. Thus, where appropriate, non-party spokespersons should expect their views on controversial issues to be given 'due weight'.

While some senior broadcasters, such as Granada's Ray Fitzwalter, felt that the Code, despite being less draconian than expected, would nevertheless compel companies to waste scarce resources on spurious 'balancing' exercises and expensive court cases, the ITC's chief TV officer declared unambiguously that it would 'not prohibit any programmes being broadcast, and would not require programmes to be conjured up which are not presently required'.[36]

In general, the initial experience of the Code's operation appears to support this more optimistic prognosis. Broadcasting journalists have not been embroiled in time-consuming and expensive legal battles on the question of impartiality, nor have they been required to produce artificial 'balancing' exercises. To this extent, the fears of Pilger, Fitzwalter, and others of a similarly pessimistic disposition have not, thus far at least, been realised.

But if the threat to the independence of British broadcast journalism posed by the ITC's impartiality Code was exaggerated, other features of the broadcasting reform process have been more damaging. For the BBC, the need to retain the government's good favour in the run-up to Charter renewal in 1996, and for C3, fundamental changes in financing and ownership, have in the view of many had a negative impact on journalistic output. It is to those 'threats' that we now turn.

# Chapter 5

# Television journalism in the 1990s

The appointment of Michael Checkland as Director-General of the BBC on February 26, 1987 signalled the corporation's intention to prioritise its news and current affairs output. In the face of government hostility, rapid technological change, and increased competition from new entrants into the market the BBC, as the 'cornerstone' of public service broadcasting, was identifying journalism as the cornerstone of its operations. Shortly after Checkland's appointment the BBC announced the formation of a News and Current Affairs Directorate, bringing the management of television and radio journalism within one structure. In March that year London Weekend Television's director of programmes, John Birt, was appointed to run the Directorate. The importance of journalism to the BBC's future was emphasised by the decision to grant Birt the additional title of Deputy Director-General.

## THE BIRT REVOLUTION

These appointments, and the restructuring of the BBC's news and current affairs output which they began, were not only the product of the changing political, economic, and technological environments surrounding the corporation as it prepared for the 1996 Charter negotiations, but also reflected the management's view that BBC journalism was weak and thus vulnerable to the kinds of attack described in the previous chapter. A little over a year after becoming Chairman of the BBC Marmaduke Hussey publicly attacked the corporation's journalism, suggesting that it had lost its reputation for 'integrity and independence'.[1] In part this was the predictable irritation of a chairman who had been appointed by the Thatcher Government for his (Conservative) political views. But it was also a criticism of the tendency of BBC journalists in the preceding years to invite Tory attack. The libel actions provoked by *Panorama*'s 'Maggie's Militant Tendency' programme and the *Rough Justice* series[2] had embarrassed the corporation and handed valuable ammunition to critics on the right.

One reason for the choice of Birt to remedy these deficiencies was his own record as a critic of television journalism, dating back to articles he had written for *The Times* in 1975 and 1976. He it was, along with co-author Peter Jay, who had coined the phrase 'bias against understanding' to refer to what he believed was the bittiness and lack of context prevalent in most TV journalism. 'Present television *news* programmes', he had argued then, 'cover a large number of stories, often more than twenty items in a space of about half an hour. As a result the focus of any one story is extremely narrow. Feature journalism' – by which was meant weekly current affairs programmes such as *World in Action* and *Panorama* – 'tends to concentrate on one aspect or one instance of a major problem rather than on the problem as a whole.'[3] 'Issue journalism', which was good in principle because it tended 'to go beyond the context provided by the feature journalist' suffered from being boring or excessively confrontational (since it relied heavily on the device of studio discussion) and in any case 'tended to be scheduled far less favourably than the very news and feature stories which issues journalism seeks to put into perspective'. At that time head of London Weekend Television's current affairs department, Birt prescribed the following remedy: 'We should redesign television news programmes so that they devote much more time than they presently do to the main stories of the day; and so that these stories are put in the fullest possible context in the time available. Feature programmes must be organised so that they are more aware of the need for a relevant focus. And the broadcasting organisations should ensure that there are more programmes which deal with issues than there are at the moment.'

As head of the BBC's News and Current Affairs Directorate Birt proceeded to apply this 'philosophy' of television journalism to the world's largest news organisation. The design and format of main news bulletins were changed in an effort to characterise

– or 'brand' – the BBC's output as more 'serious' than ITN's, while at the same time retaining its popularity and building audience share. For Tony Hall, Birt's chosen successor at the N&CA Directorate, the corporation had to 'nurture its role as the pre-eminent newsgatherer'.[4] The BBC would attempt to occupy and hold the 'high ground', developing its identity as an organisation which 'values the significant and the serious above the sensational and the merely curious. But it doesn't mean that we occupy an ivory tower, immune from the economic pressures of the broadcasting industry.'

The number of items covered in an average bulletin was reduced, while the 'depth' of coverage devoted to the main stories of the day increased. Features programmes like *Panorama* became more focused. As Birt said of *Panorama* in a press interview, 'we want to be able to look back at the end of the year and say we have covered the main stories and issues of the day on this programme.'[5]

Features output as a whole was sorted into strands. *On the Record*, presented by Jonathan Dimbleby at Sunday lunchtime, was to deal with the domestic political agenda; *Assignment* with foreign affairs; the *Money Programme* with the economy.

Increased emphasis was placed on popularity. In the interview quoted above Birt accepted that

> current affairs is not an intrinsically popular form [but] there is a significant audience for it. It should have, and will continue to have, a significant place in the peak-time schedule, both on ITV and on BBC, and any programme that is in peak-time must strive to reach out for as wide an audience as possible. But one hopes that it is not necessary, in reaching out to a wide audience, to compromise in the sort of stories that current affairs should tell. The achievement will be to tell the stories of significance but to make them accessible to the widest possible audience.

In terms of ratings 'Birtian' journalism certainly appeared to make a positive impact on the British viewing public. By late 1989, for example, the BBC's *Nine O'Clock News* was on occasion recording audiences of 12 million, as compared to 6 million for ITN's *News at Ten*, a pattern of dominance that was repeat-

*Table 5.1* Average audience figures for main news programmes, 1987-91 (millions)

| Programme | 1987 | 1988 | 1989 | 1990 | 1991 |
|---|---|---|---|---|---|
| **BBC** | | | | | |
| Nine O'Clock News | 7.5 | 7.5 | 7.9 | 7.6 | 7.2 |
| Six O'Clock News | 7 | 7.9 | 8.2 | 8 | 7.3 |
| One O'Clock News | 4.1 | 4.6 | 4.7 | 4.3 | 3.8 |
| Weekend News* | 8 | 8.3 | 8.2 | 7.7 | 7.3 |
| Newsnight | 1.3 | 1.2 | 1 | 1.1 | 1.1 |
| | | | | | |
| **ITN** | | | | | |
| News at Ten | 7.5 | 7.6 | 6.9 | 7 | 6.7 |
| Early Evening News | 8.9 | 7.5 | 6.1 | 5.8 | 5.6 |
| Lunchtime News | 2.7 | 2.3 | 2.3 | 2.7 | 2.5 |
| Weekend News* | 8 | 7.5 | 7.2 | 7.1 | 7.5 |
| Channel 4 News | 0.7 | 0.8 | 0.7 | 0.8 | 0.9 |

*Source*: *Broadcast*, May 1, 1992.
*Average of early and mid-evening bulletins, Saturday and Sunday

ed across the news schedule, though not usually in such stark form (see Table 5.1),[6] The greater popularity of BBC news programmes was particularly enhanced at moments of domestic or international crisis, such as the resignation of Margaret Thatcher as Prime Minister and Leader of the Conservative Party in November 1990.

Within the BBC itself, however, and among many of those who had worked for it in the past, the 'Birtian' approach generated intense criticism. Some of the opposition was based on nostalgia for the past, and a routine fear of change. In an affectionate goodbye to the Lime Grove studios in London (closed by Birt as part of his restructuring and efficiency drive) – 'where factual television in Britain really began' – features programme-maker Michael Cockerell recalled the milestones of television journalism which had been recorded there, and bemoaned their closing with a snipe at Birt. 'While the Directorate claims its programmes are now more rigorous and authoritative than ever, some at the BBC fear that the spirit of irreverence, originality and zest that marked the best of Lime Grove may have been consigned to the skip with the old film cans.'[7]

In an article for the *Listener* magazine Roger Bolton quoted a senior BBC journalist's view of Birt's appointment as a signal that the corporation was 'withdrawing to a defensible position' under sustained Tory pressure, and predicted that 'some of the Corporation's braver journalism is to be sacrificed in the interests of company survival'.[8]

In the same publication a week later it was argued that 'the appointment of Birt has been convenient for the governors, since his preferred analytical style defuses the normal tensions between politicians and programme-makers and leaves no room for the kind of passionate commitment that informed the work of, for example, James Cameron'.[9] Worn out by years of 'administrative hostility' on the part of the government, it was argued, and facing an uncertain and vulnerable future, the BBC governors had opted for safe, plodding journalism rather than the challenging, risk-taking sort of an earlier era. 'Today the BBC, its spirit of journalistic enquiry cowed, is effectively a state broadcasting organisation.' According to the author, 'scripts are now prepared beforehand, the logic of the argument fully worked out, and a filming structure then created to suit that . . . The time honoured definition of news as something that someone, somewhere, doesn't want to be made public has given way to a new formula in which a kind of intellectual debate is set up to examine the rhetoric of administrative affairs. This rankles with those steeped in traditional journalism, who prefer to probe the gap in public life between the rhetoric and reality.'

Opinion inside the BBC was reported to be that Birt's coming had meant an excessive centralisation of the news and current affairs operation, with a concomitant danger of increased management or governmental interference in its day-to-day running. As the above source put it, 'a centralised style of management is intrinsically more vulnerable to outside pressure than one which is discrete and scattered'.[10] In a similar vein, Roger Bolton argued, 'the danger of too much centralisation of thought and approach is that it paralyses initiative and breeds uniformity. The BBC is not *one* newspaper, it is many, and its journalism must cater for all sectors of the population and reflect a wide diversity of views and opinions. There is no one truth. [The BBC] must initiate debate as well as follow it.'[11]

Birt, of course, rejected these criticisms, and others relating to his management style, his alleged lack of commitment to and belief in the BBC's public service role, and his ambitions to privatise the corporation. All such accusations were, he suggested, the inevitable consequence of change, in which the old guard resented the new. And indeed, not all observers were critical. Even Roger Bolton, whose negative comments have already been noted, acknowledged in the same article that 'at long last, under John Birt, the [BBC's] news and current affairs departments, and radio and television journalists, have been brought together. More resources are being found, more specialists recruited, and a more rigorous, intellectual approach is being adopted. These are very positive virtues.'[12]

In 1991 a senior industry figure could observe that 'on the face of it, BBC journalism is in one of its better phases. It is well resourced, wins prizes, and acquitted itself well in the Gulf. The politicians are complaining enough to make the BBC look respectable, but not so much that it need feel threatened',[13] a view shared by Gus MacDonald of Scottish Television.

John Birt will do many progressive things for BBC news and current affairs. A solid base of responsible journalism is going to be built at the BBC, which will endure throughout the 1990s. John's got the right philosophy: it's not the social mission of the BBC to run hundreds of cutting rooms, or ensure the technical training of hundreds of grades. It seems to me that the BBC has an important social and political role to play, which means it needs a bigger head and a smaller body, and I think John understands that very clearly. More of the BBC's resources will be put into programme-making, which in BBC TV generally over the last few years has been eaten away by the growth of the institution. So I think the BBC's news and current affairs is in very good shape. Don't believe it when they say that John Birt is hostile to investigative journalism.

By 1991, of course, the Thatcher era had come to a sudden and unexpected end. A new Prime Minister was at the helm of government, and a new political mood affected the Conservative Party. For the BBC, let off rather lightly in the broadcasting reform process, this was further good news. Unlike his predecessor, John Major was reluctant to endorse the more rabid

criticisms of the BBC which emanated from his Conservative colleagues during the Gulf War. It appeared that, with Major's acces-
sion to power, a halt had been called to what one commentator
described as the 'undeclared Thatcherite war on the BBC'.[14]

Or perhaps it was merely a truce. In the run-up to the general
election of April 1992 relations between the government and the
corporation grew fraught once more, with numerous allegations
of 'bias' directed at BBC journalists by senior Tories, including
the party chairman Chris Patten. If these were attempts to discourage BBC journalists from being overcritical of the government at such a sensitive time, evidence that the Conservatives'
strategy was succeeding came when, on the eve of the election
being called, a *Panorama* special on the causes of the British economic recession – written and presented by Birt's old colleague
Peter Jay – was cancelled at the last moment on the grounds that
it was editorially inadequate to its subject. Few doubted that concern for the implications of another hostile Conservative government on the future of the corporation had influenced the decision.

## Bi-media and the BBC

What the *Guardian*'s Georgina Henry described as 'Phase 2' of the
Birt 'revolution' began in October 1991, with the BBC's
announcement that its television and radio newsgathering operations were to be merged into one. The impetus behind this development was, firstly, technological. By the early 1990s newsgathering technology had advanced to the point at which a much
greater degree of sharing of resources between different media
had become practical. The result was a move in British broadcasting towards what was termed 'bi-media', whereby journalists
and their crews would gather and produce material for use in
both television and radio programmes. Bi-media also carried the
potential of considerable cost-savings, a factor which understand-
ably endeared its adoption to the BBC's management. Although
Birt had been appointed to manage a strategic shift in BBC
resources to news and current affairs, his directorate had also
been required to make substantial cuts in staff and other costs.

In July 1991 the corporation was compelled to announce the
postponement of a major capital investment of £175 million in a

new news and current affairs headquarters. In such an environment, bi-media became even more attractive. Explaining the reasons behind the merging of TV and radio journalism, Tony Hall
argued that it would lead to 'joint planning, joint hit squads on
big stories like BCCI, a joint strategy on foreign and domestic
coverage. It means using the available technology and resources
for the benefit of both media.'[15]

The implications of bi-media for radio journalism will be
examined in the next chapter. For television, it meant a continuation of the trend towards slimmer, more efficient, less labour-
intensive newsgathering, utilising all the technological innovations
available to broadcasters. In October 1991, the BBC launched its
*Aims for the Future* document, spelling out the Directorate's
intentions in the run-up to 1996. These were further elaborated in
a series of fifteen 'Task Force' reports commissioned by Michael
Checkland in April 1991. Intended as internal discussion documents only, the Task Force reports were leaked by the BBC's staff
union BECTU on April 14, 1992, shortly after the general election. In the report dealing with the BBC's future role as information provider it was recommended that a 24-hour television
service for domestic consumption should be established; that a
new approach to current affairs should be developed; and that
BBC 1 and 2 should establish a clearer editorial focus than hitherto. The reports, though not binding on management, would
form the basis of the corporation's 'blueprint for the future'. The
government, meanwhile, having won a fourth term, announced
the preparation of a Green Paper on the future of the BBC, which
was published on Tuesday, November 24, 1992.

This document confirmed the post-Thatcherite movement in
government thinking away from privatisation and deregulation as
options for the BBC. While the Green Paper announced a period
of wide-ranging public consultation and discussion in which many
elements of the BBC's traditional operation would be up for
grabs, the fundamental necessity for, and acceptance of, public
service broadcasting principles, particularly in the sphere of journalism, was made clear.[16]

The BBC's own 'blueprint' for its future, *Extending Choice*,
was published shortly afterwards. It accepted that the coming of
multi-channel TV (and radio) would impact significantly on the

BBC in the 1990s, but reiterated the continuing importance allotted to news and current affairs in the long-term survival of the corporation as a 'distinctive' public service broadcaster.[17] All of these trends were confirmed in the government's White Paper published in July 1994.[18] The White Paper encouraged the BBC to develop the commercial aspects of its activities further, and to engage more actively in joint deals with commercial companies such as that announced with the Pearson Group in May 1994. In this deal the BBC and Pearson would work and invest together to establish two new BBC channels for the European market, and later for other parts of the world, to compete mainly with Rupert Murdoch's global TV operation. Funding of the channels would come in part from advertising. Despite concerns about the implications of such deals for the BBC's public service status, the 1994 White Paper endorsed the joint venture strategy as one part of the BBC's response to a fast-developing media environment.

Overall, the White Paper refrained from proposing radical changes to the BBC, reflecting the industry's and the government's perception that in a time of rapid introduction of information technology, the BBC required the flexibility offered by a 'wait and see' approach for some years beyond the 1996 Charter renewal. The White Paper, in accepting this, was also viewed as confirmation that the Birtian strategy of constructive engagement with the Conservative government on reform of the BBC had been successful in fending off the free market predators. As broadcaster Melvyn Bragg put it, 'in a mixed economy, a public service institution has been given a massive domestic power base, the right to alliance with media barons, the encouragement to expand globally and virtual carte blanche until 2007'.[19]

## INDEPENDENT TELEVISION NEWS

The decision to set up Independent Television News as a non-profit-making organisation owned collectively by the ITV companies to which it would provide news was taken in large part because of what Richard Collins calls 'public disquiet' (1976, p.9) about the possibility (which would otherwise have existed) of a single corporation or individual gaining control of the news output of an entire national television channel. (In 1955, of course, there were only two.) Collins also identifies strong pragmatic reasons for the decision to proceed down this path, such as 'the economies of scale accruing from centralised production' and '"insulation" of news production and information flows from pressures of ownership and profit-making'.

A further consideration was the fact that most of the regional companies set up to form ITV were strong supporters of the Conservative Party. In these circumstances the ITA felt it preferable to establish another, independent company for the supply of news to the ITV network.

The new company was remarkably successful in competing with the older and richer BBC, largely because of the many stylistic innovations which it introduced to British television journalism. Nicholas Fraser reminds us that:

> Before ITN there were no newscasters. When an employee of the BBC appeared on screen, his or her name was not revealed. No flicker of personality interfered with the austere business of delivering news. At the same time, the old news was distinguished by a grovelling posture towards the manifestations of British power. Official versions of almost everything gained willing acceptance. ITN changed all that. Suddenly, bright young men and women were standing in streets or sitting in studios reading the news or asking rude questions of politicians . . . The ITN writing style was terse and vivid. Stories came rooted in the popular experience of news without succumbing to what have become known as tabloid values.
>
> (1990, p.18)

By 1991 ITN was conservatively valued at £60 million, with a turnover of £110 million. Despite this success, however, the broadcasting reforms introduced by the Thatcher Government fundamentally changed ITN's status as a company, at the same time transforming the financial and regulatory basis of the commercial television channels in such a way that the organisation faced what would undoubtedly be the most uncertain and potentially problematic decade in its existence. While the BBC's News and Current Affairs Directorate expanded its influence and share of its parent's resources, ITN had to learn in the 1990s to live in a broadcasting environment in which its services would have to compete with others. 'The main issue', as one senior executive put it, 'is our survival.'

The main consequence of the Broadcasting Act for ITN was greatly to increase the competitive pressures on the organisation: to transform it from the 'cost-centre' which it had been for thirty-five years into a profit-making business. Under the terms of the act, ITN's status as 'nominated sole provider' of news to the C3 network would be protected for a further ten years, although its position was subject to review in five, after which time, if its customers – the C3 companies – were not satisfied, another news provider could be licensed. C3 would be obliged to continue to take three network news programmes per day, but could demand, from January 1993, more flexible scheduling arrangements. And ITN's contract with C4 would come under competitive pressure, since that channel would become self-financing after the act, and thus have a much greater incentive to 'shop around' for a good deal on its news.

With these changes in place, threats to the survival of ITN in the 1990s emerged from a number of directions. Firstly, there was the renewed struggle for audience share with the BBC initiated by John Birt which, as Table 5.1 shows, the latter was winning. On the evening of the resignation of Nigel Lawson from Margaret Thatcher's government 12 million people watched the BBC's *Nine O'Clock News*, as compared to the 6.2 million who watched *News at Ten*. Disparities on this scale were not routine, and at various times ITN equalled or surpassed BBC ratings, but the trend appeared to be towards the corporation's 'mission to explain' and away from ITN's avowedly more 'human' approach to news and current affairs.[20] In earlier times, such trends would have been worrying for ITN managers, but not life threatening for the organisation. With the broadcasting reforms, however, ITN's position as the nominated provider of news to C3 was no longer guaranteed, but would be contingent on its ability to deliver the regional companies with an affordable, high-quality, but most of all *popular* news service. The Broadcasting Act transferred ITN to the marketplace, as a company, but it also intensified the competitive pressures on the ITV companies. It would be more important than ever before for the commercial companies to deliver audiences to their advertisers. In this context, ITN's ratings battle with the BBC took on more significance than in the days of the 'comfortable duopoly'.

ITN's position was not helped by a flurry of bad publicity in 1990 and 1991. In December 1989 ITN's coverage of the downfall of Nicolae Ceausescu in Romania had won widespread acclaim. ITN reporters had been inside the Romanian capital's television studios reporting live on the death throes of the old regime, a feat not emulated by the BBC. Later events in central and eastern Europe, however, saw ITN looking decidedly amateurish. During the attempted coup against Mikhail Gorbachev in August 1991 – probably the most important single event of the late twentieth century – ITN had no correspondents in Moscow. The assassination of Rajiv Gandhi again found ITN ill-prepared and without a reporter on the spot. The debacle of ITN's attempt to cover the arrival back in Britain of released Beirut hostage John McCarthy provoked scorn for its failure to make something out of nothing.

On their own, such lapses were forgivable – the speed and unpredictability of events in post-cold war Europe made life difficult for all news organisations. But in the harsh competitive atmosphere of the times, they contributed to a public perception of crisis at ITN.

The company's response to this crisis of confidence was to re-assert the distinctiveness of its own 'brand' of television news, separating its product from others – particularly the BBC's – in the developing broadcasting marketplace. While retaining a commitment to 'high-quality' journalism – by which was meant high technical and production standards, with the greatest proportion of output comprising original, first-hand reportage (rather than material bought in from other news organisations) – ITN's distinctively human-interest-oriented approach to events was emphasised, in explicit contrast to the Birtian 'mission to explain'. As a senior manager put it, ITN were against

the tug and barge approach to journalism, where the news story is the tug at the front, pulling a huge barge of analysis behind it. Then, you lose the excitement of why that story was hot today. Yes, you must paint in some background, and make it relevant, but not to the point where you weigh it down with so much baggage, so much analysis, that people begin to yawn. There are current affairs programmes for that kind of in-depth analysis.

ITN makes different products. The *12.30 Lunchtime News* has a more social agenda for a lunchtime audience which is largely made up of women and older people, so once we've dealt with the main issues of the day we'll cover a story which is particularly relevant to that audience. The *5.40 News* is a shorter, punchier, more picture-packed programme than anything else we do. *News at Ten* tries to mop up the events of the day in a coherent manner. *Channel 4 News* is much more in depth and selective in its coverage, borne out of the fact that we're serving a different master there. On C4 we have no God-given right to produce the news. We had to win that contract, and we have to retain it. C4 wants something different from mainstream news, so we cover on C4 news areas such as the arts which don't get as much coverage on mainstream news. In general, on ITV, we probably edge more towards human interest than the BBC, but I think these definitions are quite difficult. Human interest for me is making human beings interested in what they're watching. We avoid the frivolous, because we regard our news time as pretty precious, but we don't avoid stories which might make people smile occasionally.

The BBC was not the only cloud on ITN's horizon. Perhaps more threatening still, since it directly impinged upon ITN's market, was the strong possibility of commercial competition for the contract to produce C3's and C4's news. As already noted, the Broadcasting Act created a strong incentive for the commercial companies to obtain the maximum value for money from their news suppliers. ITN's position within C3 was protected until 1995, but thereafter subject to review. Against this background, the oft-heard complaints of some C3 companies that ITN cost too much were ominous. So was the emergence of rival news organisations which might offer a cheaper service. The Visnews agency was one such potential competitor, and indeed lobbied vigorously (if unsuccessfully) for an immediate end to ITN's privileged position.

Another source of competition arose from the successful franchise bids of the GMTV and Carlton companies for the C3 break-fast and London weekday licences respectively. From January 1993 GMTV replaced TV-am in providing a rolling breakfast news and current affairs service in the morning, relying on Visnews for national and international coverage, but with regular regional opt-outs produced by the C3 companies. Visnews produced this material in cooperation with Carlton, which was based in the London Weekend Television building, and used its facilities. Thus, Carlton TV emerged as the logistical centre of an embryonic national news service, covering the UK, but with regional and international inputs. Such an organisation would be well positioned to compete with ITN for the C3 national news franchise in 1995, further intensifying the pressure on ITN to improve audience ratings and produce a more cost-efficient (from the C3 point of view) service. While LWT's Greg Dyke claimed in March 1992 that 'LWT and Carlton TV are not planning to build a news operation to challenge ITN'[21] the possibility of such a development was inevitably present in the minds of ITN managers.

In order to maintain its position in the face of such competition ITN has had to consider the way in which it packages its material for the C3 companies. The latter, under increasing ratings pressure as a consequence of the Broadcasting Act, had by 1991 expressed in public their frustration at the alleged inflexibility of ITN in matters of scheduling and packaging news. For some of the companies, ITN's reluctance to provide news at more convenient times was becoming a serious threat to their ratings. For example, the ITV network was contractually obliged to transmit ITN's main evening news bulletin at 10.00 p.m. In the context of a ratings battle with the BBC this slot was proving awkward. One of the commercial channels' key competitive strategies was the screening of major feature films, many of which had to be broadcast after the 'watershed' hour of nine o'clock because of their subject matter. It was generally accepted that the viewers would not accept films beginning after 10.30, when *News at Ten* finished. So they were shown at nine o'clock, necessitating a lengthy break for *News at Ten*, regional news, and weather bulletins. In the words of one senior regional executive, this scheduling regime was simply 'not competitive'.

Throughout 1991 ITN's management remained committed to the status quo, declaring that 'there may be changes here and there, but the basis of three network news programmes a day will stay: a) because it's a system that works, b) because they're actually watched by a lot of people, and c) because their status is now enshrined in the law, in a way that wasn't true before.'

At the beginning of 1992 ITN was showing signs of responding to the pressure for change and began a series of meetings with the ITV companies to discuss the rescheduling of the evening news bulletins from January 1, 1993, when the new ITC contracts for C3 licensees would come into force. These specified only that there should be a national news bulletin at 'peak-time', i.e. at some time between 6.00 p.m. and 10.30 p.m. ITN resisted the calls for rescheduling, however, arguing that they would 'lose the ITV companies' public recognition and commercial advantage'.[22] Despite the commercial arguments advanced by the C3 companies, lobbying by influential voices, including that of the Prime Minister himself, enabled ITN to hold out on scheduling. As of 1995 *News at Ten* was still interrupting post-watershed films.

Change of a more fundamental nature was proposed in the matter of how ITN's material (and that of any future C3 news provider) should be integrated with regional news. One of the main strategies by which the C3 companies intended to maintain their audience share in the multi-channel environment of the 1990s was vigorously to assert their regional and (in the case of Scotland and Northern Ireland) national identities. This debate will be examined more fully in Chapter 9, which deals with the future of regional journalism. At this point we can again note the frustration of many of the C3 companies at the inflexibility of their current relationship with ITN. This has obliged them not only to broadcast the programmes at certain times, but to broadcast them 'whole' and untouched, as sent down the line by ITN in London. Several of the big companies made no secret of the fact that they wanted more freedom to integrate ITN's national and international news with their own regional coverage, which had hitherto been packaged in separate programmes at the end of ITN bulletins. As with the scheduling issue, ITN's ability to maintain its position as the sole or even main supplier of news to C3 in the post-1995 period would be determined not least by its willingness to compromise on the packaging of its material and give its customers what they required.

ITN, like the BBC, would also have to compete in the 1990s with the emerging satellite providers. Despite a difficult start BSkyB's 24-hour Sky News channel had, by the late 1990s, established itself securely and become a formidable player in the UK television news marketplace, providing a unique service to a growing audience.

And, of course, while playing a fiercely competitive ratings game, ITN would also have to make profits for its shareholders. In 1991, ITN was in serious financial difficulties. The organisation's much-publicised move to a prestigious new office block in London's Gray's Inn Road had proved to be inordinately expensive. In large part due to the economic recession of the late 1980s and early 1990s, anticipated proceeds from renting out surplus space in the building had not materialised. In 1990, due to poor accounting and bad financial management, the organisation overspent on its budget by £9.8 million. Although ITN, like other broadcast news organisations, had benefited from the introduction of labour-saving electronic newsgathering (ENG) technologies, financial pressures compelled it to make 170 staff redundant. For 1991 overall, however (and despite the huge costs of its Gulf War coverage), ITN broke even, and its chief executive was reported as saying that the organisation was 'now well on its way to successfully effecting the transition from a cost-centred news service operation to a profit-centred quality news business',[23] capable of attracting investment and competing with whatever challenges the 1990s might bring. Whether such comments are regarded as predictable PR or accurate assessments of ITN's health, the organisation had by 1991 demonstrated its determination to embrace the enterprise culture.

The company entered the 1990s with a growing video business, repackaging its news material for different audiences, domestic and abroad. Its contract to supply British Airways and other airlines with in-flight news and current affairs reflected an increasing emphasis on the production of news as a commodity for sale in an expanding global market. In March 1992 it was reported that Russia's first commercial television channel, with a potential audience of 32 million households in Moscow and St Petersburg, would be taking ITN's daily international programme 'in return for two minutes of advertising airtime either side of the 30-minute bulletin'.[24]

In June 1992 ITN signed a contract to produce *Channel 4 News* until the end of 1994 (which was renewed),[25] although the company was less fortunate in its attempt to retain the Channel 4 breakfast news contract. For this, ITN had to compete with three entertainment-led breakfast TV services. In April 1992 it was announced that the contract had been won by independent producers Planet 24, although it was expected that ITN would supply the new service – to be called *The Big Breakfast* – with news bulletins.[26] More bad news for ITN came in May 1992 when, as we noted in Chapter 1, it lost the Oracle licence to Teletext UK.

In an effort to regain the offensive in the ratings battle with the BBC, and thus strengthen the commercial case for its remaining at the heart of the C3 peak-time schedule, in November 1992 ITN revamped the flagship *News at Ten* bulletin, introducing new stylistic features such as the American device of an 'anchorman', in the shape of senior newscaster Trevor McDonald. While critical response to the changes was mixed, *News at Ten*'s audience ratings increased significantly. By 1995 they were averaging 6.8 million, compared to 5.7 million for the BBC's *Nine O'Clock News*. ITN's profits rose to over £8 million in 1994, suggesting that the company had successfully weathered the post-Peacock storm.

At the same time as these stylistic changes were being implemented the regional C3 companies were involved in complex negotiations with a consortium of three of their number – Carlton Communications, London Weekend Television, and Central TV (later expanded to include Scottish, Granada, and Anglia) — who were bidding along with Reuters to buy 80% of ITN. In late November 1992 it was announced that the bid had been accepted, allowing ITN to pre-empt the possibility of future competition from other news suppliers (particularly Visnews, purchased by Reuters earlier in the year).

## BREAKFAST TV

Breakfast television services were established in Britain in 1985, reflecting the trend throughout the 1980s towards more hours of programming on television. The BBC was the first to provide a full three-hour breakfast programme, and was quickly followed by TV-am, owned by a consortium of banking and financial interests led by the Australian Bruce Gyngell, who had previously been chief executive of Australia's Channel 9. TV-am thus became the first new provider of national television journalism in the UK since ITN was established in 1954.

From the outset TV-am, like the BBC, built its service around news and current affairs, although with a markedly 'lighter' touch than the latter's more analytical, in-depth coverage. Paralleling the distinction between the BBC's Birtian approach and that of ITN, TV-am attempted to construct a distinctive brand image for its product which laid much more stress on human interest and 'lifestyle' coverage than on 'hard' news. The TV-am formula, as described in its 1991 application for the C3 breakfast time licence, was a 'live, fast-moving mixture of news, information and entertainment in short self-contained segments which viewers can dip in and out of, listen to as well as watch, as they start the day'.[27] Its style was 'warm and friendly', with a 'human face', combining regional, national, and international news feeds with cosy studio chats between Benetton-jumpered presenters and guests from the entertainment and political worlds.

Sixty-three per cent of TV-am's airtime and 75% of its programme budget was devoted to news and current affairs, supplied by foreign bureaux in Washington, Moscow, Cyprus, and Hong Kong, with local news coming from eight regional centres. Video material was supplied by Visnews.

TV-am was a highly popular service, achieving some 70% of the national audience and making substantial profits for its owners. The company's finances were greatly helped, however, by the successful outcome of its dispute with the broadcasting unions in 1988. The defeat of the ACTT made possible a re-allocation of resources from the technical side of the production process to journalism. Jeff Berliner, TV-am's head of news explained in 1991 that 'before the ACTT dispute we had 82 journalists. We've now got 120. Twenty-four per cent of TV-am's workforce are journalists. Most people at TV-am work on news and current affairs programming. Not finance, or management, or anything else.'

In this respect TV-am was a pioneer and a mould-breaker in British television news. And having 'resolved the issue of who manages the industry' with the unions, the company looked set to go into the 1990s providing what Jeff Berliner called 'a fast, accurate, credible and creditable news service, within a sensible financial base'. Unfortunately for TV-am, and to the surprise of many in the industry, the company was destined to become the most prominent victim of the changes to the procedures for allocating franchises introduced by the Broadcasting Act.

The C3 breakfast-time licence was always going to be much sought after, given the profits which it had generated for TV-am, and when invitations to tender were issued, TV-am found itself competing with two rival consortia: Daybreak Television, consisting of ITN, Carlton Communications, the *Daily Telegraph*, and NBC among others; and Sunrise (now GMTV), the majority of which was owned by the Guardian and Manchester Evening News Group, Scottish Television, London Weekend Television, and the Walt Disney Company.

Both Daybreak and Sunrise based their bids on the alleged weakness of TV-am's service. What to TV-am was 'warm and friendly' with 'a human face' was to Daybreak 'trite'.[28] TV-am's 'soft approach' to news and current affairs would, it warned, lead in the future to a loss of C3's breakfast audience and thus its advertising revenue.

Sunrise criticised TV-am for its poor regional service. Although TV-am took pride in having eight 'regional centres' feeding material which was then integrated into a national package, critics suggested that the centres – in reality remote-controlled studios on the premises of the regional companies – were 'cosmetic investments', with little input into the finished TV-am product. Sunrise proposed to farm out its regional news to the established regional companies, who would provide regular opt-out segments for viewers in different parts of the country, while the resources of LWT and Visnews would be employed to produce national and international coverage.

When the ITC allocated the C3 breakfast licence in October 1991, Sunrise emerged as its favoured candidate to provide early morning television journalism in the 1990s. To the well-publicised embarrassment of the former Prime Minister, Margaret Thatcher,

TV-am's application was deemed inferior to that of the Sunrise consortium.

As noted above, the Channel 4 breakfast franchise was won by the independent company Planet 24, offering a mix of 'middle market tabloid and mainstream Radio 1'.[29] *The Big Breakfast* launched in October 1992, to a generally positive critical reaction, while its audience ratings from the outset exceeded those of its predecessor, the *Channel 4 Daily*.

## CURRENT AFFAIRS

Channel 3 (formerly ITV) differs from the organisation of the BBC's journalism in that it has traditionally separated the production of news from that of current affairs. While news was supplied by ITN, current affairs programming was produced by the individual companies. *World in Action*, for example, was produced by Granada, *The Cook Report* by Central, and *This Week* by Thames.

For both the BBC and the commercial companies, however, current affairs provision in the 1990s will be significantly affected by the Broadcasting Act. The most controversial change – the tightening up of the 'due impartiality' obligation and the shifting of legal responsibility for meeting this obligation to the companies – was examined briefly in the previous chapter. As we saw there, opinion within the industry about the consequences of this change for C3's current affairs output was divided. Those we might describe as pessimists argued that in the 1990s companies would refrain from transmitting anything which they considered to breach the ITC Code. While there would be no pre-publication censorship of current affairs programming (on the face of it, a welcome improvement to the old regulatory structure) the fear of costly court actions *after* a programme had been transmitted would deter companies from broadcasting anything which might be vulnerable to a legal challenge.

Adherents to this view pointed out that the managements of the new companies would, in some cases, be inexperienced in fending off the political pressures which, for example, the IBA and Thames successfully resisted over the *Death on the Rock* affair, and might be tempted to give in without putting up a real fight. Others rejected this line of reasoning. David Scott, head of news and current affairs at Scottish Television, argued thus:

> I don't see that it makes any difference. I think it's healthy that individual companies should be regarded as the broadcasters, rather than the ITC. After all, a newspaper is regarded as the publisher of its own material, and I'm sure we should be responsible for what we publish. I don't think that any of the new regulatory bodies which are in place should limit one's ambition to do challenging, investigative reporting. I don't see how it can inhibit. Sure, there are additional constraints, but they're not so constraining that they might prevent you from doing the job you want to do. If you've got a network where you're obliged to take certain parts of the schedule, for example, *World in Action*, the company that makes the programme, in this case Granada, would have to indemnify everyone else who published it. At the end of the day there will have to be some assurance given by the originating company.

A further concern of the pessimists was more fundamental: that commercial imperatives would drive current affairs from C3's peak-time schedules, to be replaced by yet more soaps, game shows, and mini-series. In the 1990s, it was argued, ratings would be even more important to the maximising of advertising revenue than they had been in the past, and since current affairs was not the most popular category of programming, it would inevitably be sacrificed. In the words of Granada's Ray Fitzwalter, 'everything points to less rather than more'. In the summer of 1992 *This Week* and *World in Action* were being openly criticised for losing valuable ratings at peak viewing times. For Central TV's director of programme planning, harsh commercial logic was unstoppable: 'if you have a mass audience at 8 p.m. you don't waste it by handing it over to a less than popular current affairs programme.'[30]

An alternative argument was put by those who, while accepting the inevitability of increased commercial pressure on the companies countered that it is not simply numbers which matter in ratings terms, but also the value of the audience as a consumer market. C3 would need to deliver at least some of its advertisers an 'AB' audience, able to buy the expensive consumer goods and motor cars which they wished to sell. For this group, quality current affairs was an important programming element. As Roger Bolton put it, 'ratings are not just about numbers. Advertisers value the different kind of audience that serious documentaries can command.'[31]

No one doubted – though many regretted – that C3's current affairs would be pushed out of the early evening prime-time slots traditionally occupied by *World in Action* and *This Week*, and into later slots, after rather than before the main news bulletin. It was pointed out, however, that when BBC schedulers moved the flagship *Panorama* programme from 8.00 to 9.30 p.m. its audience ratings increased. Thus, it was argued, C3 could move its current affairs programming while retaining, perhaps even improving, its audience share.

Another safeguard would be the contractual obligations imposed on licensees by the ITC. 'When the companies bid for their franchises', points out Grampian's managing director Donald Waters, 'they said to the ITC, "these are the programmes we'll be doing for the next ten years."'

> If the revenue from advertising is in place, you can't willy nilly decide to drop programmes. You're committed to the level of programmes you've outlined in your franchise bid. That's watertight, and even if someone comes in after 1994 [when the moratorium on commercial takeovers of C3 companies expired] and buys your company on the stockmarket they're tied to the same level of programming. There would have to be a great financial catastrophe for the ITC to allow you to stop doing the programmes you promised to do, and only under those exceptional circumstances could I see programmes being reduced in number or quality.

Should a company be unable to deliver its programme commitments the ITC would be able to take measures up to and including the withdrawal of the licence. Moreover, the licences awarded in October 1991 by the ITC were not given to any company which had bid so much that its programme plans could have been jeopardised. Passing the 'quality threshold' meant not only that the programmes promised by bidders were of high quality, but also that they could be financed. The concern of some, however, was precisely that raised above: that changing economic circumstances could undermine advertising revenues and thus programming possibilities. Donald Waters concedes that

> if the whole industry runs into another recession like that of the late 1980s and early 1990s some companies will have to hold up their hands to the ITC and say 'look, the money isn't there to finance all the programmes we're committed to. We need some sort of respite.' The ITC may have to say OK. Even so, I don't think that current affairs programmes will be singled out as some kind of sacrificial lamb. They might be moved in the schedule, but that's fine. *Panorama* got a bigger audience after Grade moved it.

For the pessimists, however, 'might bes' and 'ifs' were not sufficient to guarantee the survival of current affairs journalism on C3, if economic recession and competition from other sources combined to put irresistible pressure on managers and accountants to maximise ratings. These fears were encouraged by the ITC's assessment of the first year's operation of the new C3 franchise system, which expressed serious concern about the perceived deterioration in the quality of peak-time current affairs. New series like *The Big Story* were joining *The Cook Report* in pushing the channel towards 'infotainment' rather than 'serious' current affairs. C3's management rejected these accusations, insisting that current affairs had been established as a permanent element in the new scheduling system, and that new series like *The Big Story* were not 'tabloid TV' but the outcome of legitimate efforts to update and develop the style of British television journalism. *The Big Story*, as one of its makers put it, was far from being downmarket tabloid TV but 'a new sort of current affairs – serious stories, covered stylishly, in the week they happen.'[32]

A third major consequence of the Broadcasting Act for current affairs television (and one which applies equally to the commercial sector and the BBC) was the requirement that at least 25% of output should be independently produced – bought in or commissioned, thus moving the large broadcasting organisations closer to a position where they are, in effect, publishers of material originated elsewhere.

This aspect of the broadcasting reforms was generally welcomed within the industry. Channel 4 already operated such a system for its journalistic output, with considerable success. Some influential figures within the commercial companies regarded independently produced programmes like Channel 4's *Dispatches* as the model for C3 to follow. On the other hand, concern was expressed that independent companies lacked the resources and institutional back-up to mount lengthy, risk-taking investigative journalism of the type exemplified by *World in Action* or *This Week*. Granada's Ray Fitzwalter argues that 'you need a very courageous management, and a lot of resources, to support you in that'.

The BBC, anxious to preserve its empire, was resistant at first but quickly came to accept the change. Its prestige *Question Time* programme was the first to be 'privatised', the contract to supply the programme being won by Brian Lapping Associates, who also produced the well-received *Second Russian Revolution* series.

Supporters of commissioning out argued that it would allow programme-makers more readily to take advantage of an environment in which advances in technology and the decline of the trade unions' restrictive practices would allow substantial cost-cutting. On the other hand, many of the independent companies were set up by old hands made redundant from the BBC and other established producers. Some suspected that a certain degree of nepotism would inevitably creep into the system.

## THE EXTRA-TERRESTRIALS

The late 1980s saw the coming of 24-hour, transnational television journalism transmitted by satellite from bases in the United States and western Europe. Some of these new entrants to the journalism business, like WorldNet and Cable Network News (CNN), were available outside their country of origin only to relatively small audiences, such as international business travellers and cable subscribers. In the UK, where cable had not by the early 1990s developed to the extent expected ten years before, this was particularly true. Other organisations, principally Sky News, used satellite transponders to transmit programmes made in the UK to domestic audiences. Another new entrant, World Service Television News (WSTN) was from November 1991 produced by the BBC in London for an international audience.

While at the time of writing still limited in their market share and influence, the rise of Sky News in the UK, and CNN internationally, confirms that the 1990s will be a period when satellite broadcasters become more important as information sources.

## BSB and Sky

British Satellite Broadcasting – a consortium comprising Pearson, Virgin, Granada, Anglia, and the Australian Bond Corporation – won the franchise to set up a service using one of the UK's five DBS (direct broadcasting by satellite) frequencies in December 1986. BSB would run a three-channel service, employing the technologically advanced D-Mac transmission system. Indeed, so sophisticated was the technology that BSB could not get on air before Rupert Murdoch launched his Sky channel in February 1989. Sky used the less advanced, but more reliable PAL technology, and from the moment of coming on air effectively set the pace of satellite broadcasting development in the UK (Chippindale and Franks, 1991). When BSB finally began transmitting in April 1990 it was already lagging far behind the Murdoch operation and consuming vast financial resources in an effort to catch up. These efforts proved to be in vain, and on November 3, 1990, BSB and Sky formally merged, leaving one UK-based provider of 24-hour news, the majority share of which was owned by Rupert Murdoch's News Corporation.

For the liberal broadcasting establishment in Britain, this was the worst possible outcome of the BSB–Sky struggle, since it represented the victory of the man to whom was attributed the alleged decline in the standards and ethical values of the British press (see below). Would Murdoch use BSkyB's news channel as he had used his newspapers – to propagate the values of populist Conservatism and denigrate its opponents? Would the news values of his tabloids be reproduced on television?

At first, it seemed that such concerns would be made irrelevant by the economic pressures working on BSkyB. In January 1990 the *Guardian* had estimated Sky TV's losses at £10 million, an 'intolerable cash drain on News International'[33] which was financing the venture, mainly from the profits made by the Wapping newspapers (see Chapter 7) . As late as June 1991 Sky

News was estimated to be costing £30 million a year to run, making it, in the view of City commentators, vulnerable to closure.[34]
By February 1992, however, BSkyB as a whole was able to
announce that, for the first time since its establishment, it was
making a running profit, with 2.8 million households by then having been persuaded to invest in Astra satellite receiving equipment.[35] While Sky News continued to be a substantial drain on
the overall BSkyB operation, Murdoch's Newscorp company's
profits of £105 million in the six months to June 1991 made it
more likely that the channel would survive.

And with an improved financial position Sky News was also,
by 1992, acquiring an increased, if rather begrudged, respectability as a journalistic organisation. The worst fears of 'tabloid television' had not been realised. Although a substantial proportion
of the channel's output comprised relatively inexpensive buy-ins
of variable quality, the immediacy, distinctive style, and general
standard of the 24-hour service had won many admirers. As Liz
Howell, then Sky News's managing editor, explained to *Broadcast*
magazine, the organisation had a distinctive and valid 'brand',
consisting of the absence of a rigid schedule, and no division in
programming between news and current affairs.[36] Sky News, said
Howell, explicitly rejected the Birtian 'mission to explain' as
'trite', on the grounds that 'a clear news report inevitably
explains'.

Sky News also resisted the BBC's movement towards more specialist correspondents, and unashamedly subordinated editorial
decisions on coverage to financial constraints. For Sky News
senior management, the organisation's different approach to news
values and agendas was something to be welcomed in a multi-
channel system. For the head of news, John O'Loan:

> there's nothing wrong with providing news in a different way
> to a different audience. The *Sun* provides a service to people
> who might otherwise not read a newspaper. If they didn't read
> a newspaper they'd know less about what was happening. The
> fact that the *Sun* is the way it is, and not *The Times*, doesn't
> necessarily mean that everything has to be like *The Times*, or
> like the BBC used to be, or like *Panorama*. I think the greater
> the diversity of news dissemination the better. Just because it's

presented differently doesn't mean it's wrong. We present a different style of news from the others. We are a little more relaxed. I think we take ourselves less seriously than the others do. I think that by taking yourself too seriously you can set up a barrier between yourself and the audience to the extent that instead of informing people you can be on the verge of preaching to them. What we tend to do is put the audience first, and think about what the audience would expect, what the audience is most likely to get out of what we're doing, rather than sitting in a television station and saying what the audience will get.

What we've done is to show people who were expecting downmarket tabloid television that we're not, and to people who were expecting an upmarket broadsheet that we're not, that we have quite a definite place in the TV news industry.

Resistance to Sky News remained in some quarters, however. The Royal Television Society's 1992 awards for journalism conspicuously lacked any mention of Sky News personnel. In the *Guardian*, Liz Howell asked if, given the organisation's growing reputation in the aftermath of the Gulf War, it was

forever to be ritually punished for being set up by Rupert Murdoch? I [am] well aware that Sky News' strengths were not those of *Panorama* or *This Week*. But . . . Sky News is the first and the only British 24-hour news channel. Many people would agree that it has changed the way that British journalists behave. It has forced to the forefront the issue of how to react to breaking news.[37]

By late 1992 News Corporation was sufficiently confident of Sky News's growing credibility and long-term viability to announce that it would be introducing a monthly charge of £2.99 for viewers to receive the service (the fee included reception of the Sky One entertainment channel).

### Cable Network News

Cable Network News (CNN) was launched from Atlanta, Georgia, on June 1, 1980, the brainchild of media and entertainment entrepreneur Ted Turner. As Hank Whittemore's account of the first ten years of CNN's existence describes, Turner's idea of a 24-hour cable news channel, distributed by satellite across the United States, was the beginning of a 'second age' of television in which, utilising technological innovation, the nature of news and information broadcasting would be fundamentally transformed (1990). With the established US networks committed to opulent, expensive flagship news bulletins, CNN came on air with a cheap, untried, day-long service which broke all the economic and technical 'rules' of TV news. The uniqueness of the product ensured its survival, however. As the years, and the crises, came and went, the advantages of a news channel, on the air 24 hours a day, live, were clear, and audiences quickly grew. With each key event – the TWA hijacking in 1985, the Challenger disaster of 1986, the US bombing of Libya and, of course, the Gulf War – CNN achieved an immediacy of coverage which no other organisation could match. As *Time* magazine put it, when commemorating Ted Turner's selection as 'Man of the Year', CNN had changed the definition of news from being 'something that *has* happened to something that is happening at the very moment you are hearing of it'.[38]

As CNN proved the worth – and the profit potential – of its product in the early 1980s the big US networks made several attempts to break into the 24-hour news market. None was able to repeat CNN's feat of transforming the cost structure of television news, leaving Ted Turner with the field to himself by the end of 1983. That year CNN announced its first annual profit of $20 million.

Having conquered America Turner then shifted his attentions to the rest of the world, and Europe in particular, where there was a lucrative market for 24-hour news in the expensive hotels used by business travellers. Penetration of domestic television markets abroad was initially dependent upon the degree to which a country was cabled. In Britain, where cable had failed to reach anything like the degree of household penetration Turner could tap into in America, CNN remained a minuscule player in the television news business. In April 1992, however, CNN acquired a transponder on the Astra satellite, giving it for the first time the opportunity to reach a mass audience in the UK. It seems unlikely, nevertheless, that CNN's US-dominated news agenda can achieve significant success in the United Kingdom.

## World Service Television

We have seen how the BBC entered the 1990s with a broadly expansionary posture, confident of its ability to retain a distinctive role in a rapidly changing broadcasting market. A major part of that expansion will involve the development of a global television service paralleling the established radio service. In 1986, John Tusa, as the newly appointed head of the World Service, declared his intention 'to pursue our audience by every technical means available, from short wave to medium wave, from satellite to landline, from television to cassette.'[39]

After CNN was founded and became established, the BBC began to make plans to enter the transnational TV market. Director General Michael Checkland stated to the Home Affairs Committee of the House of Commons in January 1988 that the BBC wished to produce programmes for a world audience, using the editorial staff of the External Services, and the resource base of the News and Current Affairs Directorate, thus exploiting the strengths of both. As with radio, the television service would be in English, but comprise 'international news, internationally ordered'.[40]

In keeping with the entrepreneurial spirit of the late 1980s the proposed 'World Service Television News' would be run on a commercial basis, as part of the BBC Enterprises company. This was welcomed by the Home Affairs Committee, although its final report stressed that 'commercial finance should not be allowed to cast doubt on the integrity of the news service.'[41]

The producers of WSTV argued that the distinctive features of the World Service approach to journalism (see Chapter 6) would grant it a competitive advantage over CNN, WorldNet and others. In *Conversations with the World* John Tusa pointed out that WorldNet – though 'the first substantial effort in transnational television' – had failed to win significant audiences because its 'main drive is to tell the world about America' (1990, p.16). It was, in short, too parochial and propagandistic of a particular culture, ideology, and way of life. In relation to CNN, Tusa told the author that 'we'll give much more of a world picture in news. I don't think they give a very consistent or reliable world picture. . . they're terribly American-oriented. If in doubt they go back to very localised American feature stuff. It can get very small towney indeed.' WSTV, by contrast, would operate within a news agenda which would be 'recognisable in most places of the world'. WSTV would also seek to exploit its resource advantage over the American global broadcasters. By developing bi-media in the World Service, TV and radio operations would be able to share newsgathering resources and material with each other, and with the BBC's domestic news and current affairs production.

In a speech to the Royal Television Society, John Tusa expressed the BBC's motivation in launching WSTV thus: 'who could be content to leave the domination of this immensely powerful sector of the global information market – international network news – to one company and one nation, the United States? Now there are two players in this market, BBC World Service and CNN, and there is plenty of room for both of us.'[42]

WSTV began transmitting in November 1991, using Asiasat to reach a potential audience of 38 million homes in South-east Asia. Shortly thereafter it became available in Europe, and preparations were underway for the service to reach Australia, Japan, and Africa. By the end of 1992 WSTV was fully independent of the BBC's financial structure.

As was noted earlier, in 1992 plans were announced to make a 24-hour news channel based on WSTV available to British viewers as an encrypted service on the Astra satellite. At a conference in London Michael Checkland argued that 'it would be ironic if our viewers had to be in Baghdad or Vienna or Oman to receive 24-hour news from the BBC but could not receive it at home.'[43]

In April 1991 it was reported that ITN was also considering entry into the global TV market, cooperating with ABC and NHK to launch a 24-hour speech service called Global News Network. By the time of writing, however, this project had not come to fruition.

## CONCLUSION

In the 1990s there has been more television news produced for the

UK audience than ever before. Despite the fears of some observers in the late 1980s, the traditional public service commitment to high-quality news remains written into the broadcasting legislation. While much is uncertain about the future of the BBC post-1996, it is clear that journalism will remain central to its operation. Indeed, the assertion of its public service journalistic role will be a strategic plank in its defence.

Commercial television, too, continues to be committed to quality journalism at peak-time. News is popular and therefore justifiable on purely commercial grounds. The prospects for current affairs broadcasting, particularly on C3, are less certain, because the companies' financial commitments may well dictate cuts in the quantities made, and the rescheduling of those that survive. The outcome of the regional companies' attempts to reconcile financial pressures with their proclaimed desire to maintain current affairs output will depend not least on the economic environment prevailing in the late 1990s, and the speed with which recession can be left behind.

In tandem with economic pressures, a tighter regulatory regime may lead to greater self-censorship on the part of the broadcasters and the disappearance of the risk-taking journalism which produced *Death on the Rock*. In this matter, much will depend on the will of the companies to maintain ITV's reputation for challenging current affairs programming, as well as the posture of future governments and their readiness to use the levers which, thanks to Margaret Thatcher, they now have at their disposal.

As for the extra-terrestrials, they are clearly here to stay, as distinctive and increasingly profitable elements of the British broadcasting market. The BBC, however, with WSTV now on air and the possibility of a 24-hour domestic TV news channel at some point in the future, looks well placed to compete with Sky News and CNN in the multi-channel environment of the twenty-first century.

# Chapter 6

# Radio

Radio has traditionally been viewed, by producers and audiences alike, as the 'cinderella medium' – television's poor relation. In an era of rapidly proliferating television channels, radio's presumed inferiority has frequently given rise to the view that its future is problematic, and something akin to a siege mentality has developed on the part of those who work in the medium. Fortunately, reports of radio's death have been shown to be exaggerated. Since breakfast television services began in the UK, despite the belief of many that early morning radio audiences would decline, they have in fact increased consistently. The 1990s will be a decade in which radio, like television, expands, fuelled by persistently healthy ratings and market research evidence that popular demand for radio services remains high. Radio, it would appear, retains its distinctive appeal as a form of communication which can be consumed while mobile, and while engaged in a variety of other pursuits, and whose mode of functioning is quite different from that of the visual media.

Within radio as a whole, journalism and speech services remain prominent. Question marks exist, however, over the extent to which a quantitative expansion of radio will lead in the end to a qualitative diminution of journalistic standards, particularly in the commercial sector.

## THE GREEN PAPER AND RADIO REFORM

The publication of the Conservative Party's Green Paper on reform of the radio system in February 1987[1] was greeted with initial hostility by those who feared the deleterious effects of deregulation on the existing system. As with the debate on the future of public service television, the government's opponents argued that the expansion of commercial radio, combined with a new 'light touch' system of regulation – the main thrust of the Green Paper's proposals – would reduce output to a 'lowest common denominator' of pop music and MOR, while 'quality' services such as journalism would be squeezed out of the airwaves. The BBC's head of Gaelic broadcasting, Neil Fraser, typified such concerns when he expressed the fear that the Green Paper would, among other things, threaten radio's ability to serve distinct communities such as the Gaeltacht in Scotland.[2]

In the context of what was known about the Conservatives' attitude to public services, such fears were not perhaps unreasonable. They were, however, founded on the assumption that the marketplace would be unable to sustain 'quality' radio. On the contrary, a Broadcasting Research Unit survey reported in June 1988 that audience demand for 'speech' radio was as high as that for music programming.[3] In the US, indeed, following Mark Fowler's deregulation of the radio system in the early 1980s the number of news-based networks had by 1988 increased from four to eight. The American experience suggested that deregulation did not necessarily mean the decline of radio journalism, since it was a genuinely popular service.

Reinforcing this commercial logic was the widespread perception amongst communication companies that the provision of news is a necessary component of any broadcasting service which aspires to be seen as 'quality'. To win respectability in the UK broadcasting market, one had at least to pay lip service to the provision of journalism.

Consequently, although the 1990 Broadcasting Act did not require the new national commercial networks which would shortly come into existence to provide journalism as a part of their programming, it seemed likely that all would choose to do so. John Perkins, head of Independent Radio News (IRN) – the main provider of news to the commercial radio networks – comments that 'in the old days the IBA would insist that to get the franchise you had to run a news service. That isn't the case any more. You can now set up a radio station and say, I'll ditch the news and play Madonna – but not a single licence applicant has said they will do that. All the national channels made a strong point [in their bids] of having news right up there at the top of the hour.'

In addition to legislating for the introduction of commercial network radio in the UK the government's reforms sanctioned the creation of a large number of regional and local radio stations, for which the provision of news and journalism was from the out-set an important programming element. Since the establishment of commercial radio in the 1970s there has been a relatively small number of regional stations, such as Radio Clyde and Capital Radio, but the reforms permitted the establishment of literally dozens of more localised services. While these stations were encouraged to provide journalism at their own, local level – the Broadcasting Act requires local radio to 'cater for the tastes and interests of persons living in the locality for which it would be provided . . . and to broaden the range of programmes available by way of local services to persons living in that area or locality'[4] – they were inclined to take national and international news from the London-based providers, predominantly IRN.

Taken together, the proliferation of commercial radio outlets at national, regional, and local level in the late 1980s and into the 1990s means a rapidly expanding market for companies equipped to supply radio news.

The leading player in the commercial radio news market has been, and at present remains, Independent Radio News. However, the expansion and deregulation of the industry has led new providers to attempt to enter the field and challenge what has been IRN's virtual monopoly position. In July 1991, the first network commercial radio service to be awarded a franchise under the provisions of the Broadcasting Act, First National Radio, announced that its news bulletins would be supplied by Network News Services, a company formed by former ITN jour-nalist John Davies. In February 1991, IRN had merged with ITN's much smaller radio news service to form a stronger organ-isation. Partly in response to the consequent fears of an unhealthy (and potentially expensive) monopoly developing and being consolidated in the expanding radio network, Network News Services was set up to offer an alternative source of supply.

Predictably, perhaps, IRN rejected the argument that

competition for the commercial news market would be a healthy development. Head of IRN John Perkins argues that

> there needs to be some kind of stability, some recognition that to provide a good news service – something with a bit of depth, a bit of bottom – you need resources, and money has to be provided. Otherwise what you're going to get, and what you're beginning to see – is a fragmentation of the news service. Smaller companies will set up rival news services, with even fewer resources than we have, and they'll sit there and take their material from Teletext, etc. In other words, there'll be no original or creative thought going into the process of producing a news bulletin. They will attract a bit of revenue for that, and somebody else will set up another service, so you might end up with a number of smaller, under-resourced news services, none of which is doing what a commercial radio news service should be doing – providing a comprehensive alternative to the BBC. I suspect that fragmentation of news services, and the funding of that service, is probably the biggest single problem we face.
>
> Commercial radio news was set up as an alternative to the BBC, in the same way as ITN. So there has got to be something substantial. You can run an insubstantial, top of the hour service that isn't going to satisfy the demand for in-depth, original news. A lot of news services are merely the reprocessing of other people's thought. There's no originality. If you're going to compete with the BBC you've got to have some originality and depth.

The problem of fragmentation, if problem it is, was intensified by the effects of the economic recession on the commercial radio companies' advertising revenue. On the one hand, the recession of the late 1980s and early 1990s encouraged many regional and local companies to cut their own news staff, thus making them more dependent on the national providers. On the other hand, IRN was affected by comparable cuts in *its* revenue, which is derived from the sale of the advertising space around its bulletins. Perkins points out that

> we have to sell those specific advertising slots. As our revenue

goes down, we've got more people out there expecting more from us, but we've got fewer resources to cope with it, so there's a widening gap between people's expectations of us and what we can actually provide. At the moment we do reasonably well because we have the monopoly of commercial radio stations, but if you add in a few more organisations all competing for revenue, we'll all end up with a bit of money, but frankly not enough to run a proper news service.

In facing up to the challenge of National Network News, and others such as Europe FM seeking to enter the market, IRN adopted a strategy of promoting the comprehensive nature of its news services and their flexibility. While, as we have noted, ITN resists the concept of flexible packaging of its material for the benefit of the regional companies (see also Chapter 9), IRN has always supplied news output in a form which allows it to be integrated into the buyer's own local programmes. By allowing the commercial companies to 'mix 'n' match' its material, and by providing specialised, customised services to particular clients, IRN hoped to protect its dominance of the commercial news market in the 1990s.

In March 1992, as the UK's economic recession deepened, IRN's worsening financial position led its main shareholder, Crown Communications, to sell 30% of its stake in the company. Included among the buyers were Capital Radio and Radio Clyde. The restructuring of IRN was described by Perkins as a further stage in its efforts to retain 'a strong, unified national news service to compete with the BBC'.[5]

Given such financial pressures, IRN's plans to launch a second service (IRN2) were shelved, at least temporarily. And although the Broadcasting Act specified that one of the new commercial channels should be speech-based, it seemed unlikely, while the recession continued, that there would be any serious bids for the franchise. As was noted earlier in this chapter, speech-based services in the United States have flourished since deregulation. But the advertising market there and radio's share of that market are both much larger than in the UK. In the view of senior managers in radio news, there would have to be a much larger advertising market in the UK, and radio's share of it much bigger than it is now, for a 24-hour news channel to be commercially viable. Neither development is likely to come about in the 1990s.

Responding to an increasingly competitive marketplace, in August 1992 IRN announced that it was merging with ITN, and moving into the latter's headquarters at Gray's Inn Road. From October 1, 1992, the production of IRN's news for local radio was taken over by ITN. IRN, meanwhile, successfully beat off competition from Network News to supply Classic FM with bulletins.

## THE BBC

For the same reason, examined in Chapter 5, that the BBC took a strategic decision to prioritise its news and current affairs television output in the run-up to Charter renewal, the corporation's radio journalism has entered an expansionary phase. In June 1990 the BBC's head of regional broadcasting stated his view that local radio was 'the grassroots of the BBC's journalistic network', and that he would be striving to ensure that 'every station made high quality speech and journalism the bedrock of its schedule'.[6]

In September 1991 the newly appointed regional controller Mark Byford vigorously rejected the suggestion – then being made by some on the right of the Conservative Party – that BBC radio should retreat from local journalism. 'A key activity of the BBC is to provide news and current affairs', he insisted. 'Local radio is at the very core of that news and current affairs effort at a local level. It is distinctive because it is speech-driven and based around journalism. And the market is not doing that.'[7]

As commercial radio came under increasing financial pressure the BBC was demonstrating its intention to consolidate and strengthen its historical dominance in this area of broadcasting. In 1991 Ron Neil, at that time head of the BBC's Regional Directorate, insisted that 'it's the single most important activity we have outside London. If we produce a local radio service that sounds like everybody else's, it'll get a big audience, but there'll be no justification for subsidising the licence fee . . . Our justification to be on the wavelength at all is that we work at trying to produce a high quality speech-information service.'

Network radio journalism was also growing. In early 1992 the Task Force report on the future of radio recommended that the

Radio 4 network be split, to make space for a 24-hour rolling news service of the type provided during the Gulf War.[8] To finance the new service, known after its launch as Radio 5 Live, the BBC would further develop its bi-media strategy, allowing economies of scale to be made by combining the newsgathering resources of radio and TV.

Some who work in radio were suspicious of the bi-media approach because, as one regional manager put it, 'television is by far the strongest of the two media, and when there's a clash of demand for resources, it's television which will win.' For its supporters, however, bi-media was an 'enabling approach', closely connected with the need to develop unified management structures in television and radio. As long as adequate resources continued to be provided for radio, its position relative to the BBC's TV operation would not, according to this view, be threatened. Radio 4 controller Michael Green confirmed in September 1991 that 'the provision of news and current affairs is at the core of the BBC's public service remit. The question is, how much more should we do, and at the expense of what?'[9]

## The World Service

BBC radio journalism has never been simply about the domestic audience. The BBC's World Service, with a budget of £143 million in 1992, has since its foundation as the Empire Service in 1926, been providing news, current affairs, and feature journalism to a global audience. Funded and with its output monitored by the Foreign Office, the World Service has traditionally performed the function of 'cultural diplomacy', promoting British values as well as reporting on international events.

As for other elements of the BBC's operation the 1980s were a period of uncertainty for the World Service, as it faced up at home to the Thatcherite onslaught of free market principles and, on the broader international stage, the end of the cold war and the East–West divide. The first of these challenges raised uncomfortable questions for the World Service about its long-term financial viability as a public service, while the latter raised the issue of its continuing cultural role.

An important rationale for the funding of the World Service in the post-Second World War period was the need perceived by successive British governments to provide the populations of the Soviet Union, China and other closed societies around the world with an alternative source of information to that available from their own governments. As Soviet power and that of its allies collapsed in the late 1980s and early 1990s such a need became less pressing, and the World Service's position as the pre-eminent global broadcaster could no longer be taken for granted.

A third threat to the organisation came, as we saw in the previous chapter, from the emergence of transnational television broadcasters, such as CNN and WorldNet. In such an environment, would radio retain its relevance?

## Winning the arguments

For a government deeply suspicious of public service broadcasting, as was the Thatcher Government of the 1980s, the World Service was clearly a potential target, absorbing substantial resources to produce output which was listened to by relatively few of the British people (approximately 1.5 million in 1991). In an era of unquestioning belief by government in commercial logic and the benevolent workings of the free market, the World Service might well have seemed an expensive luxury which the taxpayer could readily do without. However, management, led at that time by John Tusa, succeeded in advocating the notion that 'cultural diplomacy' was an inherently worthwhile activity for the British public service broadcaster to pursue, and demonstrating, furthermore, that the cultural diplomacy provided by the World Service was exceptionally good value for money. A considerable role in this lobbying process was played by the Foreign Office, which in the period under discussion tended to be less Thatcherite than the government as a whole, but the sound financial common sense of the World Service's pitch was crucial. In *Conversations with the World* John Tusa pointed out that

> we have 120 million regular listeners to our broadcasts. There are many millions more who listen to local relays of our broadcasts. At an all-up cost of £120 million in 1988 – capital and current – we deliver our message at a cost of two pence per lis-

tener per week, every week, every year. Not since the days of
Rowland Hill and the Penny Post has Britain had such good
value for money in the field of communication. No other medium can talk to a mass world audience so fast, so credibly, so
effectively, or anywhere near so cheaply.

(1990, p.66)

As long as the principle of cultural diplomacy was accepted, such
sentiments were difficult to resist, and the Conservative
Government had by the early 1990s abandoned any attempt to do
so, awarding the World Service a substantial increase in its budget for the triennium period 1991–3. The BBC had played its part,
by 'proving that our resource house was in order', as a senior
manager put it.[10] But in the view of the same source, 'there's an
acknowledgement now, even at the highest levels of government,
that Britain is well served by having its international service pos-
sessing such a high reputation. It's a projection, if you like, of the
quality of life on these islands, a listing of the values that the people on these islands hold dear.'

Doubts remained, nevertheless, about the long-term resourcing
of the World Service. Bob Jobbins, then head of news and current affairs at the World Service, warned in 1991 that

everything is in question because of Charter renewal. The
World Service, as a news operation, relies heavily on cooperation with the larger BBC; it gives us our editorial independence, and resources which we could never afford otherwise.
The debate about the future of the BBC after 1996 puts a huge
question mark and uncertainty beside our operation. If the
BBC Charter were not extended, or if the BBC continued but
in a significantly different form, that would cause real problems for us. I've no doubt whatsoever that our independence
and freedom for manoeuvre depends on our being part of the
BBC.

At the time of writing, however, the World Service was financially secure. Those who work within it felt confident of their continuing relevance in a world in which the cold war dichotomies of
'open' and 'closed' were losing their significance. In *Conversations
with the World* Tusa quotes approvingly the view of the past

Director-General of the BBC, William Haley, that 'the British conception of news as something coldly impersonal and objective, and which has as its only touchstone accuracy, impartiality and truth, is one of our great services to a civilisation in which speed of communication gives news an overwhelming importance it never had before' (1990, p.71).

Such assertions illustrate the extent to which the World Service has been perceived by its staff as 'idealistic' rather than 'ideological'. Unlike, for example, the Voice of America, it has always retained editorial independence from the government which allocates its resources, so that it has not in general been seen in the wider world as a mere mouthpiece for a particular political standpoint. Voice of America must carry daily editorials written for it by the US Information Agency. The World Service, while routinely broadcasting government messages for British citizens abroad, has not been required to reflect the government's view of a given international situation.

If the 'civilising message' includes the transmission of dominant British cultural values, the World Service has retained a reputation for impartiality, balance, and reliability which is the basis of its longstanding legitimacy as an information-source. In situations such as the Chernobyl disaster of 1986 and the coup of August 1991 in Moscow, it was the World Service to which the Russian people, including an imprisoned Mikhail Gorbachev himself, turned. Consequently, in a post-cold war world, the World Service has no need, its managers would argue, to change its approach to journalism.

For John Tusa, the World Service has never been 'propaganda', but a journalism equally relevant to populations all over the world, regardless of the information environment in their respective societies. So, he argues, in the post-cold war world, 'our broadcasting hasn't changed. it hasn't had to change. Something like Radio Free Europe, or Radio Liberty, has had to change.' Bob Jobbins argues that 'what's changed for us are the internal freedoms in the former communist bloc. That means more competition for us. Does it mean that we will lose our audience in those countries?' In the short term, he accepts, there may be some loss of audience. But:

In the longer term there will be a role: first, in the sense that our editorial standards remain relatively constant, whereas theirs, I think, fluctuate. They have a lot of freedom now, but not so much accuracy. They have serious problems trying to come to terms with what we could call sound journalistic practice.

We also have another selling point: our 'golden reach', the fact that we have correspondents in most places most of the time. Very few other broadcasters can say that. When the Gulf War was on we had thirty or forty correspondents in the region. But we were also able to cover events from Moscow, Africa, South America, and so on. We provide a genuine 'world service'. We have a global reach. We see the events of one country in terms of what is happening elsewhere. It's the opposite of parochial.

A further competitive advantage enjoyed by the World Service, in the view of its managers, has been that it does not construct its journalism within a British-dominated framework. While its main competitors, such as the Voice of America, broadcast a country-specific agenda, the World Service aspires to a genuinely international, global news agenda, of equal relevance to the constituent parts of a multinational audience. John Tusa insists that:

we provide something which the others don't provide: international news, the global picture of the world. And there's a demand for that even in the United States. Audiences for our programmes on American public radio increased by a factor of three during the Gulf crisis. The US is an open society, with more broadcasting, more radio stations, than anywhere else in the world. But they're so fragmented, so tiny, so tied to local communities, so driven towards particular niches of the market, that they're incapable of giving the entire world picture. That's why I think there is a continuing need, even in open societies, for this kind of service.

Elsewhere, Tusa has argued that 'our broadcasting about Britain gains in credibility because it does not give special treatment to British activities. The more narrowly you interpret the instruction to broadcast about your home country, the less appealing you are to your audience' (1990, p.15).[11]

For the World Service management, therefore, its long-term survival would be best guaranteed, given a favourable economic environment within the UK, by the quality of its journalism and the scope of its news agenda. On both criteria, it is argued, the World Service provides a unique facility to a global audience. Thus, the radio component of the service – historically the dominant one – has been earmarked for expansion. In November 1991 the head of World Service news announced a £10 million cash injection, allowing journalism for the first time to exceed 50% of total output. New technologies were permitting the expanded diffusion of programmes, first by satellite, then through local 're-broadcasting'. In Finland, for example, in 1991 there were some thirty-five FM stations re-broadcasting an hour or more of World Service programming each day. Deals were signed with the Russian Federation and other countries.

For the future, more regional specialisation is planned, while World Service English is preparing to split into two channels. Chapter 5 argued that World Service Television will become increasingly important into the next century, but radio will continue to occupy a major part of the organisation's resources. As Bob Jobbins puts it, 'I can't see radio going away. It has tremendous advantages: particularly, the fact that you can do other things while you're listening. In addition, transnational radio broadcasting is much freer from interference than television, and it is still going to be the lynchpin.'

# Chapter 7

# Before and after Wapping

## The changing political economy of the British press

Fleet Street, it has been argued – the historic centre, physically and figuratively, of the British newspaper industry — ceased to exist on January 26, 1986, 'the day on which Rupert Murdoch proved that it was possible to produce two mass circulation newspapers without a single member of his existing print force, without using the railways and with roughly one-fifth of the numbers that he had been employing before'.[1] The flight of News International's newspaper production from buildings in the City of London to a custom-built, high-technology 'fortress' at Wapping in London's Docklands was, on one level, the entirely rational and, as it turned out, highly profitable act of a ruthless and hard-headed publisher. But it also, in combination with the actions of another media entrepreneur, Eddie Shah, set in motion processes which, according to one viewpoint, revitalised a moribund, loss-making industry and created the conditions for its profitable expansion. An opposing view asserts that the 'Wapping revolution' has in fact done nothing to address the longstanding problems of the British press, particularly those of concentration of ownership, right-wing political bias, and deteriorating editorial standards.

This chapter assesses and compares these contrasting interpretations of what has happened to the British press since 1986, and considers how the industry will develop in the late 1990s, as the full fruits of the Wapping revolution are felt. Before that, however, we should perhaps answer the question, what was wrong with the British press anyway?

## THE BRITISH PRESS: A BRIEF HISTORICAL REVIEW

The story of the British press as a genuinely mass medium began with the emergence, in the late eighteenth and early nineteenth centuries, of large urban populations, descendants of the feudal peasant classes, who had been displaced from their traditional rural environment by encroaching capitalist property rights and social relations, and who were forced to make their livings by entering the rapidly developing factory system. To labour efficiently in a manufacturing, factory environment the members of this new urban proletariat were required to learn skills of numeracy and literacy, which they began to acquire from the embryonic state education service. As the masses became more educated and more literate they developed an appetite for reading material.

In the eighteenth century, as we saw in Chapter 2, newspaper readership had been limited to a relatively small elite of educated members of the bourgeoisie and upper classes, and the pro-establishment views and interests of these groups naturally predominated in the content of early newspapers. With the rise of a literate working class, likewise, a number of newspapers emerged which were targeted at the urban proletariat and which reflected their concerns. In the aftermath of the French Revolution of 1789 and in the first half of the nineteenth century, culminating in the revolutions of 1848 across Europe, these concerns were with social reform and justice. From 1815 a 'radical' press developed in Britain, which set out to shape working-class opinion and thereby influence events. By 1817 the foremost example of this press, William Cobbett's *Political Register*, was selling more than 40,000 copies a week. At the same time, trade unions were gaining in strength and reach, often using the contents of the radical press as material for political education.

For British capital, which had fought successfully for press freedom in the context of feudal authoritarianism, and thus understood the power of newspapers as disseminators of radical ideas, these were threatening developments. From 1818 libel laws began to be used more frequently to prevent radical publishers from issuing 'seditious' material, while in 1819 taxes on newspapers – Stamp Duties – were extended to cover the radical press.

These 'taxes on knowledge' were intended, as Curran and Seaton put it in their account of British press history, 'to restrict the readership of newspapers to the well-to-do by raising cover prices; and to restrict the ownership of newspapers to the propertied class by increasing publishing costs' (1991, p.12). These repressive measures failed, and instead the establishment embarked on a 'sophisticated strategy of social control', whereby the Stamp Laws were repealed and the radical press replaced by apolitical, commercial publications, read by the mass audience but in the ownership and control of capital. In these authors' view, 'the common concern of most leading supporters of the campaign [to repeal newspaper taxation] was to secure the loyalty of the working class to the social order through the expansion of the capitalist press' (ibid., p.27).

As newspapers became cheaper and the market for them expanded, capital investment, start-up, and running costs increased beyond the capacity of radical publishers to keep up. Dependence on advertising revenue increased. By the end of the nineteenth century the radical publications had either been forced out of existence, moved upmarket and to the right politically, become small specialist publications with dedicated readerships, or become financially dependent on institutions such as the Independent Labour Party and Trades Union Congress. Replacing them in the popular newspaper market were publications controlled by a small number of 'press barons' with the capital resources to found titles and build empires. By 1910 Lords Pearson, Cadbury, and Northcliffe controlled between them 67% of national daily circulation, establishing a trend of concentration of ownership which has persisted in the British newspaper industry ever since, with the exception of a brief period during and after the Second World War when state intervention in the newspaper market reduced dependence on advertising and allowed left-of-centre newspapers to strengthen their positions on the basis of readership alone.

The late 1960s saw the arrival in the United Kingdom of Rupert Murdoch and News International. In 1968 he bought the *News of the World*, and followed this by taking control of the *Sun* in 1969. Both were loss-making titles when taken over by Murdoch, and he was able to acquire them at what seem with hindsight to be knock-down prices. In the course of the 1970s they came to dominate the British tabloid market and moved into profit. They also moved to the right of the political spectrum editorially. In 1981 Murdoch bought *The Times* and *Sunday Times*, and in 1987 he took control of the *Today* newspaper.

Murdoch was the first, and to date most successful, of a new generation of press barons: interventionist rather than what Curran and Seaton call 'market-led pragmatists' (ibid., p.87). They tended to have interests in a wide variety of other media, and also in non-media sectors of industry. They were also, with the exception of Robert Maxwell, well to the right of centre in their political views, lending their support from the late 1970s onwards to the Conservative Party and its leader, Margaret Thatcher. In return for services rendered in 1979 and subsequent general elections, several of them (and their editors) received honours from the Conservative Government. The Thatcher Government also assisted the building of their empires by consistently refusing to use the Monopolies and Mergers Commission as a means of preventing excessive concentration of ownership. The most obvious beneficiary of this *laissez-faire* approach was Rupert Murdoch who, on the eve of the Wapping dispute at the end of 1985, had acquired four national titles and 33% of total national circulation. In purchasing *The Times* and *Sunday Times* Murdoch had to overcome the rule that the owner of a newspaper with sales over 500,000 was required to have a bid for another national title referred to the MMC. This could be avoided, however, if the paper (or papers) to be bought would otherwise go out of business. Despite the fact – as Murdoch himself quickly showed – that the *Times* titles were inherently economically viable, the government accepted his argument that they were not, and allowed the purchase to go ahead without reference to the MMC. The authors of a financial biography of Murdoch argue that this bending of the rules in his favour was a reward for his tabloids' loyal support of the government – and Margaret Thatcher in particular – over the years (Belfield *et al.*, 1991, p.74).

It was this overt political bias, and not merely the evidence of increasing ownership concentration, which so disturbed many observers of the British press in the 1980s. As Harold Evans put it in his published account of life as editor of *The Times*, 'the daily news in print in Britain is more brilliantly polluted by partisan judgements than the press in most other democracies and certainly by comparison with the press of the United States' (1983, p.4). Moreover, 'the arithmetic favours the Conservative Party.' The McGregor Commission on the Press stated clearly: 'there is no doubt that over most of this century the Labour movement has had less newspaper support than its right-wing opponents and that its beliefs and activities have been unfavourably reported by the majority of the press' (McGregor, 1977, p.99). Left-of-centre publications such as the *News Chronicle* and *Daily Herald* were driven out of the market in the 1960s despite relatively healthy seven-figure circulations, leaving what McGregor called 'a gap in the national press for a newspaper generally supporting left-wing parties and opinions' (ibid., p. 109). By 1985 the political affiliations of Britain's national daily newspapers were as follows: nine fully supported the Conservative Party; one, the *Financial Times*, leant heavily in that direction; leaving only the Mirror Group titles and the *Guardian* tentatively backing 'moderate' elements in the Labour Party. The *Morning Star*, of course, backed the 'hard' left, but its circulation was so small as to be negligible in terms of political influence.

Such an overwhelming bias has long been recognised to be, at the very least, unrepresentative of political opinion in the United Kingdom. Tom Baistow observes that 'the national press has never reflected the political attitudes of a large – often a major – sector of the population in any representative degree since the rise of the Labour Party after the 1914–18 war' (1985, p.3). Many of the right-wing tabloids are read by people who declare their political support for the opposition parties, but who nevertheless receive (quite willingly, it would appear) a steady diet of anti-Labour and pro-Conservative propaganda in their newspapers (see Table 7.1). This feature of the British press, it has been argued, is profoundly undemocratic, since the output of the right-wing press swings just enough working-class voters to the Conservative Party at election time to guarantee their supremacy in the context of a first-past-the-post system for parliamentary elections.

A 1991 report by the Hansard Society stated that 'research has suggested [the right-wing bias of the press] has had a significant electoral impact, with the tabloids exerting an especially strong

*Table 7.1* Political affiliations of national newspaper
readers (%)

| | Conservative | Labour | Liberal |
|---|---|---|---|
| *Sunday Telegraph* | 77 | 11 | 10 |
| *Daily Telegraph* | 71 | 13 | 15 |
| *Daily Mail* | 66 | 17 | 15 |
| *Mail on Sunday* | 62 | 18 | 18 |
| *Daily Express* | 66 | 19 | 13 |
| *Sunday Express* | 64 | 20 | 14 |
| *Times* | 61 | 18 | 17 |
| *Sunday Times* | 57 | 22 | 16 |
| *Financial Times* | 50 | 27 | 18 |
| *Independent* | 31 | 40 | 26 |
| *Independent on Sunday* | 27 | 44 | 26 |
| *Observer* | 13 | 57 | 23 |
| *Guardian* | 12 | 59 | 22 |
| *Today* | 48 | 35 | 14 |
| *Sun* | 39 | 48 | 10 |
| *News of the World* | 35 | 41 | 10 |
| *Daily Mirror* | 19 | 59 | 10 |
| *Sunday Mirror* | 24 | 61 | 13 |
| *Star* | 23 | 64 | 9 |
| *Sunday Sport* | 35 | 56 | 8 |
| *Sunday People* | 31 | 56 | 11 |

*Source*: MORI.

effect.'[2] William Miller has argued, on the basis of his study of the
1987 general election campaign, that perceptions of economic
optimism – which tend to favour the Conservative Party's election
prospects – are higher among those (even Labour supporters) who
read the right-wing press (1991, ch.7). Miller's thesis received a
boost following the outcome of the 1992 election when it was
noted that the Conservative marginal seat of Basildon was the one
which showed a particularly small swing to the Labour Party. It
was also the constituency with the highest proportion of *Sun* readers in the UK.

As we saw in Chapter 1, the suggestion that newspapers have
the power to influence voting behaviour, or any other type of
behaviour, is highly problematic. If they can, why do so many
*Sun* and *Star* readers support the Labour Party? Could it be that,

having lost to the Conservatives in four consecutive elections, Labour Party supporters found the Tory press with its overtly propagandistic and shamelessly distorted coverage of politics a convenient scapegoat? After John Major's victory on April 9, 1992 left-wingers immediately attributed their defeat to the Tory-supporting tabloids, with the tabloids themselves rigorously denying any such impact. The *Sun*, for example, despite initially taking credit for Labour's defeat, subsequently took exception to the suggestion that its readers could be so malleable and stupid as to be affected by such headlines as 'Nightmare on Kinnock Street'. The debate was not resolved in 1992 and will resurface, no doubt, at the next general election.

While the effects of political bias may be said to be unproven, the fact of its existence cannot be denied. Historically, as we have seen, the bias has been towards the right of the political spectrum in Britain – the chief beneficiary being the Conservative Party. Indeed, one of the most frequently heard justifications for the traumatic transformation of the newspaper industry which took place after 1986 was that it would give the Labour movement and the Left new opportunities to enter the market and redress this bias. As of 1995, however, it appeared that such redress might not be so urgent as it once was. Since 1992 there has been a significant, perhaps unprecedented, shift in the allegiances of the pro-Conservative press. To call many of them 'Tory', indeed, no longer seems appropriate to the reality of the situation.

'Tentative and symbolic' criticism of the Major Government was to be found in the (still) Tory press as early as the autumn of 1992,[3] but was elevated to a higher plane with the appointment of Peter Stothard as editor of *The Times* in 1993.

*The Times*'s criticism of the Major Government has been interpreted as, at least in part, a management response to falling sales and influence, in an environment where public opinion appeared to be slipping away from the Tories. More fundamentally, fiercely anti-government *Times* editorials were reported [to] 'exactly reflect the proprietor's reputed contempt for the way things have gone in Britain'.[4]

With *The Times* in the lead, other formerly Tory-supporting titles joined in, and by the summer of 1993 only the Express Group of newspapers remained truly loyal to the government. A

*Guardian* item of January 1994 surveyed journalists' views on the matter, and came up with the following explanations for why government–press relations 'have never been so bad': i) the weakness of the Labour opposition (before John Smith's death), requiring the press *de facto* to take up the opposition role; ii) the government's long period in office, leading to laziness, arrogance, and press frustration; and iii) the poor quality of the government, and Major in particular. As one former *Sun* columnist was quoted as saying: 'Everyone is agreed that John Major is a hopeless berk who must go, and that he is surrounded by a bunch of unprincipled spivs and clones.'[5]

Press hostility to the Tories continued into 1994, and Tony Blair's election as Labour leader, at which point some usually pro-Conservative newspapers began to hint at their qualified support for 'New Labour'. And once again, News International took the lead. In July 1995, to the consternation of conservatives on both the Left and the Right of the British political spectrum, Tony Blair was invited to deliver a keynote address to a conference of senior News International executives in Australia. One source interpreted Rupert Murdoch's swing to Labour as 'a combination of the group's commercial interests, a broader political assessment and a judgment on the mood of the readers.'[6] In September Henry Porter noted the dramatic improvement in News International–Labour relations.

> The bloody fight at Wapping, the favoured status that Murdoch achieved under Thatcher's administration, the viciousness of the campaign against Neil Kinnock's leadership, the persistently bruising coverage of Labour policy – all is apparently set aside in a convivial singularity of purpose.[7]

Time will reveal how far beyond the next general election this 'singularity of purpose' will last.

## SHAH, MURDOCH, AND THE NEWSPAPER REVOLUTION

The 'newspaper revolution', which began in 1983 and climaxed in the Wapping dispute of 1986 was, as in the case of the restructuring of broadcast journalism, closely related to the ascendancy of radical right-wing principles in the British government. Just as the Conservative Government in 1979 had begun a sustained attack on the public services, so too had it identified the trade unions as a major obstacle to the implementation of the Thatcherite economic project. Having come to power on an anti-union ticket, exploiting popular anger caused by the 'winter of discontent' which saw the unions locked in bitter industrial disputes with James Callaghan's Labour Government, Margaret Thatcher quickly moved to neuter the union's power by introducing a series of employment laws. The cumulative effect of legislation introduced in 1980 and 1982 was to make it extremely difficult, if not impossible, for unions to organise meaningful industrial action against determined employers. The most important measure in this respect was the outlawing of 'secondary action' – action taken by unions in support of other unions – and the tight restrictions placed on the numbers of those allowed to picket places of work. These measures made illegal the effective expression of solidarity between different groups of workers while, of course, employers could still cooperate to defeat industrial action.

This legislation established the conditions in which employers could, if they dared, engage their employees in disputes over hitherto sacrosanct staffing levels and working practices. Within the trade union movement as a whole, few groups enjoyed terms of employment which were more advantageous than the printworkers of Fleet Street. In the traditional manner of labour aristocracies, the print unions – primarily the National Graphical Association (NGA) and the Society of Graphical and Allied Trades (Sogat) – had secured relatively high wages for their skilled members, high levels of employment, tight closed shop agreements, complete control over entry to the printing trade (women were excluded from the lucrative typesetting positions, for example), and 'Spanish' working practices such as claiming payment for shifts not worked. Such terms were of course extremely expensive, and contributed substantially to the poor economic health of the industry identified by the McGregor Commission when it noted that in 1975 four of eight national dailies were in loss, and six of seven national Sundays. McGregor noted that labour was the main component of the newspaper industry's costs, since staffing levels were exceptionally high, as were wages (1977, p.31).

The ability of the printers to extract such terms from their employers was a reflection of their pivotal position in the newspaper production process, combined with the short shelf-life of news as a commodity. The 'hot metal' process, employed in Fleet Street since the nineteenth century, was heavily dependent on printers' labour which could easily be withdrawn, with damaging loss of output. In the late 1970s the printers used this power to resist the introduction of new technologies, which could have made newspapers more profitable, but at the cost of fewer print jobs. These included the techniques of photocomposition, and direct input of editorial copy by journalists into pagesetting computers.

In 1978–9 the *Times* newspapers closed for almost a year, at a cost in lost production to their owners, Thomson, of £40 million. Between 1976 and 1985 industrial action by *Times* and *Sunday Times* printworkers led to the loss of six million copies. These losses played a key part, according to Harold Evans, in persuading the Thomson Group in 1981 to sell *The Times* and *Sunday Times* to Rupert Murdoch (Evans, 1983). In 1984, with Rupert Murdoch now in control, the papers lost 11.4 million copies to industrial action.

For some on the left, such militancy on the part of the unions represented the wholly legitimate defence of their members' interests in the face of big business. Others, however, by no means unsympathetic to the goals of the Labour movement in general, argued that 'Luddism' on the part of the print unions would be counter-productive to the long-term survival of the industry, and the jobs which it provided. As Tom Baistow noted before the Wapping dispute, 'in Fleet Street the corrupting cynicism that can come with unfettered power is not the monopoly of the press barons: the erosion of journalistic standards and ethics by self-interested proprietors and their house-trained editors . . . has been paralleled down the years by an equally self-interested distortion of the economics of production by a workforce that has played its part in creating the conditions for that decline' (1985, p.77). After Wapping, Baistow again referred to a 'Fleet Street workforce that played its part in creating the conditions of decline which paved the way to Wapping . . . the whole tragic affair was much of the chapels' own making, the bitter fruits of greed and arrogance and a sectarian selfishness that betrayed the collective principles of honest trade unionism' (1989, p.65). Former industrialist and Labour peer Lord Goodman writes that 'there can have been no period in industrial history where a greater demonstration of reckless irresponsibility has been displayed by a section of organised labour . . . the behaviour of the unions prior to the Murdoch revolution can only be described as suicidal.'[8]

The print unions, like others in the Labour movement, had grown used to the status and influence bestowed upon them by the post-war social democratic consensus, and failed to recognise the extent to which Thatcherism had undermined their position. With the Employment Acts of 1980 and 1982 the legal framework was in place – backed up by political will at the highest level – to allow proprietors to begin to erode the unions' power.

The struggle began, not in Fleet Street itself, but in Warrington in the north-east of England, where from 1980 local freesheet publisher Eddie Shah had been striving to loosen the grip of the NGA on the production of his *Stockport Messenger*. The NGA resisted Shah's attempts to introduce electronic publishing technologies and thereby reduce staffing levels, leading to a dispute which culminated in November 1983 in illegal mass picketing outside Shah's Warrington plant. Shah successfully took the NGA to court, and became the first employer to 'sequestrate' – i.e. have seized by the court – a union's assets. The dispute and its outcome were enthusiastically covered by Rupert Murdoch's *Sunday Times*, whose editor Andrew Neil correctly recognised it to be a watershed in industrial relations within the British press. Shah's success in destroying the NGA's power in Warrington thus became the catalyst for News International to attempt an analogous feat – though on a much bigger scale – in Fleet Street.

Since buying into the British newspaper industry in the 1960s Rupert Murdoch had been forced, like other Fleet Street proprietors, to accept the print unions' reluctance to countenance new technologies, and absorb the consequent losses. Shah, however, showed that with the help of Conservative employment legislation the unions could be taken on and defeated. In March 1984, a stoppage at the News International plant in London's Bouverie Street cost Murdoch the loss of 23.5 million copies of the *Sun*, and three million copies of the *News of the World*. This dispute, Sogat's General Secretary was later to concede, probably convinced Murdoch that radical measures had to be taken if his newspapers were to be made profitable in the long term. And achieving such profitability was crucial to the expansion of what was, by the mid-1980s, a global media empire spanning Europe, the United States, and Australia – an empire, moreover, in some financial difficulty.

By 1985, Murdoch's new printing plant at Wapping had been constructed. He had a plant in Glasgow intended for printing Scottish and northern editions of his titles, but this lay idle because the unions would not permit the facsimile transmission of copy from London. By February of that year, Murdoch had apparently lost patience with trying to win agreement from the printers to bring these new facilities into production, and announced to his senior managers that he was making a 'dash for freedom' (Melvern, 1988, p.122).

For the rest of 1985 News International management planned and prepared for the transfer of all newspaper production from the plants at Gray's Inn Road and Bouverie Street to the new Docklands site, secretly installing an Atex computer, and putting in place a system which would enable the company to dispense with thousands of printworkers. Negotiations continued with the unions, but without success, each party blaming the other for their failure. In the unions' view, Murdoch had already decided on a course of action and had no intention of negotiating a compromise agreement. According to this view his final, unproductive meeting with the unions before the move to Wapping on January 23, 1986, was calculated to provoke a strike which, under Tory employment law, would mean that he could dismiss the printworkers without being legally required to offer expensive compensation. Murdoch, for his part, insisted that he and his managers had made every effort at conciliation over a long period of time, but that union obstinacy prevented a negotiated solution.

On January 24, 1986, following the meeting with Murdoch, the Fleet Street printers announced strike action to close down the News International titles. That evening, journalists and support staff at the two City plants were invited to turn up for work the next day at Wapping. Failure to do so would be treated as resig-

nation. At about 8.00 p.m. on Saturday, January 25, with only
one day's edition of the *Sun* lost, the production lines at Wapping
began to run and, as Linda Melvern puts it in her account of the
dispute, 'two hundred years of Fleet Street history were over'
(ibid., p.155).

News International's ensuing dispute with Sogat and the NGA
was one of the most bitter and violent in Britain's industrial relations history, but with the full weight of the government and the
state behind him, Murdoch was never in danger of losing. He
used the services of Australian haulage company Thomas
Nationwide Transport (TNT) to establish a union-proof distribution network for his titles, all of which would now be printed in
Wapping and Glasgow. Attempts at a settlement were made, but
never came to anything, and by the end of 1986 the printers had
conceded defeat. Soon thereafter, other newspapers joined the
exodus out of Fleet Street.

With the unions thus emasculated, Murdoch and the other proprietors could begin to transform their cost structures and
increase profitability. While the treatment of the unions was presented by Murdoch as a regrettable necessity for which the workers themselves were to blame, the proponents of change held out
the promise that lower labour costs and the introduction of new
technologies would lead to a more diverse, pluralistic, and financially sound print media. In the words of Cento Veljanovski (in a
book, it might be noted, published by News International itself),
'improved industrial relations [*sic*] combined with advances in
print technology have significantly lowered barriers to entry,
enabled the introduction of new enhanced graphics and colours,
and stimulated the proliferation of magazine titles and other publications' (1990, p.11). If concentration of ownership and political
bias were indeed valid concerns, the argument went, the Wapping
revolution would ease the problem by extending access to new
groups, hitherto excluded because of prohibitive start-up and
running costs.

The first proprietor to attempt to take advantage of the new
economic environment, after Murdoch himself, was, appropriate-
ly enough, Eddie Shah. Following his victory over the NGA in
Warrington, he began to make plans for the establishment of two
new national titles, *Today* and *Sunday Today*, believing that

'given the Tory union laws, a new non-union newspaper printed on greenfield sites, using colour and aimed at the middle market between the *Daily Telegraph* and the *Daily Mirror*, was now on the British agenda' (MacArthur, 1988, p.35).

Shah raised £18 million of capital in the City, and proceeded to establish a newspaper operation which would utilise direct input and satellite page transmission, with distribution by road rather than the more expensive and less reliable (because heavily unionised) rail. Given the labour savings made possible by the new relationship with the unions, it was estimated that *Today* could break even on a circulation of 330,000 and the paper duly launched on March 4, 1986, less than two months after News International's move to Wapping. Despite the new technologies, however, and the cowed state of the unions, *Today* and *Sunday Today* failed to give Shah the break into national newspaper publishing which he desired. Teething troubles with the computers used by journalists and problems with the advanced colour and graphics printing equipment led to missed production deadlines. Distribution was poor, and the printing equipment bought by Shah failed to match up to its specifications. Sales dropped quickly after the launch, and even such basic matters as revenue from newsagents proved difficult to collect. Annual running costs were estimated at £40 million, which meant that even a healthy circulation of 500,000 would be insufficient to cover the paper's costs. Four months after the launch, in June 1986, Shah sold 35% of *Today* to Lonrho (owner of the *Observer* and the *Glasgow Herald* and *Evening Times*), which quickly gained full control. *Sunday Today* ceased publication in June 1987, while *Today* continued to operate on an estimated annual loss of £28 million, before being sold to News International in July 1987, in whose hands it remained until it was closed down in October 1995 on financial grounds.

The early failure of *Today* – 'the paper that was going to revolutionise Fleet Street, put power back in the hands of journalists, and end the curse of the printers and the restrictive practices that were reducing papers to penury' (MacArthur, 1988, p.16) – is attributed by its first editor, Brian MacArthur, to weak business management, poor design, difficulties associated with the introduction of new technologies, and excessive ambition on the part of Shah. *Today*, he argues, was under-resourced to meet its production targets of one million copies daily (an output which turned out to be simply beyond the capacity of Shah's presses). But if Shah could be accused of inexperience, naivety, and overoptimism in assuming that the defeat of the print unions would enable him to challenge the dominance of the Fleet Street press barons, his 'vision of the electronic newspaper' eventually bore fruit, in MacArthur's view, in the shapes of the *Independent* and *Sunday Sport*, while his revolutionary system of distributing newspapers by road was central to the success of Rupert Murdoch's operation at Wapping (ibid., p.46).

The success of the *Independent*, the idea for which was inspired by Eddie Shah's experience (Crozier, 1988), has been attributed to the care with which, in contrast to the *Today* operation, a realistic business plan was drawn up. Another important difference between the *Independent* and *Today* was the quality of the former's personnel. As MacArthur makes clear in his account of *Today*'s setting up, Eddie Shah was suspicious not merely of Fleet Street's printers, but its journalists, seeing no reason why he should pay the (in his view) inflated salaries which would have been required to attract a sufficient number of the top names in the journalistic profession to his title. Whether or not he was correct in believing that the quality of the established journalistic superstars' writing was not appreciably higher than that of lesser-known and lower-paid hacks, he neglected to take account of the valuable status and credibility which established names could bring to a new title starting out from scratch in a fiercely competitive market. By contrast, the group of journalists, led by former *Daily Telegraph* City Editor Andreas Whittam Smith, who initiated the *Independent*, intended from the outset to attract the 'best' writers in the field.

In this task they were greatly helped by the manner and timing of News International's move to Wapping, the abruptness and uncompromising nature of which drove many of *The Times* and *Sunday Times* editorial staff out of Murdoch's employment. Unwilling to work in 'Fortress Wapping', and under siege from disgruntled printers, such influential journalists as Peter Jenkins and Isobel Hilton left News International and ran into the waiting arms of Andreas Whittam Smith. From its launch, therefore, the editorial content of the *Independent* carried a weight and authority which *Today* never achieved. It was also exceptionally well designed, while the technological glitches suffered by *Today* never afflicted the *Independent* to the same degree. By November 1987, with a total staff of only 403 (of whom 209 were editorial), the *Independent* was well on its way to being profitable, with a circulation of over 300,000. In September 1989 the *Independent on Sunday* was launched, and both titles have since become firmly established in their respective markets.[9]

The other spectacular success of the post-Wapping era was the *Sunday Sport*. Launched by pornographic-magazine publisher David Sullivan in September 1986, the *Sunday Sport* utilised only a handful of editorial staff to produce a heady downmarket mixture of sex, crime, and sport. While, as we shall see in the next chapter, some have disputed that the *Sunday Sport* could legitimately be called a newspaper, since many of its stories are fictional and its content largely soft-core pornography, it differed from the other tabloids only in the degree to which these elements predominated in its pages. With its small staff and low running costs the *Sunday Sport* was able to make a healthy profit with a circulation, in December 1986, of only 230,000 (small by tabloid standards), leading one commentator to describe it as 'the only unqualified press success' of the newspaper revolution.[10] As S. J. Taylor remarks, the *Sunday Sport* was 'the first [and to date, only] successful post-Wapping tabloid' (1991, p.376). With the defeat of the print unions by Shah and Murdoch, and the introduction of labour-saving technologies which that allowed, David Sullivan, like the founders of the *Independent*, was able radically to reduce what had hitherto been regarded as the minimum break-even circulation for a national tabloid newspaper.

One year after its launch circulation had reached 500,000, selling to a readership mainly of young males, and generating annual profits for Sullivan's Apollo group of £750,000. The financial success of the *Sunday Sport* enabled David Sullivan in 1987 to buy the *Morning Star*'s printworks in London's Farringdon Road for an estimated £2.5 million, and to seek £3 million start-up capital for a *Daily Sport*. The *Sport* launched on Wednesday, August 17, 1988, was published initially on only three days a week, but by October 1991 had become a six-day newspaper, with a profitable circulation of some 350,000.

If the five titles discussed thus far can be viewed as the success stories (or perhaps, survivors) of the Wapping revolution, others found it more difficult to exploit the new cost structures. Robert Maxwell's attempt in February 1987 to set up the *London Daily News* to compete with the *Evening Standard* failed at a cost to his company of some £30 million. Eddie Shah made a second attempt to break into national newspaper publishing with the *Post*, launched in November 1988, but despite receiving some favourable reviews, it quickly 'disappeared into a black hole'.[11]

In the second half of 1986 plans were announced for the long-awaited launch of a popular newspaper with a left-wing editorial policy – the first such to be established since the *Daily Worker* in 1930. To be called the *News on Sunday*, the paper would be launched with £6.5 million raised from trade unions, sympathetic local councils, and business. To assist in raising this capital the paper's founders commissioned market research by Research Surveys of Great Britain, which indicated a sizeable potential market for a left-wing Sunday tabloid of about three million people. This research appeared to confirm the longstanding conviction of the British left that an audience existed for a paper reflective of their opinions and agendas. With the transformation of cost structures promised by the introduction of new print technologies, it was estimated that the title could break even on a circulation of 800,000.

*News on Sunday* was launched on April 26, 1987, but failed from the outset to reach its break-even circulation target. Despite the optimistic evidence of the market research, sales of the first issue were only 500,000, not in itself a shockingly poor figure, but not enough to give *News on Sunday* the necessary kick-start which might have sustained it through the initial loss-making period experienced by every new title. Moreover, circulation declined steadily after the first issue. The final edition was published six weeks later, on June 8.

A number of explanations have been advanced for the failure of the *News on Sunday*. Chippindale and Horrie place the blame largely on a combination of bad marketing and weak management (1988). The *News on Sunday*, as they cheekily put it, was set up by, and intended for, 'Right Ons', i.e. the anti-sexist, antiracist 'new left'. This meant that its editorial policy and news agenda would have to be 'ideologically sound' and politically correct. For example, there would be no page three girls.

At the same time, however, the *News on Sunday* would have to be popular. To market the paper, advertising agency Bartle, Bogle, Hegarty were employed, on a budget of £1.3 million, to combine the necessary ingredients of political correctness and popularity within a series of advertisements which would be 'challenging, campaigning, anti-establishment and irreverent' (ibid., p.102). Exploiting the lack of page three girls, Bartle, Bogle, Hegarty designed a poster ad based on the slogan 'No Tits, but a Lot of Balls'. Another depicted Margaret Thatcher, Neil Kinnock, David Steel, and David Owen, with the caption 'These are the only tits you'll see on our page three'.

The agency's market research suggested that these posters (and others in a similar vein) would be effective in attracting the audience which *News on Sunday* was seeking. The management team rejected them, however, on the grounds that they were sexist. As one member of the management collective put it, 'at bottom the advertisers were looking for their mark, and their mark was a man. The campaign thus became one that addressed men rather than women' (ibid., p.116).

Chippindale and Horrie go on to show how marketing decisions were obfuscated and delayed as arguments went on within management – most of whom had no experience of producing newspapers – over the ideological soundness of this or that ad. As the arguments continued deadlines for booking advertising space and producing copy ran out, forcing hasty last-minute decisions to be made. As one of the paper's financial backers explained after *News on Sunday* had gone under, the advertisers had designed a campaign which 'might have proved to be very effective but was found to be offensive to the staff and to the founder of the newspaper'.[12] The strictures of political correctness won over the requirements of effective marketing.

For Peter Chippindale the failure of the paper proved, not that the idea for a left-wing tabloid was a bad one, but that 'members of the concerned middle class, essentially ignorant of journalism, cannot just wade into the arena in the belief that the moral rectitude of their brief will bring readers flocking to them . . . With little or no experience, they awarded themselves senior management posts and plunged into their obsession with putting into practice their ideas of consensual decision-making and positive discrimination with little or no thought for the realities of the newspaper business.'[13]

Ex-editor Brian Whittaker attributed the failure of *News on Sunday*, firstly, to the fact that, even with £6 million raised, it was under-capitalised from the outset. Given the much greater investment of both Eddie Shah and the *Independent* team, £6.5 million was not an especially large sum. On the question of management, he argues that 'the paper's original guiding lights were amateurs who suddenly found themselves running a public company. They were reluctant to hand over control to professionals – apparently for fear that the paper would turn into a Tory rag.'[14] In the view of Keith Sutton, another former editor, the paper suffered from the consequences of trying to apply 'a direct input system virtually untried in Britain, with a bunch of executives who had never executed anyone in their lives; seven subs; three handfuls of reporters, one staff photographer and a freelance budget that would buy Robert Maxwell lunch for a fortnight'.[15] The poor quality of management led not only to a disastrously confused marketing strategy and launch, but to a failure to obtain cost-effective deals from the print unions. The member of management responsible for employer negotiations, Alan Haylis, 'proved no match for hard-bargaining contract printers and ended up with deals that would have made a Murdoch or a Maxwell laugh'.[16]

Others have argued that the *News on Sunday* was simply a bad product editorially, the failure of which, like that of Eddie Shah's *Post* a year later, proved only that 'a bad paper, badly promoted, will rapidly meet the fate it deserves'.[17]

The *Sunday Correspondent*, by contrast, was not generally perceived as a 'bad' newspaper, but failed nevertheless, largely because it launched at a time – September 1989 – when the second great recession of the Thatcher era was just beginning to bite. When advertising revenues were falling, as they did in the late 1980s and early 1990s, sales of anything less than 600,000 were insufficient to make a Sunday newspaper such as the broadsheet *Correspondent*, standing alone in the marketplace without the support of a larger parent company, financially viable. In January

1990 the *Independent* launched its Sunday sister, inevitably eating into the *Correspondent*'s market. In addition to coping with the competitive strategies of the already established Sundays (see below) the *Correspondent* now had to find and retain readership in the face of another brand-new title.

In July 1990 the floundering *Correspondent* attempted to resolve its difficulties by relaunching as a 'quality tabloid', under a new editor more experienced in the business of popular journalism. This shift in strategy failed to make the paper profitable, and it closed in September 1990.

For some observers, the fact of these failures, and the continuing gap in the British newspaper market for popular left-of-centre titles proved that optimistic hopes of a post-Wapping future in which publications of diverse political persuasions would flourish were utopian. As James Curran has argued, the basic economic environment within which newspapers must survive has not been fundamentally transformed. Curran has noted that 'production wages comprised only 21% of Fleet Street's costs before new technology was introduced.'[18] The Fleet Street revolution had 'not significantly changed the character of the national press' since 'the basic rules of publishing have changed very little. Establishing mainstream national papers remains very expensive.' Twenty-eight per cent of the *Sunday Correspondent*'s costs when it launched at the end of 1989 were allocated to staff (although a large proportion of these would have been accounted for by journalists, as opposed to printers). After the move out of Fleet Street, start-up costs for newspapers remained high, as did running costs, making it much easier for established proprietors and corporations to launch new titles and buy up existing ones than it was for new entrants to the business. Even with £30 million Robert Maxwell's *London Daily News* failed. Eddie Shah's *Today* lost £22.5 million. Fifteen years ago, when Wapping was still a twinkle in Rupert Murdoch's eye, Lord McGregor warned that 'even if all newspapers accomplish the change [to new technologies], competition may still result in some papers closing, since the new technology does little to alter the relative position of competing titles' (1977, p.44).

The potential cost-saving benefits of new print technologies, such as they were, were substantially eroded in any case by the established proprietors' adoption of strategies specifically designed to increase the cost of production and discourage new entrants. From the late 1980s onwards, newspapers began to introduce Saturday supplements, glossy magazines, and ever increasing numbers of Sunday sections. At the same time, more money was spent on marketing and advertising. In the face of such developments new, under-resourced titles simply could not compete. Paul Foot has argued that the *News on Sunday* did not fail only because of editorial and management shortcomings, but 'also because of the insurmountable difficulties of advertising, promoting and circulating a new popular paper without any real wealth behind it'.[19] The workings of the market – if in new technological conditions – meant that 'the new technology has had no diversifying effect whatsoever. Its only real effect has been to boost the profits of the mighty media corporations at the expense of the trade unions.'[20] Belfield *et al.* agree with this assessment, arguing that 'British newspapers have not been revitalised [as a result of Wapping]. What *has* been revitalised is Murdoch's finances' (1991, p.96). As these authors point out, after Wapping the News International wage bill was cut at a stroke by £45 million per annum. As a result, pre-tax profits increased from £39.1 million in 1985 to £165 million in 1988, providing a substantial proportion of the finance for Murdoch's move into satellite television. Lord Goodman argues that 'newspapers, whose very existence was under threat, are now reaping handsome profits – something they owe largely to Rupert Murdoch – although his fellow proprietors may not enjoy acknowledging it.'[21] For Goodman, the Wapping revolution saved, among others, the *Telegraph* titles, 'now under new management, totally revitalised and apparently sailing fair out of troubled waters'. And yet, as Goodman also notes in this article, 'today the industry is more dominated by giant companies than at any previous period. The effect, of course, is to increase the risks attaching to any modest size publication, with the giants' daily increasing wealth waiting for any opportunity to wolf a straggler from the pack.'

Mick Gosling of the Campaign for Press and Broadcasting Freedom argues that unless the government is prepared to set up subsidised facilities, such as regional printing presses and other community resources, which can print newspapers at cost (perhaps financed by an advertising levy), new technology is still going to be subject to the overall economic framework of the industry. And the economics of the industry are such that the start-up costs of a daily paper are still about £20 million. You then very rapidly have to establish an advertising base, raise extra capital sums, etc. There is no automatic reason why new titles should result from that. New titles still need pre-existing media institutions to underwrite their operations.

The *Independent*'s political editor Anthony Bevins argues that 'multiplicity in itself, whether in terms of newspapers, television channels, or petrol stations, does not generate freedom . . . The predominant power will stay in the hands of the barons and their well-paid, underqualified hacks. That is the only "golden promise" of Mr Murdoch's so-called information age. More of the same. To pretend otherwise is to fly in the face of the track record, it is an insult to a free and independent intelligence' (1990, p.17).

The established players in the newspaper game of course reject, as they always have, the value of state subsidies to the press, and dispute the assertion that there is a need for them. News International's Jane Reed argues: 'everything that has happened in the media since News International confronted the unions has been about expansion, diversity and opportunity.'[22] To support her assertion she points out that ten companies share ownership of the UK's nineteen national newspapers; that Conrad Black, and not Rupert Murdoch, dominates the broadsheet market with the *Telegraph* titles; that News International and the Mirror Group command roughly equivalent circulations in the tabloid market; and that the regional newspaper market is dominated by Emap, Westminster Press and Reed International. Veljanovski argues that since 1986 the newspaper industry has become 'the exemplar of the proposition that if cost barriers are reduced, regulation is light and competition permitted, the media will grow and flourish' (1990, p.14).

Editorially, it is argued, if the majority of newspapers have traditionally been biased towards the Conservative Party, this is no longer the case. As we noted in the previous section, many of the once pro-Conservative newspapers have 'jumped ship' in apparent anticipation of a Labour victory at the next general election.

For many on the Left, nevertheless, the lack of a newspaper representative of their views continues to represent a failure of 'press freedom'. Unfortunately for them, it is not one which is likely to be rectified in the 1990s, even under a Labour government. The concept of state intervention in the financing of the press has always been treated with suspicion in the United Kingdom, and more than fifteen years ago the McGregor Commission firmly ruled it out on the oft-heard grounds that it could lead to political censorship and discrimination. With the fourth Conservative victory of 1992 the possibility of community printing presses, subsidised newsprint, or other forms of intervention common in other European countries being introduced into Britain was reduced to the level of fantasy, where Prime Minister Blair (should there ever be one) can be expected to keep it.

In any case, serious doubts must exist, given the failure of the *News on Sunday*, about the ability of the Left in Britain, as presently constituted, to produce newspapers which can sell in appreciable quantities. As the editor of one major newspaper puts it, 'one of the lessons of this whole revolution is that new technology is only the beginning. You really have to have something interesting to say – and that means good journalism – to persuade people to buy the paper.'

The austere ideological soundness which accompanied the launch of the *News on Sunday* was perhaps a forgivable response to the pro-Tory bias of Britain's national newspapers, but failures in marketing, management and, not least, in the paper's journalism, meant that it was unable to tap into what its own, expensively gathered research indicated was a large left-of-centre tabloid readership. The Left, one assumes, is as capable of producing good journalism as the Right, but has yet to learn how to reconcile political correctness with popularity. Until it does, it seems unlikely that the new publishing environment will lead to the more democratic, pluralistic press promised in the wake of Wapping.

# Chapter 8

# Competition, content, and Calcutt

In the 1980s the British press became more competitive, as more titles competed for what was a generally declining readership. As was noted in the previous chapter, the response of the broadsheets to this challenge was to increase their size in physical terms, expanding with supplements and pull-out sections (by August 1992 the *Sunday Times*, for example, comprised ten sections). With the aid of such strategies the *Sunday Times*, and other broadsheets, notably the *Guardian* and the *Telegraph*, while suffering circulation losses, nevertheless retained and even increased their market share of the newspaper-buying public. Then in July 1993, Rupert Murdoch's News International launched a newspaper price war. That month NI cut the price of the *Sun* to 20p. In September the price of *The Times* was cut to 30p, extending the price war to the broadsheet market, at a cost to NI of £45 million per year.

Murdoch's main target in this battle was Conrad Black's *Telegraph*, which followed suit in June 1994 (at an annual cost of £40 million). The *Independent* experimented with price cuts, but did not have the resources to match Murdoch or Black. The Scottish tabloids got involved in price-cutting in July 1994, and in October of that year the Sunday price war began, with the *Sunday Times* cutting its price to 50p.

As of summer 1995 the price war was still going on, with the News International and Hollinger titles clearly benefiting from reduced prices (see Table 1.1). With the cost of newsprint rising rapidly, however, and a persistent sluggishness in the economy, it seemed unlikely that even the deep pockets of Messrs Murdoch and Black could be tapped without limit. For the less wealthy titles, on the other hand, the combined effect of the price war and

increasing cost of newsprint squeezed profit margins, contributing
substantially to the changes in ownership of the *Observer* and the
*Independent* noted in Chapter 1.

The periodical sector, meanwhile, looks healthy. Since 1988 the
periodicals market has increased by 9%, attributed by industry
analysts to a sharp rise in the number of titles being published.
Between 1988 and 1992 the number of periodical titles in Britain
increased by 18%, from 2,021 to 2,394, the majority of new
entrants coming from small independent companies working in
the specialist consumer, leisure, and business sectors. While some
sections of the periodical press are doing less well than others –
magazines for teenage girls, for example, and the 'traditional'
women's magazine market – others, such as the 'new woman'
titles (*Cosmopolitan*, *Company*) and computer magazines, have in
recent years shown significant circulation increases.

For the tabloid newspapers, on the other hand, competition
and declining readerships have posed a greater threat. Peter
Dahlgren observes that 'the "serious" press as a whole seems to
be in marked decline in the contemporary world . . . The popular and tabloid press has been growing' (Dahlgren and Sparks,
1992, p.7). In Britain at least, the opposite is the case. Between
1961 and 1986, annual tabloid sales in the UK fell from 12.43 billion to 10.27 billion.[1] Between 1979 and 1986 sales increased by
only 1.2%, as compared to the broadsheets' increase of 15%.[2]

Since 1986 the decline in sales of both daily and Sunday
tabloids has continued. Aggregate tabloid readership in the UK
fell from an estimated 45 million in 1959 to around 30 million in
1992. Explanations for this vary from growing illiteracy (a substantial number of Britons still have difficulty in reading); the
steady rise in importance of television as a source of news and
entertainment (tabloid newspapers, of course, are as much about
entertaining people as informing them); higher-than-inflation
increases in the price of newspapers; and the effects of economic
recession, both short term (a factor particularly relevant to the
late 1980s and early 1990s), and long term in the sense that the
growing army of unemployed is less likely to buy a paper. Roy
Greenslade, former editor of the *Daily Mirror*, argues: 'there is little doubt that lost jobs represent lost newspaper buyers. Work is
closely bound up with the newspaper-reading habit: many people

read on their way to the factory or office or, traditionally, during their breaks. Once they stop working then newspaper buying, if not reading, gradually ceases too.'³ As we shall see in Chapter 9, changes in traditional working patterns pose a particular threat to regional evening newspapers in declining industrial heartlands such as the north of England and the west of Scotland.

The steady long-term decline in tabloid circulations, combined with the arrival on the market of new titles such as the *Daily Star* in 1978, and the *Sport/Sunday Sport* in 1987 has fuelled a furious circulation war which steadily intensified until, in the late 1980s, it led to the most vociferous calls for press regulation to be heard in Britain since the Second World War.

## YELLOW JOURNALISM: A BRIEF HISTORY

'Yellow' journalism is not a phenomenon peculiar to the contemporary era. From the very first newsbooks, publishers and readers were fascinated by stories of murders, scandals, and public executions. Louis Heren argues that 'popular journalism was created before the serious press. Moreover, papers such as *The Times* fared badly when the stamp tax was abolished in 1865; soon after the *News of the World* became the largest-selling newspaper.'⁴ And so it has remained. But if some of the distinctive features of popular tabloid journalism can be traced back to the nineteenth century the widespread perception has been that in the 1970s and 1980s the form broke qualitatively new ground, sinking to new depths of prurience and sensationalism, to the extent that traditional press freedoms in the United Kingdom have been placed at risk.

This trend in newspaper content can be said to have begun in 1968 with Rupert Murdoch's purchase of the *News of the World*, and its serialising shortly after of the memoirs of Christine Keeler, thus reviving the scandal of the Profumo Affair. Henceforth Murdoch was nicknamed the 'Dirty Digger' by the satirical magazine *Private Eye*, and acquired a reputation for sleazy journalism of a distinctly 'un-British' kind.

In order to utilise the spare printing capacity at the *News of the World*, in 1969 Murdoch's company purchased the *Sun* from the then owners of the *Daily Mirror*, International Publishing

Corporation, and proceeded to transform it from an ostensibly left-of-centre broadsheet to a daily equivalent of the *News of the World*. Preferred (with hindsight, ironically) to Robert Maxwell by the *Sun* unions (who feared the latter's warning that if he took over the paper there would be redundancies amongst printers), Murdoch launched the new tabloid *Sun* in November 1969. His objective was to turn the paper from a low circulation loss-maker (sales dropped to 650,000 at one point) into a competitor to the market-leading *Daily Mirror*.

From the outset, sex was chosen as the terrain on which the circulation war would be fought. The 'page three girl' was introduced in November 1970, and circulation quickly increased to 1.5 million, achieved not only with the help of topless models, but by the *Sun*'s pioneering use of aggressive TV advertising. In 1971 the downmarket *Daily Sketch*, owned by Lord Rothermere, was merged with the *Daily Mail*, enabling the *Sun* to pick up the *Sketch*'s readers and increase its circulation to 2 million. By 1978 it had overtaken the *Daily Mirror* in sales, and by June of that year the 4-million barrier was broken. Under the editorship of Larry Lamb the *Sun* had risen to dominate the tabloid market with a diet of what would become known as 'bonk journalism' – as opposed to the milder 'yellow' variety – defined by one commentator as 'a mixture of private investigation and porn'.[5]

The circulation war between the *Sun* and the *Daily Mirror* was complicated by the launch in 1978 of the *Daily Star*. Coming from Victor Matthews's Express Newspaper Group, the *Star* attempted to repeat the *Sun*'s trick of going downmarket in order to beat the competition. The *Star* undertook to beat the *Sun* at its own game, by printing even more explicit topless snaps and stories, keeping its cover price low, and spending vast sums on brash TV advertising. To counter the threat Rupert Murdoch replaced Larry Lamb as editor of the *Sun* in 1981 with Kelvin MacKenzie, who arrived with a brief to fight fire with fire. The move downmarket, which the *News of the World* and the *Sun* had begun, accelerated. The era of 'bonk journalism' had fully arrived.

The main constituent of bonk journalism was, as the phrase suggests, a focus on sex, preferably with a hint of scandal and involving celebrities. These could be of the major variety, such as members of the Royal Family, or the lesser stars of the music and media industries who came in the 1970s and 1980s to occupy increasing quantities of tabloid newsprint.

Closely related to bonk journalism was the category of 'yuck journalism' – graphic coverage of the bizarre, the tragic, and the pathetic, from the victims of aircrashes and disasters to the grossly obese.

The tabloids also became more overtly political, becoming for the most part willing mouthpieces of the Conservative Government as it set about the Thatcherite restructuring of British society. Jingoism and rabid anti-leftism became the norm, exemplified during the Falklands War by the *Sun*'s 'Gotcha' headline, during the 1984–5 miners' strike, and throughout the 1980s in coverage of the Labour left.

## OVER THE TOP

As already noted, a journalistic fascination with the sensational is as old as newspapers themselves, but in the 1980s the intensity of tabloid competition pushed British titles to the point at which readers, and those concerned with the long-term health of the British press, were losing patience. Key factors in the growing disenchantment of the British reader with his or her tabloid included the rise of 'cheque book journalism' – when newspapers paid the relatives of convicted criminals large sums of money to reveal personal details. In the case of Sonia Sutcliffe, wife of the mass murderer Peter Sutcliffe (the 'Yorkshire Ripper'), large sums were paid for personal details. In many cases, including this one, the payments received by criminals' relatives and friends exceeded the criminal injuries' compensation paid out to victims and their families.

A second feature of tabloid output which caused increasing concern during this period was its increasingly intrusive nature. Journalists acquired the habit of entering people's homes and gardens without permission, rummaging through dustbins for evidence of sexual deviance, and even 'setting up' public figures with prostitutes. Frequent victims of intrusion were the Royal Family, most notably the Princess of Wales, who was photographed secretly while on holiday and very obviously pregnant. Other targets included rock stars such as Rod Stewart, and soap opera actors, who frequently found their personal lives becoming the subject of intensive newspaper coverage.

A third element in the increasingly heady tabloid mix was the more primitive tool of fabrication. In the aftermath of the Falklands War the *Sun* fabricated an interview with Mrs Maria McKay, the widow of a soldier killed in action. By culling from other sources, and inventing what could not be plagiarised, the *Sun* manufactured an 'exclusive', though largely fictitious, story of Mrs McKay's personal bravery, which she disowned completely when it appeared in print.

Tabloid newspapers were heading downmarket during the 1980s in any case, but the speed of the decline increased with the launching of the *Sunday Sport* in September 1986. Owned by David Sullivan – the publisher of magazines with such titles as *Big 'Uns, Shaven Ravers*, and *The Blue Book* – the *Sunday Sport* 'established new ground rules for what is printable in a national newspaper'.[6] Where the *Sun* and the *Star* had pioneered the page three girl the *Sunday Sport* tended to report *only* those stories which had either a bonk or a yuck angle, preferably with photographs. Its advertising space was predominantly occupied by services offering phone sex or aids to lovemaking. It unashamedly printed stories which were obviously incredible, such as sightings of Elvis Presley, Second World War Lancaster bombers found on the moon, and children conceived by aliens. The *Sunday Sport*, with this coverage, was taking to its logical conclusion what the mainstream tabloids had begun, though not without its tongue firmly in its cheek. It was also importing to Britain a style pioneered by American publications like the *National Enquirer* (Taylor, 1991).

With a circulation in December 1986 of 230,000 and growing, the *Sunday Sport* (and its daily equivalent, the *Sport*, launched in 1988) posed a significant threat to the established tabloids. The newspaper revolution begun by Shah and Murdoch had created conditions in which a David Sullivan could set up with the minimum of staff and start-up capital (in August 1987 the *Sunday Sport* had only twelve full-time staff), publish a quality product, and sell it to a young, male, working-class audience (C2s, in marketing parlance) with the help of liberal quantities of tits, bums, and shock–horror stories. The advance of the *Sport* reinforced the existing tabloids' perception that commercial success demanded more of the same from them.

In this, however, they miscalculated. In the late 1980s a succession of stories, mostly attributable to the News International titles, changed the public's mood from one of amused tolerance towards the tabloids' excesses, into one of genuine distaste. These stories always involved one or more of the elements described above: intrusion into privacy; cheque book journalism; and fabrication. The *Sun*'s coverage of Elton John's alleged sexual activities with male prostitutes was one such story. Using unsubstantiated testimony, bought from a known criminal, and old personal photographs of entirely legal sex acts committed in private, the *Sun* attempted to make a public scandal of Elton John's homosexuality (which was, in any case, no secret). Not only were the details of the story untrue and libellous (to the great cost of the *Sun*, which eventually agreed to pay its victim £1 million in compensation) but they were so graphic as to shock even the readers of the *Sun*. Elton John was an exceptionally popular 'family' entertainer, for whom the Great British public felt genuine and considerable affection. The salacious nature of the *Sun*'s revelations about his private life simply turned many readers off, and led to a loss in sales. As Chippindale and Horrie relate it, 'an enormous postbag of complaints poured into Wapping from grannies downwards, with huge numbers of correspondents saying they would never read the paper again. The postbag was backed up by alarming dips in sales every time an Elton story was printed, and MacKenzie was heard moaning in the office that they had dropped on occasion by as many as 200,000 copies, only to bounce back as soon as Elton disappeared off the front page' (1990, p.268). In this case the *Sun* overestimated the capacity of its readers to enjoy the ritual humiliation of the rich and famous.

In 1987 the *Star* made a similar, but even more damaging mistake when it joined forces with David Sullivan's *Sport* to produce what was described as 'a ludicrous caricature of a tits-and-bonking tabloid'.[7] The quantity of naked breasts featured in the *Star* increased, while the age of their owners went down to the point at which the paper was verging dangerously on the paedophiliac. The 'sex and violence' content of the *Star*'s stories became noticeably more explicit. While the editor, Mike Gabbert, championed the *Star*'s unabashed 'populism', readers deserted the paper in droves. Big advertisers like Whitbreads and Tesco took fright and cancelled their lucrative contracts. Within weeks the *Star* pulled out of the joint project, and returned to its marginally less prurient style, leaving David Sullivan to continue alone in the vanguard of bonk journalism.

The key event in turning the tide of public opinion against the tabloids was their coverage of the Hillsborough disaster in April 1989. Some papers, notably the *Daily Mirror*, reproduced on their front pages photographs of dead and dying people, sometimes in colour. Others showed a similar disregard for the sensitivities of victims and relatives. The main offender in this respect was, once again, the *Sun*, with a story headed 'The Truth'. This alleged that drunken Liverpool fans had harassed the police and rescue services, and abused the bodies of the victims. In Liverpool, from where most of the Hillsborough victims had come, the story produced a ferocious reaction, with copies of the *Sun* publicly burnt, newsagents refusing to sell it, and boycotts being organised. Once again, a tabloid had alienated its readers by underestimating their sensitivity and pain. Three years later, the *Sun*'s circulation was still suffering on Merseyside from the Hillsborough fallout, as Liverpool FC manager Graeme Souness discovered when he sold an exclusive story to the paper and was nearly hounded out of Liverpool as a result. As Chippindale and Horrie put it, Hillsborough was 'an unparalleled journalistic disaster' for the *Sun*, 'with huge and continuing financial consequences' (ibid., p.277). By 1989 the paper's circulation had dropped by nearly 600,000, considerably more than its main tabloid competitor, the *Daily Mirror*. Since 1993, helped by aggressive price cutting, the *Sun* has substantially recovered its position (see Table 1.1, p.10).

## CALCUTT AND THE PRESS COMPLAINTS COMMISSION

By the late 1980s the accumulation of such incidents had begun to generate a formidable backlash of opinion against the press in general, and the tabloids in particular. In 1987 Labour MP Anne Clwyd introduced a private member's bill into Parliament, calling for legislation to give victims of the press rights of redress. In

1988 Tory MP Bill Cash introduced a Right of Privacy Bill. During the 1988–9 Parliamentary session bills on the Protection of Privacy and Right of Reply were introduced by MPs John Browne and Tony Worthington respectively.

Each of these attempts to impose legal constraints on the press failed to gain the necessary support in the House of Commons, but the frequency with which they were made, and the fact that they came from both Labour and Tory MPs, clearly shows how the content of the British tabloids had become an important political issue by the late 1980s. These bills failed, nevertheless, because of longstanding resistance in the United Kingdom to anything resembling state intervention in, or censorship of, the press. Just as it has been judged inappropriate to use public moneys dispensed by government to subsidise newspapers (see Chapter 7) the idea that the press should be prevented from saying or doing anything merely on the grounds that some sections of the population might be offended has been regarded with suspicion.

There have always been some legal constraints, of course. Journalists are not allowed to defame individuals, or they are subject to libel actions (as many of the tabloids found to their cost in the 1980s). Nor are they allowed to breach the Official Secrets Act by revealing confidential official information. Incitement to racial hatred is prohibited under race relations legislation, while there are some protections against journalistic harassment, such as the Conspiracy and Protection of Property Act. For the most part, however, newspapers have succeeded in keeping the law at a distance, on the grounds that legal constraints can be abused for political reasons. Instead, they have insisted on their ability to police their own output, and prevent the worse excesses by a system of voluntary self-regulation.

Voluntary self-regulation was introduced by the first Royal Commission on the Press in 1947, in the form of the Press Council, a 39-member committee of 'the great and the good' empowered to adjudicate on contentious press content. The Press Council was established in response to 'public and parliamentary criticism of declining press standards and fears of monopolistic tendencies in the content of the press' (Calcutt, 1990, p.58). Forty years later, by the late 1980s, such fears and concerns were still very much in evidence. Moreover, it had become clear that the Press Council was unable to allay these fears.

The failure of the Press Council, it has been argued, was due principally to the fact that it had no formal code of practice as to what the press should and should not be doing, nor any legal powers to enforce its decisions. The Council was made up of people who frequently had no professional connection with the press, and thus could exert no moral authority over it. As a result the Press Council was simply ignored for most of the time. It also lacked an independent means of finance, relying instead on the goodwill of the newspapers themselves to fund its activities. For all these reasons, the Press Council had by the 1980s come to be widely perceived as ineffectual, a 'watchdog without teeth' held in contempt by the tabloid editors as they rushed downmarket in the competitive spiral.

Meanwhile, as public debate on the content of Britain's newspapers intensified the Conservative Government lent its support to calls for action. In February 1988 Home Office Minister Timothy Renton threatened the press with statutory regulation if they failed to moderate their output. The tabloids continued as before, however, and in April 1989 the Home Secretary announced the appointment of an official committee, chaired by David Calcutt QC, to examine the possibility of the introduction of measures to prevent excessive intrusion into individuals' privacy by the press.

The Calcutt Committee's final report, published in June 1990, accepted that there was 'a wide public aversion to newspaper intrusion' but asserted 'a preference for reform by self-regulation' (ibid., p.10), as indicated by a 1989 MORI poll. Public concern had reached new heights, Calcutt suggested, because 'the past two decades have seen changes in the character of the tabloid market, with a degree of competition not present since the pre-war circulation battles. This may have led some tabloid editors to feel "let off the leash", and to become more intrusive in pursuit of competitive advantage. The content of these papers has also become less political, and more revelatory of the lives of show business personalities and royalty' (ibid., p.11). While established to challenge these undesirable trends in coverage, Calcutt made clear the committee's view that 'any additional constraints upon the press should be limited to the minimum necessary to tackle any genuine abuses' (ibid., p.5).

Having heard a large number of witnesses, including editors, journalists, and those who had been their victims – Kelvin MacKenzie, for example, gave his view that 'tabloid journalism cannot be condemned simply because it is brash or noisy or declamatory. It must only be called to order if it is false, irresponsible, or reports untruths' (ibid., p.7) – the Calcutt Committee drew back from the imposition of any legal constraints on the press's investigative activities, although it recommended that physical intrusion on private property by journalists should become a criminal offence. It also recommended that legal aid should be made available in libel cases, so that not only the rich and famous could have access to this form of redress.

Calcutt rejected the introduction of a statutory right of reply on the grounds that it was impractical. Who, for example, would determine what was or was not accurate in the hundreds of cases which would be likely to arise? Given the difficulties of introducing such a system, Calcutt recommended instead that cases of inaccurate reporting should be referred to the existing legislation on defamation, or to the new 'code of practice' proposed for the newspaper industry by the committee.

While the main thrust of the Calcutt report was for the desirability of continuing self-regulation by the press, it accepted that the 'framework of self-regulation needs substantial strengthening' (ibid., p.57). To this end Calcutt proposed that the press adopt a formal Code of Practice laying down what was and was not permissible in matters such as privacy. The press 'should be given one final chance to prove that voluntary self-regulation can be made to work . . . the Press Council should be disbanded and replaced by a new body [which] must be seen to be authoritative, independent and impartial.'

The new body would be called the Press Complaints Commission, and have similar functions and responsibilities to the Broadcasting Complaints Commission.[8] The sting in the tail of Calcutt's recommendations was his warning to the press that if they failed to take this final chance and prevent further unjustified infringements of individuals' privacy, statutory powers to do so would be introduced, similar to those enjoyed, for example, by the Advertising Standards Authority, which would enable the new PCC to demand that newspapers print corrections and pay compensation to those wronged in coverage. 'If the press', stated the report, 'wishes to retain non-statutory self-regulation, it must set up and support the Press Complaints Commission . . . Should it fail to do so, or should it at any time become clear that the reformed non-statutory mechanism is failing to perform adequately, we recommend that this should be replaced by a statutory tribunal with statutory powers and implementing a statutory code of practice' (ibid., p.74).

The Press Complaints Commission formally came into existence on January 1, 1991, chaired by Lord McGregor of Durris, a longstanding critic of the old Press Council's impotence and lack of authority. In his view, the new body would be vastly superior. It had sixteen members, as opposed to the Press Council's thirty-nine, making it much more manageable and efficient. More importantly, its members were not simply drawn from the 'great and the good', but from the industry. As McGregor puts it, 'the choice of personnel was carefully done so as to get a proper reflection of newspapers and periodicals. I made it a condition of my chairmanship that the tabloids should be strongly represented, because it's useless having a grand body of the good and the great, who are going to sit in moral judgement on the gutter press. It would have no chance of working. The tabloids caused all the trouble, and they're the people who've got to obey the rules.'

Thus, the first members of the PCC included Patsy Chapman, editor of the *News of the World*, and the editor of the *Star*, Brian Hitchen. Tabloid editors were also closely involved in drawing up the Code of Practice which would guide regulation. In McGregor's view, if self-regulation was to be the preferred method of policing newspapers' excesses, it would have a much greater chance of success if the guiding rules and codes were drawn up by the industry itself, rather than being imposed on it from without.

From the outset of the PCC's work, however, Lord McGregor had no doubt as to the main guarantor of success in controlling the press.

We are a disciplining body appointed by the press itself, to enforce a code framed by the press itself. In that way we are a proper self-regulating body, but we don't have any sanctions. The only pressure that we can bring is the pressure which the government has put on the industry by saying that if it fails to observe the PCC's adjudications, based on the Code of Practice framed by the industry, then it will legislate. That's the pressure. What is essential, from our point of view, if the PCC is to work, is that the government should maintain the threat of legislation, at least for the time being. I don't want the press lulled into a false sense of security.

Championed by its advocates as the 'last chance saloon' for the British tabloids, others regarded the Calcutt Committee and the subsequent establishment of the PCC as a cosmetic exercise by the Conservative Government, intended to head off public concern while not antagonising newspapers which were key political allies. Critics pointed out that the PCC was an unelected body, appointed in secret, operating to a Code of Practice drawn up by the very newspapers which it was intended to restrain. What, for Lord McGregor, was the strength of the Code was from this perspective evidence of the weakness of the reform. The slowness of PCC adjudications, and the secrecy in which they were conducted, was also criticised. By July 1991, only 25 of some 700 complaints had been adjudicated. Complaints upheld in the first year of the PCC's existence included that made by the Buckingham Palace press office against the *Sunday People* for publishing nude photographs of Princess Eugenie and the Duke of York. It also upheld a complaint made by newsagents against the *Sunday Sport* for running a story on cannibalism in Thailand, complete with 'explicit', 'horrific', and 'disgusting' pictures. The story was condemned as 'no more than the exploitation of an appetite for horror and necrophily' and 'an extreme breach of the code of practice and the standards which the industry sets itself'.[9]

Despite criticisms of the first year of the PCC's work, by July 1992 and the end of the eighteen-month period of 'probation' proclaimed by Calcutt there was some evidence to show that the self-regulatory path was producing results. By that stage in its existence the PCC had received some 2,069 communications from the public in regard to possible breaches of the Code of Practice (see Table 8.1). Of these, 8.4% were excluded by the PCC from its remit (i.e. they were not complaints about journalistic standards but some other aspect of press content, such as advertising), while 3.6% exceeded the time limit allowed for complaints to be made. A further 3.7% were third party complaints, specifically excluded under the terms of the PCC's establishment, while 10.7% were dropped by the complainant before they could be dealt with; 41.8% of complaints were judged not to constitute a prima facie breach of the Code and thus were not forwarded to the full PCC for adjudication (a figure which compares with the experience of similar regulatory bodies, such as the Advertising Standards Authority and the Broadcasting Complaints Commission); 23.3% were resolved between the complainant and the editor of the publication complained against, a figure which was the source of some pride to the PCC, since one of its main aims was to encourage mutually satisfactory resolutions of complaints before final adjudication became necessary.

In all, then, by the end of July 1992, only just over 5% of complaints had gone to adjudication by a full meeting of the PCC, a total of 107 complaints. Of these, fifty-one were upheld, and fifty-six rejected. Perhaps unsurprisingly, the *Sun* was the worst offender, with nine complaints against it upheld. Twenty-nine complaints were upheld against the mass-market tabloids as a whole, compared to two against the quality broadsheets. The remarkable feature of these figures, for the PCC, was just how few successful complaints there had been, given that nearly 15 million newspapers are sold in Britain every weekday. For supporters of the principle of voluntary self-regulation, they were a clear testimony to the effectiveness of the PCC in achieving the objectives demanded by the Calcutt Committee.

The probation period coincided, of course, with the run-up to a general election, the nature of which meant that newspapers could not be certain of the political complexion of government in the longer term. It was no secret that a victorious Labour Party would be inclined to introduce new legal constraints on press content and concentration of ownership and it seems reasonable to suppose that this was one factor in persuading the worst press offenders to take the PCC seriously. Conscious of the threat to their freedom which now existed, newspapers also appointed

Table 8.1 Outcome of complaints to the Press Complaints
         Commission, January 1991 – July 1992

| Outcome | Number of complaints | Percentage of total |
|---|---|---|
| Outside PCC remit | 174 | 8.4 |
| Disallowed | 152 | 7.3 |
| No prima facie breach of code | 864 | 41.8 |
| Resolved between editor and complainant | 481 | 23.3 |
| Not pursued by complainant. | 222 | 10.7 |
| Upheld | 51 | 2.5 |
| Not upheld | 56 | 2.6 |
| Still under investigation | 69 | 3.3 |
| Total | 2069 | 99.9 |

Source: Press Complaints Commission.

ombudsmen, who put complaints from the public to editorial
boards and sought redress.

The 'clean up' of the press in 1991, such as it was, was blamed
by some for the continuing decline in tabloid circulation figures,
although this was contradicted by the fact that the most prurient
tabloid of all, the *Sunday Sport*, had also by mid-1991 seen its
sales fall to around 300,000.[10]

## SHOOT-OUT AT THE LAST CHANCE SALOON

On April 9, 1992, the Conservative Party won a historic fourth
term in government. The press campaign was not noticeably more
anti-Labour than was usual although, as we saw in Chapter 7, the
Tory tabloids were blamed by Labour for its failure to make the
expected gains amongst the working class Cls and C2s of south-
east England. Shortly after the campaign ended, however, the
press presented the PCC with the first real challenge to its authority. Somewhat surprisingly, perhaps, it was a broadsheet rather
than a tabloid newspaper which was responsible for the offending
material.

On June 7, 1992, accompanied by a torrent of TV advertising,
Rupert Murdoch's *Sunday Times* published the first instalment of
its serialisation of a book by journalist Andrew Morton about
Princess Diana. The author's – and the *Sunday Times*'s – unique

selling point for the book was its allegations of Diana's personal unhappiness, attempted suicides, eating disorders, and another Royal marriage on the rocks. Other newspapers ran the story, leading to a period of several weeks in which the private lives of the Prince and Princess of Wales were debated and dissected at great length, and in the most intimate detail, in the press and on television. On Monday, June 8, the PCC issued a statement condemning press handling of the story, complaining that

> the most recent intrusion and speculative treatment by sections of the Press of the marriage of the Prince and Princess of Wales is an odious exhibition of journalists dabbling their fingers in the stuff of other people's souls in a manner which adds nothing to legitimate public interest in the situation of the heir to the throne . . . The Commission has been distressed by the reversion of some newspapers to the worst excess of the 1980s and are bound to state publicly their view that the continuance of this type of journalism will threaten the future of self-regulation just at the time when it appears to be succeeding.[11]

Journalists divided into two camps on the issue: those who agreed with the PCC, and those who supported the right of the press to expose the private problems of Royalty in the public interest. The latter, spearheaded by the *Sunday Times* itself, argued that since the marriage in question was that of the future King and Queen of the United Kingdom, the story raised important constitutional issues. Favourable comparisons were drawn with the 1930s, when King Edward VIII's relationship with an American divorcee – which ultimately led him to give up his throne – was kept virtually secret from the mass of the British people until the last moment. The *Sunday Times*, by contrast, was ensuring that no such secrecy would be permitted in the 1990s.

More pragmatically, a number of editors accused the PCC of an overhasty reaction, arguing that since the story was based on a book, and appeared to be authenticated by close friends of Princess Diana, there were no legitimate grounds for censoring it.

Critics of the *Sunday Times* argued that the paper's decision to run the story was a purely commercial one, reinforced by the staunch republican and anti-establishment tendencies of both

Rupert Murdoch and the editor, Andrew Neil. The *Sunday Times*, it was alleged, had reduced itself to the level of the gutter press.

Added piquancy was given to this debate by the fact that it came just at the end of the eighteen-month 'probationary' period allowed by David Calcutt for the press to demonstrate that it would accept and abide by the PCC's recommendations. At the end of June 1992 David Mellor, the Heritage Minister with responsibility for the media, was due to announce the government's decision on whether or not to proceed with privacy legislation. Instead, on July 10, he announced a further six-month review of press performance over the probationary period, headed again by David Calcutt. At the same time, Labour MP Clive Soley was preparing a Freedom and Responsibility of the Press Bill which would require newspapers to allow readers a right of reply to inaccuracies in coverage.

Some observers argued that journalists should not be afraid of the prospect of some legislation, but should insist that it be combined with a freedom of information law giving every citizen the right 'lawfully to obtain and to publish all official information, except when to do so would infringe the privacy of another or be gravely harmful to the security of the nation' (Lustig, 1990, p.46). In return journalists would support a right of privacy, to the effect that 'any unauthorised use or discharge of personal information calculated or intended to cause distress, annoyance or embarrassment, or damage to the reputation of another, is actionable, unless otherwise justified on the grounds of the nature of the personal information and the legitimate public interest (if any) of such information' (ibid.). Disputes as to what constitutes public interest would be settled by the courts. In July 1992 the *Guardian* reported support in the Cabinet for the implementation of legislative measures first suggested in the Calcutt Report: in particular, the creation of three new offences of journalistic trespass.[12] These measures, if implemented, would make it an offence for journalists to intrude on private property in order to obtain personal information for publication; to place bugging devices on private property for the same purpose; and to take photographs or make voice recordings on private property with the intention of rendering someone identifiable in a publication.

The Press Complaints Commission's position on legislative

change was contained in its formal submission to 'Calcutt II' (as the second Calcutt review was helpfully dubbed by the media). The document pointed to the relatively small number of complaints about breaches of the Code of Practice which had been made to the PCC in the first eighteen months of its existence (see above). It claimed success in persuading the press to take more care *before* publication, and to cooperate with the PCC and complainants *after* publication of an offending item. On these grounds the PCC's submission claimed that 'self-regulation is now working effectively',[13] and restated familiar objections to the introduction of statutory legislation on privacy and ethics: that it could be used to suppress criticism of government and other sections of the establishment; that it would be extremely difficult to apply, if not completely unworkable; and that, ultimately, it would threaten British democracy.

Many editors, including some who prided themselves on running responsible newspapers, were deeply suspicious of legislation which might hamper their ability to pursue genuine investigative journalism. In the view of Arnold Kemp, editor of the *Herald*,

> the interesting feature of press measures in the 1980s is that none of them really affected the tabloid press. They've nearly all made it more difficult for the serious press to investigate the actions of government and those in authority. These punitive libel actions have impinged on the serious press just as much as the tabloid press. That was one of the reasons why they couldn't blow the whistle on Maxwell. Exactly the same thing will occur if we get privacy legislation. We will get a set of laws designed to curb the excesses of the tabloid press, but which will in effect make it harder for the serious press to go about its legitimate business of exposing serious misconduct. I think a privacy law would be used by every rogue in town. I'm increasingly pessimistic about this curious relationship between tabloid excess and legislation impinging on the serious press.

While support for such legislation was undoubtedly growing amongst MPs in the late summer and autumn of 1992, the minister responsible, David Mellor, was known to be less than enthusiastic. Mellor's position was complicated somewhat by his own involvement in personal scandal. On Sunday, July 19, 1992 the *People* newspaper reported allegations of an affair between the minister and an actress, claiming public interest as legitimation for the invasion of his privacy, and denying that the Code of Practice had been violated. To many observers it seemed unlikely that Mellor would be able to endorse privacy legislation in the future without appearing to be vindictive.

A potential conflict of interest was avoided when, in September 1992, David Mellor resigned, to be replaced by the former Northern Ireland Secretary Peter Brooke. Brooke confirmed the government's reluctance to introduce restrictive press legislation, but stressed in interviews and statements that much would depend on the recommendations of 'Calcutt II'.

In the event, and despite continuing controversy surrounding coverage of the Royal Family, David Calcutt's review of press self-regulation, when it was published on January 14, 1993, went further than the government was prepared to go.'[14] His proposal for a statutory press tribunal to replace the PCC was rejected by ministers.

Over the next few years a number of stories kept the issue of press regulation alive: photographs of Princess Diana taken, without her permission, while she was working-out at a London gym; photographs of an ill Countess Spencer, again taken without permission; coverage of 'three-in-a-bed romps' involving Conservative MP Richard Spring; and corruption allegations against Jonathan Aitken MP. Despite these and other stories, however, the government stuck to the principle of self-regulation.

This was confirmed by the appointment in January 1995 of Lord Wakeham to the chairmanship of the PCC, replacing Lord McGregor. While the appointment was an implicit criticism of the latter (McGregor frequently commented on stories before taking time to assess them), it was also, by placing a well-known former member of the Conservative establishment at the head of the PCC, a sign that the government wished the organisation to be taken seriously. Wakeham entered his new job proclaiming the establishment of the PCC to be 'a logistical and political triumph' in the context of the criticism of the press which characterised the late 1980s. It had made mistakes, however, which should be avoided in future. In a speech to the British Press Awards on April 4, 1995, Wakeham stated that his aim as chairman of the

PCC was 'to put the maintenance of the self-regulatory system which governs the press beyond the bounds of political debate . . . to ensure that [it] is so effective that no one will want, or be able, to put anything better in its place'.

Wakeham's strategy was to 'beef up' the membership of the PCC, appointing among others the widow of John Smith.

As of April 1995 about 70 complaints a week were being made to the PCC, an increase on 1994 and, for Wakeham, evidence of increasing public awareness of, and trust in, the PCC's ability to deal with complaints. Public confidence, he acknowledged, was crucial to the survival of the self-regulatory system.

# Chapter 9

# The regional story

Previous chapters have been largely about the challenges faced by the 'national' journalistic media: those which are distributed throughout the geographical territory of the United Kingdom. But the UK is not a nation so much as a collection of nations, which are in turn divided into myriad regions and communities, each with its own distinctive characteristics. England, Northern Ireland, Scotland and Wales all possess particular cultural identities, in addition to being 'British'. In England, the North is perceived very differently from the South, while in Scotland, Glasgow, Edinburgh, and the surrounding conurbations have as much to separate as to bind them together culturally.

Throughout the UK these differences are reflected in media, so that while the country as a whole shares a common culture of 'national' news and journalism, the greatest proportion of it produced in London, each constituent part, from the national regions of Scotland and Wales down to the remote island community, has its own media covering its own issues and agendas. This chapter focuses on those media, and their future prospects.

## BROADCASTING

One of the more unexpected outcomes of the changes which have been taking place in British broadcasting is the boost they have given to regional television journalism. In the 1990s both the BBC and the commercial channels will devote more of their resources to regional news and current affairs than ever before. As the broadcasting environment becomes more competitive the established terrestrial companies have come to believe that the key to their survival lies largely in the extent to which they can meet the demands of viewers at the regional and local levels.

Audience demand for more regional broadcast journalism was identified by market research carried out for companies such as Scottish Television and Grampian in the early 1990s, and is in itself perhaps unsurprising, since information about one's own locality, whether in printed or broadcast form, performs a number of important social functions, from the banal of knowing which roads are open to such matters as local crime and factory closures. National news suppliers, by definition, are ill equipped to cover local news, except when it has national repercussions, and no one has ever expected them to do so. As a result the ITV companies have always maintained the facilities to produce local journalism, which has traditionally been broadcast in the early evening, with shorter bulletins at other times of the day, usually following ITN's national news. As for the BBC, its Regional Directorate, set up in 1987, now maintains six regional news and current affairs operations, each with substantial budgets.

While regional news and current affairs has tended to be seen as a less glamorous poor relation in the television journalism industry, the developments in broadcasting examined in previous chapters have revealed its potential contribution to the financial health and long-term survival of the organisations which produce it. The emergence of satellite television represents a significant addition to the number of hours of broadcast journalism available to the British viewer. More choice for the viewer (disregarding, for the moment, the quality of what is on offer) will inevitably mean more competition for the audiences on which, for the commercial companies especially, income depends. And the satellite providers have some important advantages in the ratings war: notably, their ability to stay on air twenty-four hours a day, and to be there, live, as the cruise missiles fly through downtown Baghdad (or wherever the newsworthy event of the day may be). The regional companies, on the other hand, have nothing but their 'regionalness' on which to sell their product.

A regional director of the ITC argues that 'in future there will be many more sources of national and international news than there are at present, and I think that the way for local regional companies to build up a reputation for themselves, to interest their viewers, to get their viewers and to keep them, is to provide a good local or regional news service.' It seems likely that regional news and current affairs provision will be strengthened in the next few years, not least because the success or failure of the independent television companies will depend on the quality of the journalism they can provide. The above source believes that 'news and current affairs has an extremely large part in the commercial companies' future plans. Whether it will draw huge audiences is another matter, but it will give credibility to a station, and once you've got the credibility, the people will tend to watch you more.'

As noted above, the companies' own market research has convinced them that regional journalism can and will draw audiences, and is thus justified on commercial, as well as 'quality' criteria.[1] For Stuart Prebble of Granada:

> the reality is that for any local station the main point of contact with the viewer is the main evening news programme. Some years ago we took the view that with the proliferation of satellite, cable, C5 at some point, the thing we should concentrate on is the one thing those channels couldn't give them – local news. You don't get real local news on cable, because they don't have the resources, nor will they in the foreseeable future. So we've invested a lot of money in news by way of increasing staff, more cameras on the road, more editing equipment, more bulletins, and so on.

This essentially commercial logic connects with a profound cultural shift towards greater decentralisation of economic and political decision-making, and of cultural production. The trend is global, and underpins one of the Conservative Party's main arguments for opening up the UK television system to the market. Audiences, it is argued, are fragmenting into ever more heterogeneous groups, separated by class, lifestyle, region and, in the case of Britain, nation. The era of London-centred UK media is coming to an end.

Stuart Prebble, who has played a key role in the debate about the future of regional TV journalism, identifies trends pulling in two different directions. On the one hand, news coverage is becoming more global in nature, so that 'it's not unusual for us to see *News at Ten* being presented from the middle of the Sahara Desert, and we're quite relaxed about the idea of seeing the newscaster standing in Riyadh and introducing reports from South Carolina where the Americans are getting ready to go to the Gulf, and flipping over to Tel Aviv where they're expecting the missiles to come in – only a few years ago that would have been unthinkable, but now it's routine.' Satellite newsgathering and transmission, in this sense, endows TV news with an increasingly international 'footprint'. For Prebble, however, and those who agree with him, this merely enhances the need for news which is more parochial, in the best sense of the term, making it incumbent on those with a local focus to consolidate that strength and give viewers a picture of the world seen from where they live. Says Prebble, 'I think that will become the key to ITV's position as the competition [from Sky, the BBC, CNN, etc.] gets stronger.'

From this point of view the regional companies' news production is seen as potentially their most popular local output, providing a distinctive service which the large national and international broadcasters cannot, thus attracting audiences and advertising revenue. The C3 companies' ability to address local audiences with a local news agenda becomes, in this analysis, their unique selling proposition. In short, it is precisely what some commentators have termed the 'globalisation' of television culture occasioned by the advent of satellite broadcasting which has thrust on to regional journalism a heightened role.[2]

As we saw in Chapter 5, this development has thrown the C3 companies into conflict with the producers of networked television news, ITN, centred on the desire of the former to meet more effectively what they see as a demand for local coverage. The critics of the status quo argue that ITN's programmes, which the companies have been obliged to take in their entirety, are inadequate competitors, not only to the new satellite providers, but to the BBC, as evidenced by the latter's consistently higher ratings. In a straight fight over the terrain of national news the BBC, as 'the voice of the nation', would always win. Commercial news, therefore, should direct its resources into local coverage. National news would not be abandoned, but repackaged into a form capable of being combined with the regional news agenda of each individual company. Stuart Prebble, whose name has been most associated with this position, argues that if you look back to the beginning of ITV it made sense, since all the ITV companies individually didn't have the resources to set up their own national and international newsgathering operation, to pool their resources and have a service provided by one organisation. The price you pay for that is that if you live anywhere in the country other than London, you have to accept that there is a metropolitan perspective on the news you get. It's pre-digested in that sense, and therefore remote from your interests. I think that advances in newsgathering technology, and an increased understanding of regionalism have made possible what would sensibly have been done in the first place, if common sense rather than economics and logistics had determined decisions. There is now no reason why it's not possible to see the world from the perspective of a place much closer to where you live. The present system was born not because it's the best system, but because that was the only way available to us to do it. Things have moved on.

What Prebble and his supporters proposed was, in simple terms, the transformation of ITN from being a supplier of news programmes (which are transmitted live in their entirety) into an agency supplying national and international footage, which could then be taken by the regional companies, integrated with their own local stories, and presented by a local anchorperson. The formal division between the national international and local agendas would cease to exist, being replaced by a more flexible format in which the main evening news could lead with a local story, to be followed by a national or international story, before returning to local events. A national story concerning, for example, the council tax, could be treated from a local perspective. Crucially, the regional production team, rather than ITN's editors in London, would decide the running order of items, based on their own judgements of newsworthiness.

In October 1990, Prebble called for the ITV companies to move towards 'a mixed national/international/local news magazine to replace ITN's early evening news bulletin',[3] implying that the late evening *News at Ten* could retain its present position in the schedules. He also predicted that by 1997 'ITN will be providing additional hourly news bulletins' but that its 'weekday

early evening news programmes will be replaced by locally produced news magazine shows'. A regional manager who supports
the 'Prebble plan' explains that

> I might want to run *News at Ten* the way it runs at the
> moment. But what we would do is work on the early evening
> news, which is less substantial, and also more of a problem,
> because so many people miss it. I want to try and use the hour
> rather the way they do it in America, so that you give stature
> to your local newscasters by having them package a rolling
> hour of news, maybe between six and seven. That would be
> one of the options we would look at. Then you could have a
> late all-UK bulletin.

ITN, as one would expect, have expressed fierce resistance to any
proposals of this kind. On the one hand, the company has a clear
commercial interest in maintaining the status quo. But its managers make two specific criticisms of the 'Prebble plan': firstly,
that the demand for integrated news of this type has been overstated; and secondly, that it will threaten C3's ability to fulfil its
contractual obligation to provide 'quality' competition to the
BBC's news and current affairs output. A senior manager of ITN
argued in 1991, before the new C3 franchises were awarded by the
ITC, that

> it's not true that a lot of ITV companies are putting pressure
> on us to offer them a more flexible package of news material.
> One ITV company [Granada] has and even then, you could
> narrow it down to one individual within an ITV company
> [Prebble], who has got an awful lot of publicity out of this par-
> ticular cause. That doesn't invalidate it, and it is perfectly
> proper to raise the issues, but the consensus, so far as we can
> judge, not only from the existing franchise holders, but from
> the applications of challengers for the new franchises, is that
> the vast majority are happy with the ITN service as it is. So
> I'm not sympathetic to the notion that there is a demand for
> more flexibility in packaging ITN's product. I'm very sympa-
> thetic, in the particular case of STV, with their natural desire
> to serve a nation properly and adequately with news, and if
> they judge that they should include in their package national

and international events which have a particular relevance to Scotland, and may wish to make them more relevant to Scotland, I think that's a wholly laudable thing for them to do.

Indeed, Scottish Television by 1990 was already broadcasting such a programme, *Scottish International*, which combined ITN and Visnews footage of international events with locally produced analysis and discussion. Such programmes would form a significant element in STV's journalism output in the 1990s, according to the successful franchise application, which emphasised the importance to the company of 'reporting from a Scottish perspective on European and other events'.[4]

Concerning C3's legal obligation to provide quality news, ITN sources pointed out that the Broadcasting Act in effect dictates that there must be a properly resourced news provider in the commercial sector of UK public service broadcasting, able to compete with the BBC; and furthermore, that there should continue to be national and international bulletins on the traditional model. Beyond that, it was argued, the companies were free, as STV had done, to produce additional programmes of the type demanded by supporters of the Prebble plan. 'There's absolutely nothing to stop them,' as one senior ITN source put it. 'They can take a satellite from anywhere in the world, and put it on their programmes. We can't stop them even if we wish to, and we don't. But that should not be – and this is where a mistake is made in the analogy with America – at the expense of a national networked programme dealing with national and international news. In the US there's still network news, although many of the affiliates do a mix of news.'

It was also argued that if ITN were to lose its guaranteed market its experienced journalists and technical crews would lose their commitment to producing a distinctive, identifiable product.

Stuart Purvis, ITN's editor-in-chief, made the further point that if the C3 companies 'had to package national and international news, they would have fewer resources for covering local and regional news'.[5]

One could be tempted (given the market research evidence brandished by STV, Grampian and others) to dismiss these arguments as having more to do with ITN's commercial self-interest than the needs of the regional television audience, but it is certainly true that not all of the C3 companies share the enthusiasm of Granada, STV and others for the 'Prebble plan'. Laurie Upshon, Central TV's controller of news, argues that 'regional news is strong because it is regional. If you put your national news in a regional context it would put the BBC at an advantage.'[6]

Others objected to the Prebble plan on economic grounds. The smallest companies, such as Grampian, serving the vast north of Scotland, would simply be unable to meet the costs of such a development, and fear that if ITN were damaged in the process they would also suffer a loss of quality in their national and international news. Gus MacDonald of STV concedes that 'I certainly wouldn't want a situation where in Scotland we ended up with an inferior product simply because of national pride. We'd have to make sure that we could cope with the costs and technicalities of it.' Here, however, new technology appears to be on the side of the Prebble plan. As Prebble himself argues, 'satellite time gets very cheap indeed if C3 makes a block booking, so we're actually talking about relatively small amounts of money, and some changes in working practices. And we're entering a situation where an improved competitive position turns directly into money.' According to Gus MacDonald:

> With the new video equipment, some of which is very cheap indeed, you can get images of the same quality that you used to have to buy at great cost, and which can be edited quite quickly. More importantly, you can get out of the studio. Until the late 1980s, local TV meant studio TV – people talked at you in the studio. Now you can send people out, so you can start to patch together the equivalent of a very expensive ITN bulletin with all its one minute thirty second bits patched in. You can achieve the same pace [as ITN] and the same quality of picture. There's not the incompatibility which there used to be in suddenly going from ITN pictures to local pictures. And with the American experience you can see the way that city stations do patch in international, national and local news. One of the problems in Britain is that it has always looked as though professionalism resided in London, and the provincials were all rather incompetent. That's no longer the case.

Tunstall and Dunford note that the falling price of satellite links means 'regional presenters in Manchester and Birmingham will soon be routinely conducting line interviews with politicians and others in Milan and Brussels' (1991, p.21). In such an environment ITN's attempt to preserve editorial control over the use to which national and international coverage is put by the regional companies will become increasingly difficult as the decade progresses.

For some companies, though, particularly those with relatively small populations spread across large territories, even the savings available from the adoption of satellite newsgathering techniques are unlikely to make it feasible for them to produce the hour-long combinations of local, national, and international news favoured by STV and Granada. They would have to take the programmes produced by a larger neighbouring company. On these grounds Prebble's plan was attacked by Yorkshire, Westcountry, Central, and Border when the companies met to discuss the future of regional news in January 1992, asserting that it would 'detract from the strong identity of their existing regional programmes'.[7] By then, however, some form of change to the status quo was inevitable. By January 1992 Granada's *Granada Tonight* regional news magazine was incorporating a sixty-second round up of international news supplied by Visnews via satellite, with three other companies reported to be interested in similar deals. For ITN, the message was clear: adapt to the changing demands of the customers, or be supplanted by rivals entering the marketplace.

## The BBC

In early 1991 the BBC placed advertisements in the press for a battery of new appointments, part of an investment of £3 million in its regional journalism. This was one clear signal that, as for the C3 companies, regional journalism was going to play an important role in the BBC's future. As Ron Neil, the head of the Regional Directorate put it, 'we are choosing to make journalism our number one priority in regional broadcasting. I'm putting my share of the savings we made from *Funding the Future*[8] into journalism and creating more jobs, because I think it's the single most important activity we have outside London. I think the licence payers should be able to expect decent local and regional information from the BBC.'

Although the bulk of the BBC's regional journalistic resources are placed in its radio service, which we examined in Chapter 6, its regional television journalism is also expanding, if the creation of the Regional Directorate and the recent investments can be taken as reliable indicators of corporate strategy. The strategy reflects the perception, articulated by Ron Neil, that 'all our lives are becoming more regional. The policy centre is shifting to Brussels, and I think the regionalisation of society will be reflected in broadcasting.'

At present, the commercial companies clearly dominate regional television journalism in the UK. As we have seen, the C3 companies, in the process of winning their franchises, reasserted the importance of journalism to their operations, and have committed themselves to appropriate levels of investment. The C3 network has twenty-one news centres run by twelve regional companies, as compared to the BBC's six regions (including the 'national' regions of Scotland, Wales, and Northern Ireland).

Rather than attempt to match the C3 network's greater number of regional splits, the BBC's Regional Directorate has adopted a strategy which attempts, on the one hand, to replicate 'Birtian' principles (see Chapter 5) at the regional level, and on the other, to maximise the advantages to be gained from having substantial television and radio departments in the regions. Jack Regan of BBC Scotland points out that one of the differences between the regional journalism of the C3 companies and that of his own organisation is that 'they invest more in camera power, in order to get more [and more local] stories on screen. We will increasingly invest more into the quality and expertise end, so that you may find your local C3 station offering 23 stories in 28 minutes, while we offer seven or eight.'

Local journalism, in short, like national and international coverage, will increasingly be produced by informed, specialist correspondents, capable of finding stories and breaking them, rather than merely reacting to them. For the BBC's senior management, branding their regional journalism as 'authoritative' is the key to competing with what they see as the C3 companies' 'smash and grab' approach. As one regional controller puts it, 'what we're about is being the authoritative voice, a high-quality dependable service which also has to be popular.'

The second key element in the BBC's regional strategy has been to develop its bi-media resources. Just as the C3 companies are moving towards a greater integration of their newsgathering operation the BBC will tend in the 1990s to combine television newsgathering with the needs of radio and vice versa. In June 1991 it was reported that 'all ten main regional centres in England will have a local government specialist correspondent serving both local radio and regional television. A network of specialist correspondents will also be built up in the regions covering industry, business, transport, environment and community affairs.'[9]

In an echo of the C3 companies' dispute with ITN about news, the BBC regions were at the beginning of the 1990s increasingly expressing their desire for more freedom to opt out of network programming, in favour of locally produced current affairs. Some regions – BBC Scotland, for example – already had substantial opt-out powers, based on their special status as 'nations', but some observers expressed doubts that this freedom could be maintained, let alone increased, beyond 1996. One management source identifies 'a body of opinion in London that BBC1 should be a network with no opt-outs, and that all the opt-outs should be on BBC2'. Those who defended BBC1's currently more liberal attitude argued that locally produced opt-out programmes frequently attract bigger audiences for BBC1 than networked programmes.

Hanging over these plans, and belying the enthusiasm and self-confidence with which they have been put, has been the renewal of the Charter in 1996 and the activities of an influential lobby which asks if the BBC should be involved in any regional journalism at all. Such questions are put mainly in the context of radio, but there is little doubt that the C3 companies' current strength in local television journalism could be used as an argument for divesting the BBC of its production, as part of the wider process of 'slimming down' the corporation which will inevitably take place in the 1990s.

## Feeding back

Both the C3 companies and the BBC regions are part of a greater whole. And for both, relationships with those who run the network are issues of great concern for the future. In the case of C3, as we have seen, there are tensions concerning the integration of national, international, and local news, and the desire of the regional companies to acquire more freedom in how they package ITN's material. A different problem exists for at least some of the C3 companies, whose managements complain of the difficulties they experience in gaining access to the network for their own regionally produced programmes. With the exception of the largest companies, notably Granada and Central, regional current affairs has traditionally been excluded from the network (one notable exception being Grampian's *Rescue* series, which followed the activities of a North Sea rescue team and included the rescue operations which accompanied the Piper Alpha oil rig disaster). STV's head Gus MacDonald describes how he felt on coming to Scotland, having been head of ITV's factual programming, 'to suddenly be locked out of the network':

> There's no way for Scottish Television's current affairs and documentaries to get onto ITV. It's blocked off by the old majors which still have a de facto guarantee on these slots. There's a big job to be performed in getting Scotland onto the UK commercial network. I think it's very unhealthy that inside a union of these countries only 1% of what the English see on their screens at peak-time comes from Scotland, and it's the same for Ireland and Wales. If you look at the statistics you'll find that maybe 5% of programming on UK screens comes from Scotland, but close inspection shows that most of that 5% comes well out of peak-time – afternoons, mornings, religious slots, etc. Given that 75% of what we see comes from England, Australia and America, I think that the English should make much more effort to encourage Scottish programming. There's nothing more marginalising than the idea that the Scots only contribute to the UK network something 'Scottish', which means that 'Britishness' is monopolised by the English companies. 'Britishness' is ceded to the English companies, and we're marginalised by our own sense of identity. The Irish and the

Welsh suffer from the same thing, and its got to be fought against.

For the C3 companies, this problem may be solved by the appointment of a 'central scheduler' whose job is to arbitrate and seek to establish a more accessible system. MacDonald is optimistic: 'This brutal shake-up of ITV, which in some ways has been vindictive, ill-conceived and badly done, has been beneficial for a country like Scotland, because we had such a dreadful position before, and were so neglected and excluded by the old system. We're going to come out of it, I think, much stronger.'

The problem of marginalisation also exists for the BBC regions which, like the C3 companies, may have more than adequate resources to produce quality regional journalism, but feel frozen out of the BBC network when it comes to current affairs. Patrick Chalmers, former controller of BBC Scotland, argues that 'the biggest problem we have is maintaining our place representing Scotland within the culture of the UK. We are in grave danger of being homogenised out of existence. They [the BBC's management in London] are quite happy to ghettoise you, but it seems to me that if you're reflecting the UK, which after all is what the BBC should be about, it's not enough to say "off you go boys, do your own thing".'

In 1991 BBC Scotland made approximately 3% of networked BBC programmes, with 75–80% made in London and the Southeast. There were virtually no networked current affairs television programmes made outside London. In the face of such statistics Kenneth Cargill, head of BBC Scotland's TV news and current affairs operation, has argued that while the investments described above are a welcome sign of the BBC's commitment to regional TV journalism

> what hasn't been satisfactorily addressed yet is how we can get regional journalism across to the metropolitan audience. Those of us working in the regions are very concerned about the provincialism of London. We want to get some more of our perspectives on important stories across to the London audience, and we believe that significant numbers of current affairs programmes currently made in London should be devolved to the regions. We think that there should be a greater decentral-

isation of programme making, because it's just as valid to make programmes outside London as inside it, and it's also cheaper.

There have always been occasional regional contributions to networked current affairs strands, but the demand here is for a more systematic and substantial regional input, to balance what Cargill calls 'the metropolitan bias':

A parallel can be drawn in this respect between the situation of the regional organisations (BBC and C3) and that of the independent production companies. The Broadcasting Act decreed that the BBC and commercial television should move towards a position in which at least 25% of current affairs output was independently produced. Could not the regional producers, it has been suggested, be allocated a quota of network programming, whether in the form of entire current affairs strands or individual editions of programmes such as *Panorama*? Perhaps in response to such calls Channel 4's commissioning editor for news and current affairs, David Lloyd, announced in July 1992 that the channel would be introducing a new current affairs strand in 1993, with a specific remit to broadcast work by 'independent producers based outside London and the south-east with local stories that would interest a national audience'.[10] Of a £250,000 initial budget, £150,000 would go to Scottish producers.

While the pressures for increased access to the network are greatest in the case of the 'national' regions of Scotland, Northern Ireland, and Wales, they are felt also in the English regions of the BBC, and appear to be acknowledged by the Corporation's senior management. In September 1991 the newly appointed regional controller, Mark Byford, explicitly called for more regional input to the network, and announced another opt-out slot, at 7.30 on a Thursday evening, for each individual region to broadcast a locally produced current affairs programme.[11]

## THE PRESS

In the hierarchy of print journalism the press outside London have traditionally been regarded as low status, second-class newspapers by those who work on the major nationals. The regional journalists are relatively low paid, on average; their work is by definition parochial (as it has to be to serve the local market); and it is generally assumed that the more successful among them will automatically graduate to the big London titles. To some extent this is a correct assumption, if only because provincial publishers are often unable or unwilling to pay the larger salaries common on national newspapers.

The regional press, however, occupies a distinctive and important role in the British journalism industry, supplying local communities with news and information in a way which no other medium can. Regional titles have the inherent advantage of being first and arguably best in their reportage of local stories. They can also boast a high degree of reader loyalty, as would-be new entrants to the market such as the *Sunday Scot* in 1991 have found to their cost. The value of the services which they provide – local news and information – guarantees readers and attracts advertisers. Indeed, it is often the information contained in classified advertisements on theatre openings, second-hand cars for sale, and so on, which gives the local newspaper its competitive advantage over the national titles. The regional press is of course vulnerable, like other sectors of the journalism industry, to booms and slumps in the wider economy – in the 1960s and 1970s, for example, regional newspapers were generally profitable, while in the recessionary 1980s and 1990s times have been more difficult.

If, as is suggested, the demand for regional and local news is essentially healthy, there are nevertheless a number of ways – and media – through which local information can be delivered to the audience. By far the dominant medium of local news has been, until now, the 'paid for' newspaper, published daily or weekly, and deriving its income from sales and advertising revenue. Since the 1960s, however, the 'paid-fors' have been joined in the market by 'freesheets', distributed free to all households within a particular geographical area, and entirely dependent on advertising revenue. The 'frees' have grown steadily in number and in the share of the regional advertising market which they attract.

A further challenge to the paid-fors has emerged in the late 1980s, as the new printing technologies and distribution systems described in Chapter 7 have permitted national titles to attempt to enter regional markets and cream off some of the substantial advertising revenues which are available. We shall deal with each of these developments in turn.

## The challenge of the frees

As Table 9.1 shows, in 1970 free newspapers received a mere 1.4% of all advertising revenue in the regional press. By 1990 the figure had risen to 35%, more than the 19.5% share claimed by the paid-for weeklies. In 1975 there were 185 frees publishing in the UK, as compared to 1,140 paid-fors. By 1986 the balance was 842 frees to 867 paid-fors.[12] A 1986 Target Group Index survey found that 75% of all adults in the UK read a free newspaper, while only 49% read a paid-for weekly. In the first quarter of 1987, freesheet circulation reached 36 million copies, compared to 13 million in the paid-for sector.

What these figures clearly show is the rapid growth of a new medium, which has risen to threaten the traditional place of the paid-fors in local communities, particularly the paid-for weeklies (since the vast majority of frees are not published daily). In Scotland, where population densities are lower, and the economics of distribution rather more unfavourable, the expansion of free newspapers has been less marked, but in the UK as a whole, their rise has been inexorable.

Their success has been based on the belief of advertisers that they can reach consumers more effectively by this means than by others. The freesheet, it is argued by its proponents, will have an almost 100% penetration of households in the locality to which it is distributed, since it is pushed through the door whether one wants it or not. There is some doubt as to whether newspapers delivered in this way are actually read, or are binned along with the rest of the junk mail, but advertisers are satisfied that they *are* read, at least by enough people to make them effective promotional media. In the view of one advertiser, 'free papers are almost three times more cost-efficient than the average paid-for weekly.'[13] The editor of the *Birmingham Daily News*, Britain's first 'metro morning' (mass distribution free newspapers delivered each morning in major metropolitan centres) describes them as 'a new genre of newspaper which combines editorial excellence with all

*Table 9.1*    Share of advertising revenue in the regional press,
1970–90 (%)

|       | Daily/Sunday | Weekly | Free |
|-------|--------------|--------|------|
| 1970  | 62.9         | 35.7   | 1.4  |
| 1971  | 61.8         | 36.2   | 2    |
| 1972  | 63.3         | 34     | 2.7  |
| 1973  | 62.6         | 32.3   | 5.1  |
| 1974  | 62.4         | 31.4   | 6.2  |
| 1975  | 62.2         | 31.4   | 6.4  |
| 1976  | 61.6         | 31.4   | 6.9  |
| 1977  | 61.6         | 31.1   | 7.3  |
| 1978  | 61.7         | 31.1   | 7.2  |
| 1979  | 60.5         | 30.5   | 8.9  |
| 1980  | 59.1         | 27.8   | 13.1 |
| 1981  | 57.5         | 27.3   | 15.2 |
| 1982  | 55           | 26.6   | 18.5 |
| 1983  | 52.6         | 25.3   | 22   |
| 1984  | 51.5         | 24.2   | 24.3 |
| 1985  | 50.4         | 23.3   | 26.2 |
| 1986  | 49.4         | 22     | 28.5 |
| 1987  | 47.3         | 21.1   | 31.6 |
| 1988  | 45.4         | 20.8   | 33.8 |
| 1989  | 45.8         | 19.9   | 34.4 |
| 1990  | 45.5         | 19.5   | 35   |

*Source*: Advertising Statistics Yearbook, 1991.

the advantages of precision targeting in a mass market'. They give
advertisers 'massive penetration of households in a major metropolitan area over an extremely short timespan'.[14]

The *Birmingham Daily News*, launched in October 1984, now
claims to reach 80% of Birmingham's households. In this sense,
the rise of the freesheet is a reflection of the extent to which newspapers are increasingly viewed as 'product', the main use-value of
which is to deliver audiences to advertisers. Free newspapers have
the advantage in this respect of 'micro-marketing' – the ability to
deliver advertising messages to very precise demographic groups,
as opposed to the more diffuse spread of TV, radio, and national press advertising. In addition, many free newspapers are part
of a chain, allowing advertisers to 'micro-market' on a country-
wide scale.

The majority of the early frees were set up by independent pub-

lishers, like Eddie Shah in Warrington, and initially provoked a
hostile response from the regional publishing establishment. Early
examples of the genre were filled mainly with press releases, public relations material, and advertisements. Since their main function, and only means of survival, was 'to provide a service for
advertisers . . . effectively to deliver an advertiser's message at a
lower cost to competing media',[15] the quality of the journalism
which they provided was not necessarily their first priority. For
this reason, journalists working in the paid-for sector were frequently dismissive of their rivals on the frees. The editor of the
paid-for *Birmingham Post* typified this position when he warned
that 'free publications will be unable to maintain the best tra-
ditions of community newspapers, partly because there is now only
one customer, the advertiser, but mainly because of the inevitable
trimming of editorial resource if times get tough . . . More companies will find it easier and cheaper to produce entertaining local
magazines than to reflect every aspect of a community.'[16]

This was undoubtedly true, but has not stopped the rise of the
freesheets, and the concomitant decline of the paid-for weeklies.
In response the regional newspapers adopted a policy which
might be best summarised as, 'if you can't beat 'em, buy 'em'.
Thomson Regional Newspapers (TRN), Reed Regional
Newspapers (RRN) and others began to buy into the free sector,
and to establish new free titles of their own. This produced a shift
from the view of freesheets as low-quality imposters in the regional journalism business to one which saw them as 'an integral part
of the product mix'.[17] Freesheets came to be seen as comple-
mentary to, rather than threatening of, paid-for titles. Companies
began to strive towards a situation where they published both
types of titles in a given locality. Freesheets could be used to trail
a paid-for's news features, and to give a taste of what the latter
might offer.

In keeping with this shift in thinking TRN increased the number of its frees from thirteen in 1983 to one hundred in 1989,
claiming a total distribution of five million copies. To achieve this,
TRN purchased the *Herald* and *Post* chains owned by independent publishers, merging the titles to create a new chain of *Herald
and Post* freesheets. Packaged with and around its paid-for titles,
TRN announced its ambition eventually to have 17 million

Table 9.2  Average circulation of regional dailies, 1986–91*

| | 1986 | 1987 | 1988 | 1989 | 1990 | 1991 |
|---|---|---|---|---|---|---|
| Bristol Evening Post | 111,304 | 110,617 | 109,790 | 105,184 | 104,317 | 107,684 |
| Hull Daily Mail | 107,113 | 107,176 | 108,342 | 109,102 | 107,142 | 101,528 |
| Yorkshire Evening Post | 149,405 | 146,964 | 142,175 | 141,630 | 139,148 | 133,652 |
| Leicester Mercury | 153,340 | 150,044 | 149,010 | 145,013 | 141,297 | 134,328 |
| Liverpool Echo | 211,213 | 211,852 | 204,202 | 207,013 | 202,236 | 195,845 |
| Manchester Evening News | 310,682 | 300,978 | 289,528 | 283,521 | 267,400 | 256,109 |
| Evening Chronicle (Newcastle) | 148,683 | 147,788 | 147,691 | 144,436 | 144,275 | 137,472 |
| Sheffield Star | 149,259 | 144,271 | 140,683 | 140,392 | 133,688 | 127,418 |
| Evening Sentinel (Stoke) | 111,676 | 110,347 | 107,504 | 107,816 | 106,422 | 101,168 |
| Press and Journal (Aberdeen) | 112,862 | 108,904 | 108,137 | 109,035 | 105,079 | 104,953 |
| Daily Record (Glasgow) | 763,866 | 767,485 | 768,364 | 775,018 | 777,434 | 761,434 |
| Dundee Courier and Advertiser | 129,605 | 127,012 | 124,551 | 121,554 | 119,425 | 117,299 |
| Edinburgh Evening News | 123,356 | 119,186 | 113,785 | 106,874 | 105,873 | 102,033 |
| Glasgow Evening Times | 191,910 | 187,091 | 181,361 | 172,455 | 171,909 | 164,329 |
| Glasgow Herald | 127,636 | 123,720 | 122,931 | 124,725 | 123,656 | 122,101 |
| Belfast Telegraph | 149,377 | 147,470 | 146,572 | 144,941 | 141,310 | 133,914 |
| South Wales Echo | 96,599 | 96,328 | 96,599 | 91,085 | 87,478 | 83,728 |

Source: Audit Bureau of Circulation.
*Averages for January–June in each year.

*Herald and Posts* delivered weekly to every household in the UK, combining localisation and micro-marketing with a corporate TRN identity.

RRN, the largest regional publisher, had by 1989 more frees than paid-fors in its product mix. By late 1986 it could be reported that 'every old-established regional press publisher now operates in both the paid and free sectors of the business'.[18]

For regional publishers the economic benefits accruing from merging the two sectors were clear. As Table 9.2 shows, the late 1980s were generally a period of gradual (though not catastrophic) decline in the circulation of paid-for newspapers, a trend at least partly associated with the rise of the freesheets. By swallowing the predators whole, the companies could afford to be more relaxed about the relative position of the paid-for and free titles. As long as they controlled both, one could boost and reinforce the readership of the other. As a result, in the late 1980s, the regional press as a whole, incorporating both paid-fors and frees, increased its advertising revenue in absolute terms, and its share of total advertising revenue as against TV, radio, and the national press. There were casualties of the integration process, with both paid-for and free titles going under, but by exploiting economies of scale and the introduction of new print technologies (in which regional proprietors frequently outpaced the nationals) the regional press had by the beginning of 1990 successfully incorporated the free-sheet phenomenon, without appreciable damage to the paid-for sector. In 1989 2.6 billion regional papers were sold, and 2 billion free weeklies distributed, attracting a total classified advertising revenue of £2.25 billion.[19]

With the increasing revenues and investment which came with incorporation and integration into the big chains the frees were able to improve their editorial content and to become more like 'real' newspapers, with substantial newsgathering resources, prestigious columnists, and award-winning designs. The success of the regional proprietors in combining paid-for and freesheet publishing prompted Roy Greenslade to observe in 1994 that 'there has been a quiet, sustained revitalisation of the provincial press in recent years'.[20]

**Enter the nationals**

By 1989 TRN chairman Bill Heeps could state that 'the enemy [of
the regional press] is no longer the predatory free newspaper but
increasingly competitors for the advertising pound – local TV,
local radio, local editions of national newspapers, and new electronic media.'[21] Competition for finite advertising revenue has
always existed, of course, but in the late 1980s changes in the
national press produced new challenges to the regionals. Chapter
7 described how, after the Wapping revolution, the proprietors of
national newspapers quickly introduced new printing technologies
into their production processes. This enabled them not only to cut
costs and increase profitability, but also made it much easier for
them to 'editionise' their production – to produce multiple editions of a national title, tailored to the particular characteristics
of populations in different parts of the country. From his plant in
Glasgow Rupert Murdoch adopted an aggressive strategy of editionising the *Sunday Times* and *Sun* titles, in a bid to break into
the Scottish market. The practical results of the policy were seen
when, in the period before the 1992 general election, the *Sun*'s
Scottish edition ran with the headline 'Rise and be a Nation
Again', in distinct contrast to the pro-unionist, pro-Conservative
editorial line adopted by News International titles in England.
And it was successful, doubling the *Sun*'s Scottish circulation to
around 400,000 over a seven-year period. In late 1994, therefore,
the *Daily Mail* and *Daily Express* followed News International in
launching Scottish editions. As this book went to press it was
too early to assess the impact on the Scottish market of these
developments.

Some dispute the value of editionising the London-based titles,
however. The editor of one large circulation Scottish title notes
that 'for the tabloid and middle market papers new technologies
have been quite significant – the *Sun* with its late sports editions,
the *Scottish Sunday Express* putting more Scottish content in, but
in the quality market people tend to buy London papers for the
non-Scottish content. They don't buy them to see Scottish news.
Most London editors would say that localised content doesn't
give them much of a return. It's quite expensive to get. I think
they feel they're better to go on their strengths as London papers.'

In response to the nationals' challenge, regional newspapers adopted a number of competitive strategies. Firstly, like the nationals, they have turned the new technologies to their advantage. Regional publishers were in the vanguard of 'the newspaper revolution', and were thus well placed to reap its benefits at the end of the 1980s and into the new decade. By late 1987, for example, TRN had almost completed the process of introducing direct input technology into its ten provincial printing centres. In 1988 the company announced a further £75 million programme of investment and acquisitions. In Glasgow, Tiny Rowland's Lonrho invested heavily in new colour presses for its *Herald* and *Evening Times* titles, before selling them to a management-led consortium in 1992.

Such investment enabled the regionals to improve their design and colour printing techniques. It also enabled them to editionise to a greater extent than had been possible before (editionising has long been conventional practice for local evening papers). By 1990 virtually all of the UK's larger evening regionals were editionising 'to provide a distinct editorial and advertising service for the various communities into which their massive circulation areas have been subdivided'.[22] The Glasgow *Evening Times*, for example, would produce three editions between early afternoon and evening. As of July 1992 the *Aberdeen Press and Journal* had nine editions in circulation, each targeted at specific geographical areas in northern Scotland, such as the Highlands, Shetland, Kincardine and Deeside, and Aberdeen city. As a TRN editor puts it, 'the nationals have had a go at editionising, but it's not at the same level as the regional press. National newspapers will never be able to produce that number of editions.'

Because of new technologies, a greater share of resources could be invested in 'editorial quality', i.e. journalism. By paying higher salaries regional newspapers could retain more and better journalists, thus slowing down the brain drain to London (a process assisted by the high cost of property in southern England in recent years). Traditionally, Fleet Street journalists earned on average double the salaries of their colleagues in the provinces, leading inevitably to a one-way flow of talent heading south. In Scotland, where journalists' earnings have always been higher than in the English provinces, more people read local papers (62.5% of adults read a paid-for weekly in Scotland, as opposed to 48.7% in the UK as a whole)[23] two facts which are probably connected. A 1988 report by the Henley Centre for Economic Forecasting, commissioned by the Newspaper Society (the major association of regional proprietors), urged regional papers not to respond to the nationals' challenge by chasing them downmarket, but to 'adopt a serious tabloid format to provide readers with local news, information and lifestyle features which they are unlikely to get from the national press or television'.[24] To achieve this required money spent on journalism.

Thus, by increasing the number of editions, improving design and presentation, and strengthening 'editorial resource', the regionals have taken the nationals' challenge on, recognising that the new technologies which have threatened them (by making the nationals more attractive in regional markets) can also work for them. For this reason, the concentration of regional ownership which has occurred in recent years may be viewed as a necessary evil.[25] Large chains with extensive resources, it is argued, can respond more effectively, and invest more heavily, than small independents, isolated and impoverished. In any case, as Alistair Hetherington observes in his study of regional news, 'regional and local newspapers are less subject to political pressure than the nationals . . . Nor does there appear to be much political direction from proprietors' (1989, p.6). If it is true that more and more regional titles are being incorporated into fewer and fewer companies, it also appears to be the case that they retain a much greater degree of editorial independence than the majority of London-based titles. In July 1995 one of Britain's biggest regional proprietors, TRN, owned by the Canadian-based Thomson Corporation, announced that it was selling its British titles. Citing declining advertising revenues and the need to raise investment capital, the Thomson Corporation's announcement set in motion a process of restructuring in the British regional press. Thomson's English and Irish titles were sold to the Liverpool-based Trinity International Holdings, while the Scottish titles (principally the *Scotsman* and the *Aberdeen Press and Journal*) were divided between the reclusive and enigmatic Barclay brothers (owners of the *European* and Associated Newspapers). As this edition went to press, the long-term consequences of these developments for the Scottish newspaper industry were not clear.

## Marketing the regionals

Another element of the regionals' defensive strategy in the face of competitive challenges has addressed a traditional weakness in the marketing of their product – the failure to provide advertisers with sufficiently accurate data on readership. As we saw above, the paid-for regionals' share of advertising has tended to decline, partly due to the fact that, until 1989, the regional press did not employ particularly efficient audience measurement techniques, and lost advertising revenue to those media which did. By 1989, however, in conjunction with advertisers, they had established the Joint Industry Committee for Regional Press Readership (JICReg), a database designed to provide extremely accurate information about who reads what in precisely defined geographical areas and, of particular importance to advertisers, the effectiveness of their advertising messages. In 1991 thirteen regional publishers formed the Alliance of Regional Publishers for Effective Advertising (AREA), in an attempt to offer advertisers nationally coordinated local packages which could compete more effectively with national media. The 'Mosaic' system for identifying readers and analysing their consumption characteristics was employed.[26] Under the auspices of the Regional Daily Advertising Council seventy-three regional dailies combined to launch themselves as a 'national' medium with a single ratecard. The package offered advertisers access to a total circulation of about 5.3 million. TRN now operates a media sales division in London, enabling the company to offer advertisers 3 million readers throughout the UK for a single advertisement. In these ways, by the early 1990s the regional press was, from the advertisers' viewpoint, steadily improving its product.

Underpinning the strategies described thus far was that of exploiting the regionals' key competitive advantage: their very 'regionalness' or 'localness'. We began this chapter by noting that the demand for local news and information – in all media – is increasing. It has also been argued that the news audience is fragmenting into groups divided not only by geography but demography and lifestyle. This cultural shift is one which the regional newspapers are optimally equipped to exploit. On the one hand, readerships are becoming more narrowly focused, while on the other new technologies allow publishers to target them more precisely. Huw Stevenson of Westminster Press has argued that 'the UK's great regional dailies are mainly the product of an industrial revolution which turned our society from rural to urban living but now it's moving in the other direction. What I think this means for the prospects of the regional press is a proliferation of smaller communities which are now large enough to be viable publishing centres in their own right, some even on a daily basis.'[27]

Brian MacArthur argues that 'with union power curbed and the almost universal use of electronic editing, the cost of entry is so much lower that there are still many towns where evening papers could flourish and earn a profit on circulations of 5,000–7,000.'[28]

Changing demographics looked like being a double-edged sword for some regional newspapers, however. The Henley Centre notes that the regional newspapers face 'a disintegration of their traditional urban markets. The self-contained city [is] changing into a network of inter-linked towns and cities as the middle class moves out to the surrounding villages and country towns.'[29] For evening papers in particular this development, when combined with other long-term trends in lifestyle, and the increasing role of television in people's lives, presents a serious threat to their readership. George McKechnie, editor of the Glasgow *Evening Times*, explains that 'evening papers were very strong in the days when we worked longer hours, and the only time that some people had to read was in the evening. Those days have gone, plus there are other ways of getting information.' Arnold Kemp, former editor of the *Evening Times*'s sister publication, the Glasgow *Herald*, agrees that social change, alongside shifts in the nationals' marketing strategy, have created a potential crisis for the regional evenings:

> The tabloid morning papers have changed. They now sell throughout the day as entertainment packages – their reps top up supplies throughout the day. So the *Evening Times* is now competing with the *Daily Record*, the *Sun*, and the other tabloids in a way that is quite new. Even five years ago newsagents would have exhausted their morning supplies by lunchtime. Now the morning tabloids are still being sold at four o'clock in the afternoon, because they're less rooted in

news. People buy them for showbiz chat and sport.

In addition, the old industrial society is disappearing. The city centre is losing population. The bourgeois dormitory suburbs are growing, but the old industrial parts are uniformly in rapid decline. Any paper which is targeted on that particular segment of the population is going to be in difficulties, whereas quality papers are targeted on the more affluent sectors of the economy – the growing professional classes.

George McKechnie observes that

there is a long-term decline in the sales of evening newspapers. The major factor involved in that is cultural and social change; dramatic change in the jobs market; change in the reasons why people purchase an evening newspaper. At one time in this city you were selling about 400,000 copies of an evening newspaper. At the moment our circulation varies between 150,000 and 170,000, and that drop is in keeping with other evening newspapers elsewhere in the UK. Go round Glasgow and Edinburgh at six o'clock at night and see how quickly the city empties. At one time between 4.30 and 6 you had all these factories, shipyards, etc. spewing out people. They're not there anymore. Glasgow's population has fallen from 1.1 million just after the Second World War to just over 700,000, and it's predicted to go down even further. People don't use public transport to the same extent anymore.

The evenings must respond to this challenge by

turning their attention to the things they can do best, like 'need to know' news – what's on, where, when, what it costs – all the things which are difficult for the electronic media to do. People no longer buy evening papers to get the first bite of news, because they've probably heard it somewhere else – radio, TV – but to find out what that news means to *them*. The evening paper can best cover that.

The Henley Centre advises that regional newspapers should 'focus their editorial and marketing policies more sharply on key groups – the newly affluent, the retired, working women and the "household formation group" in the 25–44 age group. There [is] a need for newspapers to cope with the shift towards "communities of interest" and the relative decline of geographically based communities.'[30] The regionals in the 1990s, according to this view, must not only 'cope' with these cultural changes but view them as opportunities to hold and even increase their share of the newspaper-reading public.

## The Press Association

The British regional press has much to be optimistic about. Their product has a clear and growing market, and the regional titles appear to be in a strong position to retain their share of it. As commercial broadcasting fragments with the expansion of satellite and cable, this will be even more true. There are, of course, some clouds on the horizon. As this edition went to press the United Kingdom was still in the grip of the longest economic recession of the post-war period, with no end in sight. Advertising revenues were down and regional newspapers, like other sections of the media dependent on advertising, were going through relatively hard times. The need for cost-cutting had forced regional newspapers to shut down their offices in London, the last of which, TRN's, closed in March 1990. At the same time as becoming more reliant on news agencies, however, the regionals began to put pressure on the Press Association, which has traditionally monopolised the supply of national and international news to the regional press, to provide a more flexible, and cheaper service. In July 1991 the 'Birmingham Eight' – a consortium of regional publishers led by TRN – met to discuss the setting up of an alternative to the PA, arguing that the £2,000–5,000 weekly cost of the service to subscribers was unjustified when only one in ten items might be used, and when 'the editorial emphasis is increasingly switching to local news'.[31] Editors, it was reported, wanted the ability 'to shop off the [PA] shelf, to pick and choose the service they want without paying for 400,000 words a day'. Some editors were concerned, however, about the implications for the quality of regional journalism should the PA go bust or be seriously undermined. In the view of the *Herald*'s Arnold Kemp:

There's a subtext to this. There's been quite a successful

attempt in the English regional press, and parts of the Scottish press, to disable the National Union of Journalists and drive down journalists' wages and conditions. I think that the attack on the PA is part of the same movement. The Press Association is an expensive service, because it's a good service. On the whole it's reliable and authoritative, and that kind of journalism doesn't come cheap. Also, I think there's been a loss of interest in serious news by the evening papers, in England particularly. So quite a large chunk of the PA market – basically the regional evenings in England – have lost interest in the traditional job they've been doing, which has been to provide good staple news.

This particular movement has been led by the people in Birmingham who had a management buy-out, which within the industry was regarded as being for an excessive price, so their interest is driven by a need to cut costs. What it means is, instead of sending a qualified journalist to cover a court case, you send some kid who's only on £8,000 a year, and who's probably only got five minutes to pick up the threads of the story.

I think it's quite a serious trend, because the more that people pull out of the PA, the higher the unit cost of the service, and the cost of subscription, will be. At the moment we're committed to supporting them. We find it expensive, and although the service has been eroded slightly by these pressures, we still think it's a pretty good service for staple news. It's also pumping out a lot more tabloid-style trivia, which it never used to do, but I don't have any confidence in a rival alternative at the moment.

After an acrimonious dispute with echoes in the ITN/C3 debate described earlier, an attempt was made to set up an alternative supplier to the PA, named the Independent News Consortium. INC failed because of the regional publishers' reluctance, when it came to it, to part company with a tried and trusted news supplier, but the PA had been served with a clear warning. As the editorial director of TRN noted after the collapse of INC, 'as time goes by we will get more specialist operations offering services to newspapers on a low-cost basis. The days of one monolithic organisation supplying one service to 200 newspapers are on their way out.'[32] Around the same time it was reported that several TRN titles would be taking 'entertainment and leisure' material from an independent agency, World Entertainment Network News. In September 1992 the Press Association announced that it was shedding a further sixty-six posts, with obvious implications for its ability to service its regional and other customers.

## CONCLUSION

The pressure on regional newspapers to cut costs was an inevitable consequence of economic recession, but given the underlying strength of the industry – the result of the fundamental resilience of the market for local journalism, as well as the adoption of strategies described in this chapter – their fortunes seemed certain to improve when, and if, the economy recovered. While some newspapers, paid-fors and frees, had gone under in the harsh economic climate (the *Sunday Scot*, for example) others have prospered. In the period July–December 1991 *Wales on Sunday* increased its circulation by 16%, *Scotland on Sunday* by 10.1 %, and Belfast's *Sunday Life* by 7.6%.[33] So rosy, indeed, were the prospects for the regional press that in September 1992 David Sullivan launched a new Sunday title, the *Sunday News and Echo*, in an attempt to join the ranks of the regional publishing companies. It would be a middle-market tabloid, aimed at the north-west of England, pitching its editorial content somewhere between the *News of the World* and the *Mail on Sunday*. At the same time, Westminster Press launched its *Yorkshire on Sunday*, demonstrating that at least some publishers had confidence in an end to the recession. Only time will tell if that confidence was well placed.

# Chapter 10

# Conclusion

## Issues for the 1990s

The 1980s were a period in which the principle of public service broadcasting was subject to assault from two directions: the ideology of right-wing Conservatism; and the erosion of wavelength scarcity which had historically inhibited the growth of broadcasting in the United Kingdom. Although it took ten years of Thatcherism to weaken the public service and prepare the ground for radical change, by 1990 a Broadcasting Act had been introduced which would push broadcasting in the 1990s down an unashamedly commercial path. The British population's last chance to put a brake on the commercialisation of broadcasting – the general election of 1992 – resulted in the further endorsement of the Conservatives' approach, and an end to serious opposition. Thus, the 1990s have seen a continuing retreat of public service principles from the four terrestrial TV channels, as from BBC and commercial radio. The provision of mass information in the form of news and journalism has been further subject to the logic of the marketplace and the cash nexus. ITN – since 1954 a cost centre with a remit to provide quality competition to the BBC's television journalism – has become a commercial company like any other, competing against Visnews, Carlton TV, and others as yet unknown to supply a commodity to the C3 licensees, while at the same time providing its largely non-broadcasting shareholders with regular dividends. The C3 companies, having taken forty years to establish a worldwide reputation for challenging and innovative current affairs television, have found that their peak-time slots and the audiences they command have become too valuable to be wasted on journalism. More and more of the BBC's information-gathering resources are employed in the production of wealth-generating subscription services.

In all these respects the 1990s have seen, as media sociologists predicted in the 1980s, 'the creation of a two-tier market divided between the information-rich, provided with high-cost specialised information and cultural services and the information-poor, provided with increasingly homogenised entertainment services' (Garnham, 1986, p.38). Although the concept of public service broadcasting has proved more resilient than might have been feared in the 1980s, we have seen 'a shift from the [currently] dominant definition of public information from that of a public good to that of a privately appropriable commodity' (ibid., p.39).

So what?, one might ask. Print journalism has been circulating in commodity form for more than two hundred years. Now that we have the technology, why shouldn't broadcast journalism enter the realm of market relations, in which people choose to watch and listen from a proliferation of terrestrial, cable, and satellite sources, rather than be fed from a limited number of outlets produced and managed by a London-based cultural elite? The answer to this question depends above all on one thing: the extent to which the BBC, for all that it embraces the enterprise culture, is permitted to retain a measure of autonomy from commercial pressures, and to continue producing a bedrock of what we might call 'quality journalism'. This implies some extension of the traditional public service principle – universality of access to adequately resourced broadcasting – beyond 1996, even if on fewer channels of radio and television than at present. The commercial providers of news will, as the UK broadcasting environment becomes more competitive and audiences fragment, be forced into news and information programming dominated, as Steve Barnett has warned, 'by the tenets of good entertainment rather than good journalism' (1989, p.55). The two things are not mutually exclusive, of course, but the standard of broadcast journalism will undoubtedly remain higher in the commercial sector – and on C3 in particular – if the BBC is allowed to maintain its reputation as the world's pre-eminent news organisation.

In the first edition of this book I suggested that 'the omens in this respect are not wholly discouraging' since, in government report after government report in the 1980s, the more extreme adherents of a commercialised, deregulated broadcasting system for the UK were defeated in favour of a continuing commitment to PSB. The government of John Major had, by late 1992, shown no indication of returning to the Thatcherite path in media policy. The most likely option for the post-1996 period looked like being a slimmed-down BBC, but with journalism remaining at the heart of its operations. Some of these would be pay-per-view subscription services, but a substantial *public* service would remain, including a 24-hour speech channel on Radio 5. In this sense the decade-long debate about the relative merits of the public service versus the market looked like being resolved in a compromise between the two, in which the BBC would represent a smaller proportion of a larger broadcasting system. In this system a variety of 'brands' of journalism would compete for different segments of the audience, rather as newspapers have always done, but with many of the BBC's services continuing to be universally available. Confirmation that such a compromise would emerge came in the government's White Paper of July 1994. The document revealed the government's intention not to force the BBC to seek advertising revenue, and to permit the licence fee to continue to be the main source of the Corporation's income.

There will, of course, continue to be a struggle to prevent the BBC being 'ghettoised' in the manner of the American public service channel, but the Corporation's deep roots in British culture should assist that effort.

A second key issue for broadcasting discussed in this book has been the complex and curious inter-relationship between the 'globalisation' of information media, on the one hand, and 'localisation' on the other. Cornford and Robins argue that 'if the policy agenda of the 1980s was about "public service versus the market" . . . this is being overlaid with – or perhaps even supplanted by – a new geographical agenda concerned with the scales of broadcasting, with the relation between the global, local and national services' (1990, p.5). As we saw in Chapter 5 new and established broadcasters – including the BBC – are quickly developing a genuinely global journalism, through which the population of the planet as a whole is coming to share a common agenda and experience. CNN were the pioneers in this respect, but there can be no doubt that the BBC intends, through its

World Service Television Network, to compete seriously in this arena and establish a televisual equivalent of its World Service radio journalism.

For some observers the globalisation of journalism carries with it the threat of cultural imperialism – the dissemination across the planet of a journalism dominated largely by North American values, agendas, and ideological assumptions. The BBC indeed exploits this concern by explicitly defining its own global journalism as 'not American', and comprising an agenda 'recognisable in most places of the world' (see Chapter 6). The 1990s and beyond will be a period in which these two competing visions of global news culture struggle for dominance. Other organisations, most probably Rupert Murdoch's Sky, may join in the race, offering a mixture of both.

The growth of global journalism, as we saw in Chapter 9, has coincided with, and indeed encouraged the domestic broadcasters' efforts to 'brand' their own journalism with increasingly local characteristics. Sound commercial logic dictates that in a world where transnational 24-hour television news is becoming available to a mass audience local broadcasters must focus on what they are exclusively equipped to do – the detailed coverage of local news and current affairs. The demands of commerce coincide, moreover, with a cultural movement – seen throughout Europe – away from the nation-state towards identification with smaller communities and collectivities. What has led to war in post-communist eastern Europe has its healthier manifestation in the desire of western European populations to view events and processes from their own local perspectives, rather than those of the dominant metropolitan centres. In Britain, these communities include the nations of England, Northern Ireland, Scotland, and Wales, and within them smaller communities still, shaped by such factors as industrial history and political culture. In Britain the movement, led by Granada TV in the north-west of England, to enable coverage of national and international news to be constructed from the viewpoint of the local community is unstoppable, posing considerable problems, as we have seen, for the established suppliers of national and international news, ITN. The BBC, too, has committed itself to the expansion of regional journalism.

The trend towards localisation is also impinging upon the British press. For print journalists, like the broadcasters, audiences are fragmenting, and markets becoming smaller. New printing technologies have allowed newspapers to respond to these trends by more precise targeting of readerships, while maintaining and even increasing their profitability.

Some sections of the press, on the other hand – in particular the regional evening papers – are finding that the emergence of the post-industrial city and the dispersal of populations to the suburbs – a process which has occurred throughout Britain, but is most evident in the huge industrial conurbations such as Glasgow – are eroding traditional markets. In London, where a captive commuter market will continue to exist for the foreseeable future, the *Evening Standard* is secure, but many in the industry doubt that the institution of the evening regional paper will survive long into the twenty-first century.

What *will* survive is the 'freesheet', that curious hybrid of advertising and journalism. Once seen as a threat to 'real' newspapers, it has become an essential element of the regional publishers' product mix. Assuming that the economic recession of the early 1990s ever ends, the 'freesheet' sector will continue to prosper alongside the 'paid-fors'.

The national press, as Chapter 9 described, have made their own attempts to break into local markets, by using such techniques as facsimile transmission and editionising, but without significant success if measured by increased circulations. National newspapers have been successful in making the transition from being over-staffed, loss-carrying organisations to lean, profit-making ones. The Wapping revolution led, as Chapter 7 showed, to a transformation in the fortunes of the established proprietors, such as Rupert Murdoch and Conrad Black. It also permitted the entry into the market of some new ones, such as David Sullivan and the founders of the *Independent*. As was argued in Chapter 7, however, the cost-cutting potential of new technologies has to a large extent been negated by the established proprietors' strategies of printing more pages and spending more on advertising and marketing. For this reason, with the exceptions of the *Independent* and *Sport* titles, new entrants to the national newspaper business have been notable by their absence. The economics of newspaper publishing remain weighted against newcomers, whether of the left, like the *News on Sunday*; the centre, like the *Sunday Correspondent*; or the right, like Eddie Shah's *Post*. Consequently, the problems of concentration of ownership identified in Chapter 7 will remain for the foreseeable future, notwithstanding the proposals contained in the Green Paper on cross-media ownership. These, if they are implemented, will shape the pattern of ownership of Britain's media, but not seriously weaken the positions of the established players.

On the important issue of political bias, as was noted in Chapter 7, the shifting allegiances of the former Tory-supporting press have introduced an unforeseen element of unpredictability into the equation. Time will tell if such unusual and refreshing editorial diversity survives the next general election campaign, to be held in May 1997 at the latest. As Chapter 8 described, by the summer of 1995, it appeared that there was a very real possibility of protection of privacy legislation being introduced to deal with what some regarded as excesses on the part of both tabloid and broadsheet newspapers. While John Major was known to be against legislation, pressure was building from backbench MPs of all parties for some legal constraints to be imposed on the journalists' right to investigate and report on individuals' private lives. When David Calcutt's review of press self-regulation reported in January 1993 its main recommendation – the replacement of the Press Complaints Commission by a statutory press tribunal – was not endorsed by the government. Ministers let it be known, however, that some changes to the law on privacy were inevitable. At the same time, Clive Soley's private member's bill on Freedom and Responsibility of the Press was given a second reading in the House of Commons.

As this book went to press, the future of press regulation in the United Kingdom was still far from being resolved. Editors and journalists faced a further period of uncertainty as they waited to find out the scope and severity of the legal restrictions which would finally be imposed on them.

# Notes

## 1 Why journalism matters

1 *BBC Guide 1991*, London: BBC. See also Barnett, S., 'The BBC after the Cold War', *Guardian*, April 8, 1991. For a useful guide to the history and structure of British broadcast media see MacDonald (1988).

2 *Application for Channel 3 Licence for Central Scotland: Summary* Scottish Television, 1991.

3 See Chippindale and Franks (1991) for an account of the brief life of BSB. An account of the merger negotiations is contained in Chippindale, P. and Franks, S., 'How Sky fell on BSB', *Guardian*, November 11, 1991.

4 Shamoon, S., 'BSkyB in the black by March', *Observer*, January 26, 1992.

5 MacNamara, M., 'Consulting the Oracle', *UK Press Gazette*, August 19, 1991.

6 Higham, N., 'Fine tuning radio's future', *Broadcast*, April 24, 1992.

7 *BBC Guide 1991*.

8 Kavanagh, M., 'World Service put under the microscope', *Broadcast* July 10, 1992.

9 Reported in the *Guardian*, April 15, 1992.

10 *Media ownership: The Government's Proposals*, Cmd. 2872, 1995, London, HMSO.

11 Slattery, J., 'Dorrell loosens the media shackles', *UKPG*, May 29, 1995.

12 Editorial, *British Journalism Review* 2(1), p.4. The study in question was undertaken by MORI and published in Worcester and Jacobs (1990).

13 William DeGeorge identifies three levels at which agenda-setting might work (if it works). Firstly, the level of audience awareness, whereby 'the public is primarily aware of those issues or topics which are reported by the media'; secondly, the level of *priorities*, where 'the [media's] agenda of events, in proper-rank, will be transferred to the public largely intact'; and thirdly, the level of *salience*, where 'the public assigns high or low importance to topics as held by the media' (DeGeorge, 1981, p.222).

## 2 Journalism and the critique of objectivity

1 Noam Chomsky quotes a recent restatement of the liberal pluralist principle by US Supreme Court Justice Powell: 'no individual can obtain for himself the information needed for the intelligent discharge of his political responsibilities . . . By enabling the public to assert meaningful control over the political process, the press performs a crucial function' (1989, p.13).
2 From the *BBC Guide 1990*, London: BBC.
3 For a detailed discussion of Soviet news values, see McNair (1991).
4 See Lichtenberg (1991) for a defence of objectivity as seen from the journalists' perspective.
5 See Harrison (1985) and Philo (1987) for further discussion of the methodological issues raised by the GUMG's work.

## 3 Explaining content: current debates in the sociology of journalism

1 See Schudson (1989) and Curran (1990) for comparative analyses of these approaches.
2 Morgan, R., 'Disease that's all in the minders', *Guardian*, July 15, 1991.
3 *Guardian*, March 5, 1990.
4 The author's own study of news coverage of the USSR in the 1980s argues that the 'ideological bias' of individual journalists was less important in explaining western news images of the Soviet Union than the professional constraints routinely faced by Moscow correspondents (McNair, 1988).
5 For a discussion of British television news coverage of the KAL 007 incident, see McNair (1988).
6 McNair, B., 'Accidents don't just happen', *New Statesman and Society*, July 15, 1988.

## 4 Broadcast journalism: the changing environment

1 See Leapman (1987) and Milne (1988).
2 For an account of the making of the programme and its aftermath, see Bolton (1990).
3 See *Index on Censorship* 16(3) March 1987 for the documents.
4 *Report of the Committee on the Future of Broadcast*ing, Cmd. 9824, 1986, London: HMSO, p.44.
5 Ibid., p.80.
6 Ibid.,p.151.
7 Fiddick, P., 'Time to cut the Peacock cackle', *Guardian*, July 28, 1986.
8 The BBC's journalism received some criticism when the report alleged

that 'today, entertainment values at times appear to have taken over in some news and current affairs programmes with the inevitable consequences of triviality and dilution of information' (p.131).

9  *The Future of Broadcasting*, HC 262, 1988, London: HMSO, p.xlviii.
10  Ibid., p.viii.
11  Ibid., p.xliii.
12  Ibid., p.xiv.
13  Ibid.
14  Ibid., p.xxvi.
15  *Broadcasting in the 90s: Competition, Choice and Quality*, Cm 517, 1988, London: HMSO, p.10.
16  He declared that 'operators of Channels 3, 4, and 5 will be expected to show high-quality news and current affairs programmes dealing with national and international matters, and to show the news, and possibly also current affairs, in main viewing periods' (*Hansard*, vol. 140, c.30).
17  *Broadcasting in the 90s*, p.22.
18  Lynn, M. and Olins, R., 'Media giants switch onto Channel 5 race', *Sunday Times*, April 9, 1995.
19  Parliamentary Debates, Standing Committee F (Home Affairs Select Committee), House of Commons Official Report, 1990, London: HMSO.
20  Ibid.
21  Ibid.
22  Ibid.
23  Ibid.
24  Ibid. Darling recognised the dangers in such an approach, however. 'I do not want a television company to use the loophole and provide its own local television service simply by lifting items off the Press Association, so providing a cheap second-rate news service. There is the risk that a company may opt out, not bother to pay for ITN, thinking that people in its area do not want to know what is going on in Romania, eastern Europe and South Africa, and just lift news items from the PA and read them out. That would be a disaster. I am talking about a high-quality national and international news service that has regard to the area it serves.'
25  Ibid.
26  Ibid.
27  Other issues of great relevance to the future of British broadcast journalism raised by Standing Committee F included the bill's provisions to increase the powers of the police to confiscate journalists' materials in pursuit of criminal investigations; the bill's failure to remove the government's power to censor broadcast material (such as the statements of Sinn Fein members); and the alleged weakness of its restrictions on cross-media ownership.

28 *Broadcasting Act*, 1990, London: HMSO, p.7.
29 *Hansard*, vol.521, c.380.
30 *Broadcasting Act*, p.7.
31 Pilger, J., 'A code for charlatans', *Guardian*, October 8, 1990.
32 Here, and throughout, unless otherwise indicated in the notes, statements attributed to media professionals were obtained in interviews conducted by the author.
33 Snoddy, R., 'Broadcasters attack new rules', *Financial Times*, July 6, 1990.
34 Mellor, D., 'Free from bias of any kind', *Guardian*, October 8, 1990.
35 Independent Television Commission, Programme Code, 1991, p.19.
36 Burnett, C., 'ITC faces legal action over impartiality code', *Broadcast*, March 8, 1991.

## 5 Television journalism in the 1990s

1 From a speech to the Institute of Directors delivered on February 23, 1986.
2 In both cases the BBC was required to make public apologies for reporting errors.
3 Birt I., 'Bias: where TV is guilty', reprinted in *The Times*, March 23, 1987.
4 Hall, T., 'A voice worth listening to', *Broadcast*, August 16, 1991.
5 Fiddick, P., 'John, the apostle of change', *Guardian*, March 21, 1988.
6 *Guardian*, November 11, 1989.
7 Cockerell, M., 'Lime Grove Blues', *Guardian*, July 1, 1991.
8 Bolton, R., 'Year zero shouldn't mean zero confidence', *Listener*, March 3, 1988.
9 Wolfinden, B., 'Has BBC journalism lost its spirit of enquiry?', *Listener*, March 10, 1988.
10 Ibid.
11 Bolton, 'Year zero'.
12 Ibid.
13 Cox, B., 'Journalism without ceremony', *Broadcast*, July 26, 1991.
14 Barnett, S., 'The BBC after the cold war', *Guardian*, April 8, 1991.
15 Quoted in Henry, G., 'Gameplan for a Beeb team spirit', *Guardian*, October 7, 1991.
16 *The Future of the BBC*, Cm 2098, November 1992, London: HMSO.
17 *Extending Choice*, London: BBC, 1992.
18 *The Future of the BBC*, Cm 2621, 1994, London: HMSO.
19 Reported in *Guardian*, July 11, 1994.
20 See Phillips, W., 'Have I got news for you?', *Broadcast*, May 1,1992, for a detailed analysis of viewing trends.
21 Reported in *Broadcast*, March 20, 1992.
22 Henry, G., 'ITV ponders time change for news', *Guardian*, January

24, 1992.
23 Reported in *Broadcast*, August 16, 1991.
24 Reported in *Broadcast*, March 20, 1992.
25 Stoddart, P., 'Breakfast for Four', *Broadcast*, June 19, 1992.
26 Reported in *Broadcast*, June 19, 1992.
27 *Application for the National Channel 3 Breakfast-time Licence: Summary*, TV-am, 1991, p.4.
28 *Application for the National Channel 3 Breakfast-time Licence: In-Brief*, Daybreak, 1991, p.3.
29 Stoddart, P., 'Breakfast for Four', *Broadcast*, June 19, 1992.
30 Reported in *Broadcast*, June 19, 1992.
31 Bolton, 'Year zero'.
32 Miles, C., 'The hot air over the *Big Story*', *Guardian*, January 10, 1994.
33 *Guardian*, January 29, 1990.
34 Reported in *Broadcast*, June 21, 1991. The importance of Sky News to Murdoch is observed in Chippindale and Frank's account of British Satellite Broadcasting. In 1990, when Murdoch employed Australian media manager Sam Chisholm to carry out a major cost-cutting exercise at Sky Channel, it was suggested that Sky News be closed down. 'Murdoch disagreed. Not only was he pleased with its achievements but he told Chisholm there were overriding reasons of prestige and politics for keeping it. The final hurdle of the Broadcasting Bill had still to be overcome and the case being mounted in the Lords for the acceptability of Sky would collapse if suddenly there was no News Channel' (1991, p.262).
35 Reported in *UK Press Gazette*, February 17, 1992.
36 *Broadcast*, November 23, 1990.
37 Howell, L., 'Broadcast news dues', *Guardian*, March 2, 1992.
38 *Time*, January 6, 1992.
39 *Guardian*, September 9, 1986.
40 *The Future of Broadcasting*, HC 262, 1988, London: HMSO.
41 Ibid., p.xli.
42 Howell, L., 'Broadcast news dues'. Tusa added: 'This market is so vital for the global flow of information that I believe it should not be the prerogative of the two existing players. Cultural and political pluralism demands that there should be at least a third competitor in this field, in the interests of diversity of opinion and information. Who will it be?' Few in his audience doubted that Rupert Murdoch's Sky News would be a serious contender.
43 Burnett, C., 'Sky faces BBC challenge', *Broadcast*, February 21, 1992.

## 6 Radio

1 *Choices and Opportunities*, Cm 92, 1987, London: HMSO.
2 Reported in *Guardian*, July 6, 1987.

3 Reported in *Guardian*, June 13, 1988.
4 *Broadcasting Act*, 1990, London: HMSO, p.96.
5 *Broadcast*, March 3, 1992.
6 *Broadcast*, June 8, 1990.
7 *UK Press Gazette*, September 30, 1991.
8 Kavanagh, M., 'Task force inflicts superficial wounds', *Broadcast*, March 6, 1992.
9 *Guardian*, September 2, 1991.
10 In June 1992, a National Audit Office report favourably assessed the World Service's overall performance (Kavanagh, M., 'World Service put under the microscope', *Broadcast*, July 10, 1992).
11 Andrew Joynes, head of English-language current affairs at the World Service, argues further that

> with the barriers coming down, with new definitions of what constitutes an appropriate world order, with the emphasis upon the individual's rights as a citizen of the world, as much as a citizen of a country, with new global threats to the environment, what is going to be needed above all is information. The new emphasis will be upon putting different parts of the world in touch with each other. Just as there's been a rebirth of the idea of the United Nations and its potential, so I think we're at the threshold of a new awareness of the potential of international broadcasting as a means of putting people in touch with each other.

## 7 Before and after Wapping: the changing political economy of the British press

1 Wintour, P., 'Life at the longest funeral', *Guardian*, June 26, 1987.
2 Reported in *UK Press Gazette*, September 23, 1991.
3 Porter, H., 'Thunderer versus the blunderer', *Guardian*, June 28, 1993.
4 Ibid.
5 'It's War', *Guardian*, January 17, 1994.
6 McKie, R., 'Five heads with a single mind' *Guardian*, August 15, 1994.
7 Porter, H., 'The Murdoch Wooing Game', *Guardian*, September 26, 1994.
8 Goodman, A., 'Tradition and talent in an age of transition', *UK Press Gazette*, June 13, 1988.
9 In 1991 the *Independent on Sunday* went through a period of financial difficulty. During the worst advertising recession for twenty years, and with a circulation of close to 350,000 the *Independent on Sunday* was making a loss, draining the profitable daily title. For some time, industry observers speculated that it would close. Instead, effective cost-cutting and restructuring measures were applied and, at the time of writing, the title had regained long-term security.
10 Kavanagh, G., 'Busting into the dailies', *Guardian*, August 24, 1987.

11 *Guardian*, November 10, 1988.
12 Horsley, N., 'News that didn't fit', *Guardian*, June 26, 1987.
13 Chippindale, P., 'Mercy killing', *UK Press Gazette*, November 30, 1987.
14 Whittaker, B., 'Will the cactus flower!', *Guardian*, September 7, 1987.
15 Sutton, K., 'Rounded corner logos are politically Tory', *UK Press Gazette*, June 15, 1987.
16 Whittaker, 'Will the cactus flower!'.
17 Minogue, T., 'Sleazy does it', *Guardian*, January 25, 1989.
18 Curran, J., 'Fleet Street: No Entry', *Guardian*, April 11, 1988.
19 Foot, P., 'Never has so much been owned by so few', *UK Press Gazette*, December 21–8, 1987.
20 Ibid.
21 Goodman, 'Tradition and talent'.
22 Reed, I., 'The Murdoch Empire Strikes Back', *Guardian*, June 19, 1989.

## 8 Competition, content, and Calcutt

1 Reported in the *Guardian*, February 17, 1986.
2 Halcrow, M., 'Views in paler shades of blue', *Guardian*, November 17, 1986.
3 Greenslade, R., 'The lost readers', *Guardian*, October 19, 1992.
4 Heren L., 'When pops are tops', *Guardian*, April 3, 1989.
5 Rusbridger, A., 'Ten times a night is not enough', *Guardian*, August 1, 1988. See Chippindale and Horrie (1990) for a lively account of the history of the *Sun*. S.J. Taylor's *Shock! Horror! The Tabloids in Action* (1991) reviews the development of tabloid journalism in Britain and America.
6 Reported in the *Guardian*, December 15, 1986.
7 Reported in the *Guardian*, September 7, 1987.
8 Louis Blom-Cooper, the last Chairman of the Press Council, argues that the Council had already decided to reform itself in any case, and that the reforms were precisely those proposed as guidelines for the new PCC. The Press Council was disbanded, rather than being reformed, in Blom-Cooper's view, because 'Mr Calcutt and his colleagues considered that whatever the Chairman and many Council members would accept of the proposed additional reforms – and the Chairman [i.e. Blom-Cooper himself] for his part would have avidly accepted all of them – there was within the membership of the Press Council a sub-culture which would thwart the Chairman's lead' (1991, p.38).
9 Press Complaints Commission adjudication released on October 6, 1991.
10 Greenslade, R., 'Tabloids doom horror', *Guardian*, July 1, 1991.
11 Reported in the *UK Press Gazette*, June 15, 1992.

12 Henry, G., 'Press pass to be trespass?', *Guardian*, July 27, 1992.
13 *Submission to the Review of Press Self-Regulation*, Press Complaints Commission, October 1992, p.5.
14 Calcutt, D., *Review of Press Self-Regulation*, Cm 2135, 1993, London: HMSO.

## 9 The regional story

1 As Donald Waters of Grampian TV puts it, referring to Scotland in particular, 'people get fed up about ITN's being too metropolitan, too English-oriented. Our market research shows it.'
2 For a discussion of globalisation and its implications for television journalism, see Gurevitch and Levy (1990) and Gurevitch (1991).
3 Reported in *Broadcast*, October 12, 1990.
4 Scottish Television application for Channel 3 licence, Summary.
5 Reported in *Broadcast*, November 16, 1990.
6 Quoted in Goodwin, P., 'ITN exclusive', *Broadcast*, January 10, 1992.
7 *Broadcast*, January 24, 1992.
8 The BBC's declaration of its long-term financial strategy.
9 *Broadcast*, June 14, 1991.
10 Reported in the *UK Press Gazette*, July 13, 1992.
11 MacNamara, M., 'Regional network call', *UK Press Gazette*, September 30, 1991.
12 Garner, S., 'Free and proud of it: the new establishment line', *UK Press Gazette*, September 15, 1986.
13 Ibid.
14 Ward, M., 'Daily News: up and running well', *UK Press Gazette*, October 5, 1987.
15 Radburn, P., 'On the road to a community press', *UK Press Gazette*, October 5, 1987.
16 Garner, 'Free and proud of it'.
17 Ibid.
18 Garth, A., 'The free concept which paid off', *UK Press Gazette*, August 15, 1988.
19 *UK Press Gazette*, February 25, 1991.
20 Greenslade, R., 'Community service', *Guardian*, July 18, 1994.
21 Quoted in Lawrence, C., 'Frees for all', *UK Press Gazette*, September 15, 1989.
22 Marks, N., 'Distilling the community spirit', *UK Press Gazette*, March 12, 1990.
23 Morgan, J., 'It's so bonny to be working in Scotland', *UK Press Gazette*, March 14, 1988.
24 *UK Press Gazette*, June 27, 1988.
25 The *UK Press Gazette* has observed that 'more and more [regional] newspapers are being concentrated in fewer and fewer hands' (June 6, 1988).

26  Morris, R., 'Hitting the right target', *UK Press Gazette*, November 5, 1990.
27  Slattery, J., 'Regional press prospects are good, says Stevenson', *UK Press Gazette*, June 18, 1990.
28  MacArthur, B., 'Lessons in survival', *UK Press Gazette*, November 19, 1990.
29  Slattery, J., 'Regionals warned of threat from specialists', *UK Press Gazette*, September 5, 1988.
30  Ibid.
31  MacArthur, B., 'Birmingham 8 cabal discusses rival to PA', *UK Press Gazette*, July 1, 1991.
32  Slattery, J., 'Regional apathy kills off INC news service plans', *UK Press Gazette*, June 8, 1992.
33  Morgan, J., 'Sundays turn tide in sales', *UK Press Gazette*, June 8, 1992.

# Bibliography

Alexander, J. (1981) 'The mass news media in systemic, historical and comparative perspective', in E. Katz and T. Szecsko (eds) *Mass Media and Social Change*, London: Sage, pp. 17–51.

Altschull, H. (1984) *Agents of Power*, New York: Longman.

Anderson, D. and Sharrock, W. (1979) 'Biasing the news: technical issues in media studies', *British Journal of Sociology* 13(3): 367–85.

Baistow, T. (1985) *Fourth-rate Estate: An Anatomy of Fleet Street*, London: Comedia.

—— (1989) 'The predator's press', in N. Buchan and T. Sumner (eds) *Glasnost in Britain?*, London: Macmillan, pp. 53–69.

Barnett, S. (1989) 'Broadcast News', *British Journalism Review* 1(1): 49–56.

Belfield, R., Hird, C., and Kelly, S. (1991) *Murdoch: The Decline of an Empire*, London: Macdonald.

Bevins, A. (1990) 'The crippling of the scribes' *British Journalism Review* 1(2): 13–17.

Blanchard, S. (ed.) (1990) *The Challenge of Channel Five*, London: BFI.

Blom-Cooper, L. (1991) 'The last days of the Press Council', *British Journalism Review* 2(3): 34–9.

Bolton, R. (1990) *Death on the Rock and Other Stories*, London: W. H. Allen.

Bruhn-Jensen, K. (1986) *Making Sense of the News*, Aarhus: Aarhus University Press.

Buchan, N. and Sumner, T. (eds) (1989) *Glasnost in Britain?*, London: Macmillan.

Calcutt, D. (1990) *Report of the Committee on Privacy and Related Matters*, London: HMSO.

—— (1993) *Review of Press Self-Regulation*, London: HMSO.

Chippindale, P. and Franks, S. (1991) *Dished! The Rise and Fall of British Satellite Broadcasting*, London: Simon & Schuster.

Chippindale, R. and Horrie, C. (1988) *Disaster*, London: Sphere.

—— (1990) *Stick it up your Punter*, London: Heinemann.

Chomsky, N. (1989) *Necessary Illusions*, London: Pluto.

Chomsky, N. and Herman, E. (1979) *The Political Economy of Human*

*Rights*, volume 1, Boston: South End Press.

Cohen, S., (ed.) (1971) *Images of Deviance*, Harmondsworth: Penguin.

Cohen, S. and Young, J. (eds) (1973) *The Manufacture of News*, London: Constable.

Collins, R. (1976) *Television News*, London: BFI.

—— (1990) *Television: Policy and Culture*, London: Unwin & Hyman.

Cornford, J. and Robins K. (1990) 'Questions of geography', in S. Blanchard, (ed.) *The Challenge of Channel Five*, London: BFI, pp. 3–21.

Cranfield, G.A. (1978) *The Press and Society*, London: Longman.

Crozier, B. (1988) *The Making of the Independent*, London: Gordon Fraser.

Cumberbatch, G., McGregor, R., Brown, B., and Morrison, D. (1986) *Television and the Miners' Strike*, London: Broadcasting Research Unit.

Curran, J. (1989) 'Culturalist perspectives of news organizations: a reappraisal and a case study', in M. Ferguson (ed.) *Public Communication*, London: Sage, pp. 114–34.

—— (1990) 'The new revisionism in mass communication research: a reappraisal', *European Journal of Communication* 5: 135–64.

Curran, J. and Gurevitch, M. (eds) (1991) *Mass Media and Society*, London: Edward Arnold.

Curran, J. and Seaton, J. (1991) *Power Without Responsibility*, 4th edition, London: Routledge.

Dahlgren, P. and Sparks, C. (eds) (1992) *Journalism and Popular Culture*, London: Sage.

Davies, D. (1990) 'News and politics', in D. Swanson and D. Nimmo (eds) *New Directions in Political Communication*, London: Sage, pp. 147–84

DeGeorge, W. (1981) 'Conceptualisation and measurement of audience agenda', in G. Wilhoit and H. de Bock (eds) *Mass Communication Review Yearbook*, volume 2, London: Sage, pp. 219–24.

Dunnett, P. (1990) *The World Television Industry: An Economic Analysis*, London: Routledge.

Elliot, P., Halloran J. and Murdock, G. (1970) *Demonstrations and Communication*, Harmondsworth: Penguin.

Ericson, R.V., Baranek, P.M. and Chan, J.B.L. (1990) *Representing Order*, Toronto: Open University Press.

Evans, H. (1983) *Good Times, Bad Times*, London: Weidenfeld & Nicolson.

Ferguson, M. (ed.) (1989) *Public Communication*, London: Sage.

Fiske, J. (1987) *Television Culture*, London: Methuen.

Fowler, R. (1991) *Language in the News*, London: Routledge.

Fraser, N. (1990) 'The grand design for ITN', *British Journalism Review* 2(1): 17–21.

Galtung, J. and Ruge, M. (1973) 'Structuring and selecting news', in S.

Cohen and J. Young (eds) *The Manufacture of News*, London: Constable, pp. 62–72.

Garnham, N. (1986) 'The media and the public sphere', in P. Golding, G. Murdock and P. Schlesinger (eds) *Communicating Politics*, Leicester: Leicester University Press, pp. 37–54.

—— (1989) 'Has public service broadcasting failed?' in Millar and Norris (eds) op. cit.: 17–35.

Glasgow University Media Group (1976) *Bad News*, London: Routledge & Kegan Paul.

—— (1980) *More Bad News*, London: Routledge & Kegan Paul.

—— (1986) *War and Peace News*, Milton Keynes: Open University Press.

Golding, P., Murdock, G. and Schlesinger, P. (eds) (1986) *Communicating Politics*, Leicester: Leicester University Press.

Gunter, B. (1987) *Poor Reception*, New Jersey: Lawrence Erlbaum Associates.

Gurevitch, M. (1991) 'The globalisation of electronic journalism', in J. Curran and M. Gurevitch (eds) *Mass Media and Society*, London: Edward Arnold, pp. 178–93.

Gurevitch, M. and Levy, M. (1990) 'The global newsroom', *British Journalism Review* 2(1): 27–37.

Hall, S., Critcher, S., Jefferson, T., Clarke, J. and Roberts, B. (1978) *Policing the Crisis*, London: Macmillan.

Hallin, D. (1986) *The Uncensored War*, Oxford: Oxford University Press.

Harrison, M. (1985) *TV News: Whose Bias?*, Hermitage: Policy Journals.

Hartley, J. (1982) *Understanding News*, London: Routledge.

Herman, E. (1982) *The Real Terror Network: Terrorism in Fact and Fiction*, Boston: South End Press.

—— (1986) 'Gatekeeper versus propaganda models: a critical American perspective', in P. Golding, G. Murdock and P. Schlesinger (eds) *Communicating Politics*, Leicester: Leicester University Press, pp. 171–95.

Hetherington, A. (1989) *News in the Regions*, London: Macmillan.

Iyengar, S. and Kinder, D.R. (1987) *News that Matters*, Chicago: University of Chicago Press.

Katz, E. and Szecsko, T. (eds) (1981) *Mass Media and Social Change*, London: Sage.

Keane, J. (1991) *The Media and Democracy*, Oxford: Polity Press.

Leapman, M. (1987) *The Last Days of the Beeb*, London: Coronet.

Lichtenberg, J. (1991) 'In defence of objectivity', in J. Curran and M. Gurevitch (eds) *Mass Media and Society*, London: Edward Arnold, pp. 216–31.

Lustig, R. (1990) 'Promises are no longer enough', *British Journalism Review* 1(2): 44–8.

MacArthur, B. (1988) *Eddie Shah: Today and the Newspaper Revolution*, London: David & Charles.

MacCabe, C. and Stewart, O. (eds) (1986) *The BBC and Public Service Broadcasting*, Manchester: Manchester University Press.

McCombs, M. (1981) 'Setting the agenda for agenda-setting research', in G. Wilhoit and H. de Bock (eds) *Mass Communication Review Yearbook*, volume 2, London: Sage, pp. 209–19.

MacDonald, B. (1988) *Broadcasting in the United Kingdom*, London: Mansell Publishing Limited.

McGregor, O.R. (1977) *Royal Commission on the Press*, Final Report, Cmnd. 6810, London: HMSO.

McNair, B. (1988) *Images of the Enemy*, London: Routledge.

—— (1991) *Glasnost, Perestroika and the Soviet Media*, London: Routledge.

—— (1995) *Introduction to Political Communication*, London: Routledge.

McQuail, D. (1987) *Mass Communication Theory*, London: Sage.

Melvern, L. (1988) *The End of the Street*, London: Methuen.

Miliband, R. (1972) *The State in Capitalist Society*, London: Quartet.

Millar, N. and Morris, C. (eds) (1989) *Life After the Broadcasting Bill*, Manchester: Manchester Monographs.

Miller, W. (1991) *Media and Voters*, London: Clarendon Press.

Milne, A. (1988) *D.G.: Memoirs of a British Broadcaster*, London: Hodder and Stoughton.

Morley, D. (1990) 'The construction of everyday life', in D. Swanson and D. Nimmo (eds) *New Directions in Political Communication*, London: Sage, pp.123–6.

Murdock, G. (1973) 'Political deviance: the press presentation of a militant mass demonstration', in S. Cohen and J. Young (eds) *The Manufacture of News*, London: Constable, pp. 156–75.

Peacock, A. (1986) *Broadcasting in the 1990s*, London: HMSO.

Philo, G. (1987) 'Whose news?', *Media, Culture and Society* 9(4): 397–406.

—— (1990) *Seeing and Believing*, London: Routledge.

Ranney, A. (1983) *Channels of Power*, New York: Basic Books.

Robinson, J.P. and Levy, M.R. (1986) *The Main Source*, London: Sage.

Rock, P. (1973) 'News as eternal recurrence', in S. Cohen and J. Young (eds) *The Manufacture of News*, London: Constable, pp. 73–80.

Scannell, P.(1989) 'Public service broadcasting and modern public life', *Media, Culture and Society* 11(2) 136–64.

Scannell, P. and Cardiff, D. (1991) *A Social History of British Broadcasting*, volume I, Oxford: Basil Blackwell.

Schiller, D. (1981) *Objectivity and the News*, Philadelphia: University of Pennsylvania Press.

Schlesinger, P. (1978) *Putting Reality Together*, London: Constable.

—— (1989) 'From production to propaganda', *Media, Culture and Society* 11(3): 283–306.

—— (1991) *Media, State and Nation*, London: Sage.

Schlesinger, P., Murdock, G. and Elliot, P. (1983) *Televising Terrorism*,

London: Comedia.

Schudson, M. (1978) *Discovering News*, New York: Basic Books.

—— (1989) 'The sociology of news production', *Media, Culture and Society* 11(3): 263–82.

Siebert, F. (1956) *Four Theories of the Press*, Urbana: University of Illinois Press.

Swanson, D. and Nimmo, D. (eds) (1990) *New Directions in Political Communication*, London: Sage.

Taylor, S.J. (1991) *Shock! Horror! The Tabloids in Action*, London: Bantam.

Tiffen, R. (1989) *News and Power*, Sydney: Allen & Unwin.

Tuchman, G. (1972) 'Objectivity as strategic ritual: an examination of newsmen's notions of objectivity', *American Journal of Sociology* 77(4): 660–70.

Tunstall, J. and Dunford, M. (1991) *The ITC and the Future of Regional and National Television News*, London: Communications Policy Research Centre.

Tusa, J. (1990) *Conversations with the World*, London: BBC Books.

Van Dijk, T. A. (1988) *News Analysis*, New Jersey: LEA.

Veljanovski, C. (1990) *The Media in Britain Today*, London: News International.

Whittemore, H. (1990) *CNN: The Inside Story*, Boston: Little, Brown.

Wilhoit, G. and de Bock, H. (eds) (1981) *Mass Communication Review Yearbook*, volume 2, London: Sage.

Willis, P. (1971) 'What is news?', *Working Papers in Cultural Studies* 1(1).

# Index